Developing Creativity in the Primary School

Developing Creativity in the Primary School

Jill Jesson

Open University Press

Open University Press
McGraw-Hill Education
McGraw-Hill House
Shoppenhangers Road
Maidenhead
Berkshire
England
SL6 2QL

email: enquiries@openup.co.uk
world wide web: www.openup.co.uk

and Two Penn Plaza, New York, NY 10121-2289, USA

First published 2012

A catalogue record of this book is available from the British Library

ISBN-13: 978-0-33-524463-8 (pb)
ISBN-10: 0-33-524463-7 (pb)
eISBN: 978-0-33-524464-5

Library of Congress Cataloging-in-Publication Data
CIP data applied for

Typesetting and e-book compilations by
RefineCatch Limited, Bungay, Suffolk
Printed by Bell and Bain Ltd, Glasgow

Fictitious names of companies, products, people, characters and/or data that may be used herein (in case studies or in examples) are not intended to represent any real individual, company, product or event.

MIX
Paper from
responsible sources
FSC® C007785
FSC
www.fsc.org

The *McGraw·Hill* Companies

For my sister Alison.

Contents

Preface

This book has arisen from a lifetime of seeing creativity not as a set of skills to be acquired but as an attitude towards life which enriches it. From many years teaching in the primary school and later, working with trainee teachers, I felt that unless the teachers were confident in their own creativity, there was little they could do to develop the creativity of their pupils. Many students and teachers associate the term creative exclusively with the arts and with artistic standards they feel unable to attain. They are challenged with developing the potential of individuals while faced with groups with differing needs.

The book looks first at what experts in this field suggest is covered by the term creativity, together with the benefits and problems it can bring. Second, it suggests ways to develop the creativity of the teacher, as without a creative outlook on life, it is hard to respond to and enjoy the changing challenges of the teaching profession and without enjoyment come frustration and disillusion. Third, it considers the characteristics of individual and group creativity and how each can be developed in six Areas of Creative Endeavour (ACE), which include technical, artistic, mathematical, linguistic, physical and natural philosophical aspects of learning. The latter includes scientific and religious ideas. There are practical suggestions for developing the creativity of the teacher, the group and the individual in each of these areas. It looks at ways of developing creative teaching and learning across the curriculum and through subject teaching. This is a handbook for anyone concerned with developing their own creative potential and the creativity of those with whom they work, from the parent, student teacher and teaching assistant, to the head teacher and advisory teacher. It is for all who are concerned with developing educational practice and helping people to widen their horizons and make the most of their talents.

Acknowledgements

Thanks in particular to Carole Hill for her generosity in sharing so many of her creative ideas.

Many thanks to my husband and critical friend, Graham Peacock for his endless patience and proof reading.

Thanks also to:

- Anna Craft and Routledge for the Creative cycle diagram;
- Belle Wallace for permission to reproduce The TASC wheel © 2010;
- Joe Novak for the Concept diagram;
- Andrew Wilcox for the Thinking Hats diagram.

Every effort has been made to trace copyright holders and obtain their permission for the use of copyright material. The publisher and author would be grateful for information enabling them to rectify any error or omission in subsequent editions.

1   What is creativity?

Introduction

In this chapter we will look first at how the elusive notion of creativity has been identified and defined through the ages. The five creative behaviours (Figure 1.1), as outlined by QCA (2004), are referred to throughout this book as these are the behaviours which cultivate creativity in ourselves and in those we teach. The skills which feed these behaviours are used to build activities which will contribute to the creative development of the teacher, the group and the individual in all curriculum areas.

The benefits and problems which developing the creativity of pupils may bring to a school are considered. We then look at the attributes of creative people and what is needed to promote them. Problems involved with planning for both the individual as well as the group are discussed in the light of the differences between group and personal creativity. Factors which promote or hinder creative development in schools are outlined before analysing the creative process to understand the skills or environmental conditions required at each stage.

Finally, a rationale and methodology are given to identify six curriculum areas where creative development can be demonstrated, taught, promoted and assessed. Examples of creative outcomes and the skills required for each Area of Creative Endeavour (ACE) are suggested.

- Questioning and challenging
- Making connections and seeing relationships
- Envisaging alternatives/seeing things in new ways
- Exploring ideas and keeping options
- Reflecting critically on ideas and outcomes

Figure 1.1   The five QCA Creative Behaviours.
Source: QCA (2004) (The icons are my own.)

Creativity through the ages

Human beings have been developing their creativity for the last two million years but only recently have we decided to formally analyse the characteristics of this aspect of ourselves and what helps to promote it. In early civilizations creativity was not viewed in the way it is today. In Ancient Greece, a time we now recognize as particularly creative in the arts and architecture, as well as in natural philosophy, maths and technology, people who followed those professions were considered gifted, perhaps inspirational, but not creative. These artists and craftsmen followed set rules in their trades and the Greeks had no word for 'to create', only 'to make'. This term was applied only to the writings of poets who were much admired while artists and architects were thought to imitate nature and so were less highly regarded. The Romans reserved the term 'creative' for the activities of gods who were credited with being able to create from nothing. Right through the Middle Ages, domains which people today would consider creative, were designated as craft which was not to be confused with creation. St. Augustine insisted, 'creatura non potest creare' – the creature who has been created cannot himself create, and this view was widely held until the sixteenth century. Only in Renaissance times, a period of exploration and innovation in the arts, and sciences, when people first began to promote novelty, and analyse what was necessary for people to bring something new into existence, was the word creativity used to describe human accomplishments. The first person to apply the term 'creative' to human work was a poet, Sarbiewski (1595–1640), who wrote that a poet 'invents . . . *creates anew* . . . in the manner of God' (Tatarkiewicz 1980: 248).

By the eighteenth century, as people became more interested in the possibilities involved in projects arising from the imagination, art was linked with the concept of creativity, although it was not until the twentieth century that it was linked with technology and the sciences. Galton (1869) is credited with the first systematic study of creativity, although in his study of eminent achievers of the day, he was in fact looking at the attributes of genius and whether they were passed on by heredity.

As long ago as 1926 Wallas looked at the creative process and suggested that it has four stages: *preparation*, where the problem is looked at from different perspectives; *incubation*, where the problem is left to unconscious development; *illumination*, the emergence of a solution and *verification*, when the idea is tried out and checked for value and refined. However, the modern study of creativity is usually attributed to 1950 when an American psychologist, J.P. Guilford, made a speech to the American Psychological Association, challenging them to consider creativity as an area worthy of study. Guilford was puzzled by the way intelligent aircraft pilots were often unsuccessful in completing their training and realized that intelligence involved more than the tests of the day could measure. The pilots who were most effective at problem-solving in a crisis were not always those with the highest IQ scores, and he argued that scientists put too much emphasis on convergent thinking skills at the expense of divergent ones. Guilford believed that creativity should lead to something useful and listed the characteristics of creativity as:

1 *fluency*: the ability to produce a great number of ideas or solutions in a short period of time;

2 *flexibility*: the ability to find a variety of approaches to a problem;
3 *originality*: the ability to produce innovative, original ideas;
4 *elaboration*: the ability to systematize and organize ideas mentally and then carry them out.

In education, the Montessori method, which was pioneered in Italy from 1907 and took off in the USA during the 1960s, is an approach to developing the potential and creativity of the individual which has been claimed to be effective in developing life-long creative skills (Dantus 1999; Cane 1999, cited in Craft 2001). The Reggio Emilia approach to educating the young child, which developed in Italy after the Second World War, proposed as a fundamental that children should have many ways and opportunities to express themselves (see Chapter 9). Advocates found this way of teaching to be particularly successful in promoting children's creativity (Leach 2001, cited in Craft 2001).

During the 1950s and 1960s there were many attempts to identify and measure the characteristics of creativity and the creative process, for example, Torrance (1974), and what was involved in its development. When Rhodes (1961) suggested that creativity involved a *person, a product, a process and a press* (place), he recognized that the context was crucial to the development of the creative process and that in order for it to have value, an outcome which he called a product was important as well. A product may not be a tangible outcome but a process, system or theory. Other angles on research into creativity looked at the influence of personality, on cognition and on the best ways to stimulate creativity in individuals (Craft 2001). At this stage, the individuals studied tended to be the gifted and those identified as being especially innovative in some way.

Meanwhile primary education was under review and the Plowden Report in 1967 recommended child-centred and experiential pedagogies which focussed on the creative development of pupils and in particular through the arts. This led to a somewhat arts-based, product-orientated view of creativity which is still found among many teachers and students today. Twenty years after the Plowden Report (Plowden 1967), concern that the rigour of teaching the basics in education had been lost led to calls for a back to basics curriculum which culminated in the publication of a National Curriculum for England and Wales in 1989 which listed what was to be taught. When this was reframed in 1999, although creativity was listed as one of the cross-curricular key skills, there were only brief references to it elsewhere in the document. From the 1970s, through the 1980s and into the 1990s research into personality continued. This included studies concentrating on the development of the individual creative mind and the influence of social and environmental factors on the creative process. Spindler (1983) noted that in the West the emphasis is on the 'novel product' view of creativity which is judged in a social context where individuality and originality are valued, whereas some Asian cultures have traditionally valued conformity over individuality.

Many experts have tried to define the nature of creativity as well as the processes involved. Amabile (1988) and Hennessey (1996) looked at what blocked or enabled the creative process. Gardner (1993) distinguished between the 'big C' creativity of genius, and society-changing innovation and that of 'little c' everyday creativity. Craft (2002) looked at the 'little c' problem-solving creativity of ordinary people. Fryer (1996) and Craft (1996) considered the best ways to develop teacher creativity while Beetlestone (1998a) examined creativity in the Early Years. During this time, the methodology of research shifted from large-scale quantitative surveys to small-scale qualitative studies which focussed on the context and process as well as the philosophical nature of creativity.

All this work resulted in a growing recognition that the development of creativity in both pupils and their teachers is an essential element in successful education and a competent and contented society. In 1999, the National Curriculum review by the National Advisory Committee on Creative and Cultural Education (NACCCE), entitled *All Our Futures* recognized that everyone has the ability to be creative if they are given appropriate opportunities, knowledge and skills, and stated that this should be a function of education. It categorized levels of creativity as:

1 historic (genius level) Big C;
2 relative (to that of peers) Little c;
3 individual (relating to previous ideas) Little c.

(NACCCE 1999: 30)

Several government reports, fuelled both by researchers and educators in the classroom, have been crucial in taking creativity education forward into the twenty-first century recognizing that creative development is an important part of education. Towards the end of the 1990s, best practice research scholarships (BPRS) enabled practising teachers to carry our small-scale research projects in their schools which focussed on creative issues. These were replaced in 2004 by Creative Action Research Awards (CARA) and Creative Action Research in Schools projects (CARIS) where schools worked with professional artists and crafts people to develop the creative abilities of pupils.

In 1997, 'education, education, education' was a priority for the new Labour government and as service industries and e-commerce took off and workers in the East started to take over some of the manufacturing roles of the West, people with creative skills and outlooks were increasingly required for a new jobs market in an era of change. 'Our aim must be to create a nation where the creative talents of all the people are used to build a true enterprise economy for the twenty-first century – where we compete on brains, not brawn' (Blair 1999, cited in NACCCE 1999: 5).

As Seltzer and Bentley agreed:

> To thrive in our economy . . . we must be able to do more than absorb and feed back information. Learners and workers must draw on their entire spectrum of learning experiences and apply what they have learned in new and creative ways. A central challenge for the education system is therefore to find ways of embedding learning in a range of meaningful contexts, where students can use their knowledge and skills creatively to make an impact on the world around them.
>
> (1999: 9–10)

Since the end of the 1990s there has been an increased focus on English and mathematics in the form of the national literacy and numeracy strategies. Alongside this, advice from QCA (1998) stated that schools must maintain a broad and balanced curriculum but that priority should be given to the core subjects, ICT and RE. Soon schools were encouraged to prioritize, combine or reduce skills and content in the Foundation subjects. The result was that many schools severely cut time for subjects such as science, music and D&T. Since many people equate creativity with these subjects, the profile of creativity in schools became particularly low.

The NACCCE report (also known as the Robinson Report after Ken Robinson who chaired it), had suggested that developing individual pupil creativity contributes to the cultural development of society. While acknowledging the importance of individual creative development, Robinson agreed that the basics should be taught to inform and develop it. The report noted that creativity can be developed in *all* areas of the school curriculum, including the sciences as well as the expressive arts. This was a response to fears expressed by teachers, parents and employers that the National Curriculum's heavy focus on mathematics and literacy was driving out opportunities for creativity in education and that children's creativity needed to be encouraged in order for them to be fit for the challenges of the modern world of work. The report led to the establishment of Creative Partnerships in 2002, an organization that mentored school projects with creative professionals. These projects started with the needs of the school and pupils and with the help of creative practitioners working across and beyond the curriculum, to find new ways for teachers to teach and for young people to learn. Often, however, this involved arts-based projects more than scientific, mathematical or technological ones.

In 2000, the Early Years curriculum (revised in 2007) identified creative development as one of the Early Learning Goals for pre-school children and, in the same year, creativity in Key Stages 1 and 2 was supported by the *Creativity: Find it! Promote it* materials (QCA 2004), now archived. These made it explicit that creativity was much more than an exploration of artistic ideas and the following five creative behaviours were identified and promoted in all curriculum areas. Teachers were challenged to promote the five creative behaviours:

The five creative behaviours

1   Questioning and challenging

2   Making connections and seeing relationships

3   Envisaging alternatives/seeing things in new ways

4   Exploring ideas and keeping options open

5   Reflecting critically on ideas and outcomes.

OFSTED encouraged artistic creative development as part of the curriculum in 2003 in two reports on *Improving City Schools: How the Arts Can Help* and *Raising Achievement Through the Arts*, though sadly other aspects of creativity were not given such prominence, compounding the exclusive association between arts and creativity. The same year, the DfES published *Excellence and Enjoyment* instructing schools to give creativity a higher profile. Another OFSTED survey in 2003 identifying current good practice in promoting creativity in schools was entitled *Expecting the Unexpected: Developing Creativity in Primary and Secondary Schools*. This report found that high quality creative work was to be found in all age groups, and across all subject areas and noted that barriers to learning could be overcome if teachers are committed to the promotion of creativity, possess good subject knowledge and have a sufficiently broad range of pedagogical skills to foster creativity in all pupils, whatever their ability. 'The best primary schools have developed timetables and teaching plans that combine creativity with strong teaching in the basics' (2003c: 15). Teachers were urged to make learning vivid and real: and to 'develop understanding through enquiry, creativity, e-learning and group problem solving' (2003c: 25). In 2004, the DfES also funded a number of research, development and continuing personal development (CPD) initiatives including a series of creative citizenship conferences and introduced the notion of 'personalized learning'. In 2005, they developed materials for creativity CPD for the Foundation Stage through to KS3. In the same year, the National College for School Leadership developed the notion of Creative Leadership building on the document *Emerging Good Practice in Promoting Creativity*, published by Her Majesty's Inspectorate in March 2006 (DfEE 2006). Meanwhile, research by the 'Higher Education, the Arts and Schools' group (HEARTS), explored ways to use creative partners and non-academic locations, to develop creative skills in learners. This project aimed to revitalize the place of the arts in the experience of people studying to become primary teachers and to prompt questions about the teacher training curriculum. The subsequent report by Downing, Lamont and Newby (2007) noted that while cross-disciplinary work may involve logistical problems and even a blurring of aims, the benefits of such co-operation can re-enthuse both individuals and departments as teachers see that the evolution of democratic pedagogies is exciting and can expose both teachers and learners to new possibilities in education.

In Wales, creative skills are one of the seven requirements of the curriculum, while in Northern Ireland, an important feature of the area's work on creativity is the emphasis on harnessing new developments in ICT. In Scotland, *A Curriculum for Excellence* was published in 2004 as the first stage of a review of the 3–18 curriculum. The review identified the principal purpose of education as enabling all children and young people to become successful learners, confident individuals, responsible citizens and effective contributors. Among the skills required for successful learners was noted the ability to 'think creatively and independently' while effective contributors should be able to 'create and develop'.

In 2009, the Independent Cambridge Review stated that 'Creativity and imaginative activity must inform teaching and learning across the curriculum' (Alexander 2009: 23). By this time, in the same year, the government of the day was planning a complete review of the National Curriculum. The government commissioned the Rose Review, also published in 2009, which included suggestions for a new National Curriculum which supported creativity, and the importance of creative thinking and problem-solving. This was subsequently withdrawn by the following Conservative government who favoured a slimmed down and possibly cheaper curriculum which is still under construction. It is interesting that the last two reviews mentioned, were led by Robin Alexander and Jim Rose, two of the 'three wise men' whose earlier reports advocated a more back-to-basics approach with less emphasis on creativity!

Despite all these reviews and reports, in my many recent visits to school and exhibitions of creative work, discussions with teachers and trainees have revealed that although there is now more emphasis on creative teaching, there is still scant evidence that pupils are being helped to develop real personal creativity beyond a little creative writing, drama and art-based lessons. Trainee teachers asked to give examples of pupil creativity during their final practice are often unable to do more than describe the results of fairly prescribed actions. Pupils involved with enterprise education talk about what they have mass produced, rather than what they have learned, and with some excellent exceptions, display boards show a multitude of very similar results.

So what is creativity?

Creativity is hard to define as it does not exist as quality or outcome apart from the people, process or products involved in its inception. Many have tried to define its elusive qualities and many facets. Some have seen creativity as a quality owned only by the expert, genius or Nobel Prize-winner; the Big C creativity of Gardner (1993) and Csikszentmihalyi (1996b). Others believe in the more egalitarian view that we all have creative potential (NACCCE 1999; Craft 2000). The reality is probably somewhere on a sliding scale between the two, in that we may all have some potential, but not everyone develops it. Whether we view creativity as an innate gift which cannot be taught but only nourished, or a basic human attribute, or as a set of skills to be learned and developed in everyone, our viewpoint will affect the way we teach and the way we value what our pupils do.

Spendlove (2005) notes that our creative capacity is what separates us from other species and that the development of people's creativity has paralleled the evolution of our culture and society from the use of fire and the wheel to space flight and nanotechnology: 'Whether from an elitist or egalitarian perspective, creativity remains the elusive and ultimate goal of education; central to an individual's well being' (Spendlove 2005: 9). He reminds us also that our inventions and genius do not always result in positive outcomes. War, torture, pollution and deforestation all owe their origins to our creative capacity. Some teachers and politicians fear that if we teach pupils to think and behave originally, we may start to lose control of them in school, and later in society.

Exploring the five creative behaviours involves questioning current rules, exploring different perspectives and practices and trying out ideas which are not always comfortable, convenient or popular. In the twenty-first century, creativity has become an in-word, a fashionable term used not only in education, but in the popular press in advertising and many aspects of our culture. It is a term over-used but often undefined, misunderstood, and often interchanged inappropriately for related terms such as enterprise, innovation or different. So what exactly does it involve?

The characteristics of creativity

Mackinnon (1962), as cited in Feldhusen and Goh (1995), said that creative outcomes must be novel, must solve a problem and involve evaluation and elaboration of an original insight. He suggested that it is a process characterized by originality, adaptiveness and realization, which implies that one person's creativity may build on another's ideas, but also that it should be a conscious and reflective process, rather than an accidental variation.

Bruner (1962), as reported in Spendlove (2005), thought that true creativity involves the process of achieving surprise in the beholder, bringing the evaluation of another into the process.

Lytton (1971), discussed in Compton (2010), distinguished between objective and subjective creativity. The former related to the rare creation of an original outcome appropriate for, and transformative of its context, while the latter occurred more frequently, as the novelty was only new to that individual.

Heinlett (1974), noted in Cropley (2001), made the distinction between self-indulgent 'pseudocreativity' and novelty which meets external standards of effectiveness which he termed 'quasicreativity'. Here again, the judgements of domain experts are recognized, though it should be noted that these may change over time. There are many instances of artists, musicians and writers being rejected by one age but applauded by another. Copernican theory was rejected for many years. Henry Ford was told that the car would never replace the horse, while Raphael was unappreciated in his lifetime and has gone in and out of fashion as a creative painter several times since then.

Shallcross (1981), cited in Craft (2000), also felt that the term could be applied to creative outcomes which are new to the learner, even if they have existed before, ensuring that some children's innovations and originality should be recognized even if it is not of wider significance.

In 1990, Smith, also cited in Craft (2000), considered the relationship that creativity may have with the notion of the skill involved and said:

> Creativeness is not a skill, but that skills are involved in expressing creativeness. You do not learn to be creative by creativeness exercises, but you learn to capitalize on creativeness through mastery of a medium . . . Creativeness necessarily fails when its expression is thwarted by ignorance, inexperience, or feebleness of intention.
>
> (Smith, cited in Craft 2000: 89)

This suggests that the skills are external to the creative process, but also that the creative process cannot be developed without them.

In 1996, Csikszentmihalyi wrote: 'Creativity is any act, idea, or product that changes an existing domain, or that transforms an existing domain into a new one.' Using this definition suggests that a creative contribution must be recognized by expert members of the domain as significant and transformative for the domain. In this view, creativity has major socio-cultural implications through interactions between creator, domain and cultural institutions.

Gardner (1997) claimed that creativity is 'the ability to solve problems and fashion products and to raise new questions'. Here the outcome of a new question may be the starting point for a new discovery. It is worth noting that the emphasis here is on non-product outcomes such as problem-solving which might involve systems as well as products as well as new ideas implied by the questions raised.

Seltzer and Bentley (1999) and Claxton (2003) usefully define what they believed creativity is *not* and remind us that it is not just involved with artistic sensibilities. It is not equivalent to brilliance; it does not imply talent, or a particular skill or techniques to be performed well on command. It is not easy, wacky, not lodged in one side of the brain and may not be comfortable.

The NACCCE definition of creativity as 'imaginative activity fashioned so as to produce outcomes that are both original and of value' (1999: 29) is one which has been widely adopted for its simplicity and relevance to education.

Spendlove (2005) comments on Simonton's (2003) idea that creativity is what makes us productive, adaptive and efficient and that it should therefore not be considered optional, but embedded in all activities.

Cropley (2001: 28) considered that the constant factor was novelty. He believed that children's inexperience contributed to their ability to see new solutions and divided creativity into 'everyday' and 'sublime' while defining the three key elements as: novelty, effectiveness and ethicality. The latter emphasized that the term creativity was used for positive outcomes rather than destructive behaviour, though many would argue that it is hard to deny that the ingenious and inventive minds which have developed bombs and methods of torture were certainly creative.

Lucas defined creativity as 'A state of mind in which all our intelligences are working together' (2001: 38). This suggests not only a belief in more than one type of intelligence, but that creativity might be a unifying process for them. He notes that although it is often found in the creative arts, creativity can be demonstrated in any subject at school or in any aspect of life.

Fisher (2007) agreed with Rhodes (1961) that creativity is a property of the interaction of person, process and product and press, the latter covering environmental influence. Fisher also said that the processes of creative evolution are generation, variation and originality and he talks about degrees of originality whether they are individual, social or universal.

Craft (2001) developed the notion of possibility thinking at the heart of little c creativity, and problem-solving, emphasizing the mental processes involved as well as the accessibility of creativity for the ordinary mind. While big C refers to a highly novel response or ideas which result in changes in the outlook of a domain, or which affects how others live their lives, little c deals with incremental change, problem-solving and the ability to adapt to change. It involves problem-finding as well as problem-solving.

Fisher (2007) points out that we need both critical and creative thinking, both analysis and synthesis. We need creative thinking to generate new ideas, and critical thinking to judge their value.

Wegerif (2010) sees the development of creative thinking as a dialogic process achieved by encouraging learners to develop ideas through discussion and reflection. He argues that 'creativity originates in the capacity to "let go" of the self into a shared place of multiple perspectives and possibilities that is first found in playful relationships' (2010: 37).

Summary

To summarize, while some experts see creativity as being domain-specific and others view it as a general characteristic of personality, it is generally agreed that creativity does not take place in a vacuum. It requires the imaginative application of thought, effort and skill. It is a term which can be applied on a sliding scale from the 'little c' creativity which involves personal novelty for the learner to the 'big C' creativity recognized as being of value by specialists or even society as a whole. All definitions of creativity involve a component of originality. A creative outcome typically includes a new idea, perspective, interpretation, or contribution. Purposefulness and reflection are other recognized characteristics of creativity; the creative act must be intentional and considered, not accidental. The case of a writer such as e e cummings, who bends the rules of punctuation in the service of creative expression, is different from children using incorrect punctuation because they do not know any better. A creative outcome may be an innovative idea, a novel system, a new act or original product. Problem seeking and problem-solving, perhaps building on and adapting the ideas of others by asking 'What if?', can result in original outcomes which may involve further questions and which will require reflection and evaluation of results. The process entails intelligence, but is not a measure of it. There is general agreement that it is not just a term to be used in artistic contexts and that it is a quality which all of us can develop to some degree. To be recognized as creative, an innovation needs to be more than imaginative reproduction or production, it should have value and purpose as well so that critical thinking is an essential part of creative thought.

A personal view

For me, creativity is an attitude towards life: a lens through which to view the processes and products of our world with both playfulness and purpose, always looking for development and new areas of interest (Figure 1.2). Creativity is a positive view of the planet, not just a problem-solving strategy, but one which is simultaneously puzzle-seeking and solution unravelling. It is an approach which looks for the beneficial, the unusual, or just the engaging, takes risks, explores options and builds on them. All experiences, including problematical situations, are opportunities to question the status quo and to develop new ideas.

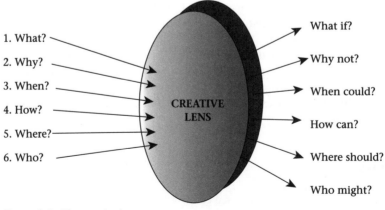

Figure 1.2   The creative lens

> **Creative Challenge!**
> Ask your classes what activities they see as being creative. Ask them to explain their
> ideas. Help them to see that creativity involves more than the creative arts.

What are the benefits of creativity to groups and individuals?

The development of creativity in pupils is important for the development of their intellect, confidence, knowledge and skills base (Figure 1.3). On an individual level the creative process can be enjoyable, motivating and empowering. When a child creates their first play den or make-believe story, they are using their imagination to invent something which is theirs, with which they are involved and over which they have control. Involvement is crucial to development and all forms of learning and it is widely accepted that when people feel in control of what they are doing, they are motivated, happy and likely to work well. These emotional conditions are the same as those required for learning, so if we can engage children in activities which are creative for them, they are more likely to be successful learners. The creative skills of *asking questions, making connections, exploring ideas, seeing things in new ways and reflecting*, are those which help people to think independently and solve problems. They give personal relevance to activities, whether of their own design, or at the suggestion of others.

Creativity, or the lack of it, is important to the individual, the group and the species. Individuals with creative lives are likely to be interested and interesting people who engage with the world around them, seeking out the unexpected, the unexplored and the unknown. They welcome opportunities to try new experiences, to develop new skills and engage with problems. Those without creative skills and interests, both in school and later in society, are likely to be bored, unexcited and unlikely to make the most of their potential. This does not mean that if an individual is not a practising artist, she is likely to be unfulfilled. But if a person has no experience of activities which require adaptation and ingenuity, such as cooking or gardening, or playing games or sports, solving puzzles or being challenged by problems to which they can find solutions, they are less likely to lead rich and interesting lives. It is not just a question of intelligence or academic achievement. Generations of people have enriched their lives and the lives of their families by inventing stories, running up toys from odds and ends, or improvising gadgets which perform a necessary job. This is creativity in everyday life which empowers and enriches the lives of those who experience it. For the individual, creative activity is rewarding at an emotional level as well as a practical or economic one. The materials given in *Creativity: Find it, Promote it* (QCA 2004) describe how promoting pupils' creativity can:

- improve pupils' self-esteem, motivation and achievement;
- develop skills for adult life;
- develop the talent of the individual.

Robert Sternberg's (1999) research showed that when students are assessed in ways which recognize their creative abilities, their academic performance improves.

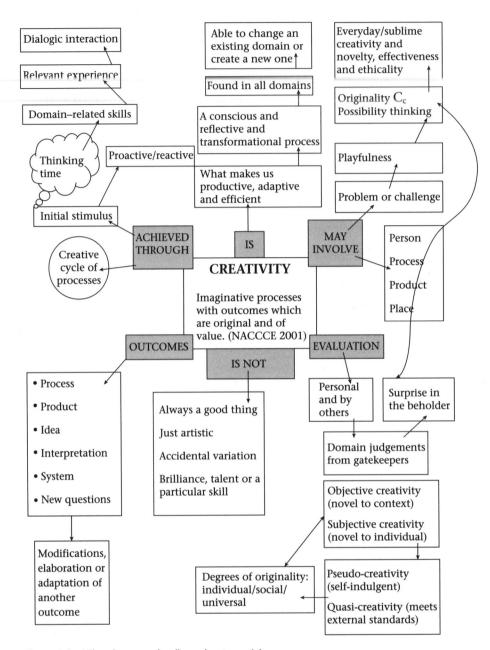

Figure 1.3 What the research tells us about creativity

The following reports concur with this view:

- NACCCE (1999: 7) noted that, 'When individuals find their creative strengths, it can have an enormous impact on self-esteem and on overall achievement.'
- *Excellence and Enjoyment* (DfES 2003: 27) urged teachers to make learning vivid and real by developing understanding through enquiry, creativity, e-learning and group problem-solving because pupils' literacy and numeracy skills were enhanced in this way. The report noted that 'Promoting creativity is a powerful way of engaging pupils with their learning.'
- OFSTED (2010: 21) reported that 'in the schools which deliberately set out to encourage independence, adaptability, imagination and curiosity, most of the pupils had very positive attitudes to learning. In all but two of the 44 schools visited, the survey found pupils' personal development, in terms of the activities and attitudes characterising creative learning, to be good or outstanding.'

Groups perform best when they involve people with a variety of creative talents who are prepared to share them. The village show, the local council and the primary school all need people with the determination to improve existing conditions, tackle challenges, and solve problems in new ways, and this will sometimes involve taking some risks. 'A ship in harbour is safe – but that is not what ships are built for' (John Shedd 1928). Problems in a community require new skills and fresh attitudes, people with imagination and creative minds to adapt to change. School is where these skills must be nurtured.

Progress as a species comes as a result of purposeful exploratory and innovative activity, or of recognizing the benefits of accidental variation. We have to adapt to be able to succeed in a changing world. We have to be able to solve the problems of population growth and the need for food on a planet where, in most countries, they are not making any more land. Our society needs people who can cope with new circumstances, take responsibility and think autonomously. The world of work is changing fast and we have to educate a generation for change both in terms of jobs they may do, leisure facilities and interests they may follow and ways they interact with members of other societies. 'The focus of education must be on creating people who are capable of thinking and doing new things, not simply repeating what past generations have done, but equipped for a world of challenge and change' (Fisher and Williams 2004: 11).

Finding ways to develop the creative skills and attitudes of children in school is vital for motivating them and enabling them to learn in an enjoyable and personal way. School is a place where they should be able to take risks and learn that failure in a task is not a failure in them. Not trying is the only failure. Things not working out the way they hope or expect may be disappointing, but it is an important part of the learning process. I often say to my students, 'Tell me what you have learned today from what has *not* gone as you expected. I apologize to those who have had no failure at all today, because then I'll merely have confirmed your suspicions, rather than taught you something new.'

2   Developing creativity in schools

What are the problems with developing creativity in schools?

There are several problems with developing what is becoming widely regarded as a beneficial and enjoyable set of skills and a particular mindset. The greatest hindrance to the development of creativity in pupils is probably the lack of time in a crowded curriculum to experiment, innovate and think about ideas. There are tensions between the conflicting demands of target-led curriculum and government reports such as NACCCE report (1999), *Excellence and Enjoyment* (DfES 2003) and the Rose Report (2009) that schools should be places devoted to creative learning.

Teachers need to decide:

- which skills to develop;
- how and when to develop them.

As professionals, we are all so afraid of standards appearing to fall or not getting through the right number of tick boxes, that we are tempted to keep feeding our classes with information, rather than help them develop ideas, imagination and creative thinking skills. Lack of time for creativity is seen as a huge problem. As OFSTED (2010: 11) noted: 'Allowing pupils to explore ideas through a creative process of trial, error and revision generally proved more time-consuming than firmly teacher-directed activities.' Other problems arise from the fact that creativity is so hard to identify or define, that even the experts do not always agree on what it comprises. Sometimes it has been over-associated with the arts or perceived by males as just a feminine trait. One must remember that creativity *per se* is neither good nor bad, but can be used for cruel or immoral purposes as well as beneficial ones. Weapons of mass destruction, as well as cruel playground jibes, can arise from a creative imagination.

There are further tensions for teachers who may not recognize their own creativity or who will feel that they may not have the appropriate skills to promote creative learning in a particular domain. Developing the creative potential of pupils is a problem for those who are unfamiliar with current theoretical perspectives on creativity and do not recognize the relevant skills to develop. As a result, creative professionals may be called in to implement often artistic designs where pupils act as little more than drones on a project which is not of their initiation.

With a truly creative project or even small pieces of work where pupils are able to develop their own ideas and take risks, the teacher may end up feeling out of control. Novel work may take a lot of time or require unusual resources or even new ways of working and collaborating across subject disciplines or class boundaries. Extra time spent on experimental work by pupils in one area, could involve lack of progress in others. Creative outcomes cannot be guaranteed as outcomes can be in more standard lessons. Failure is part of the process and teachers need the confidence and skill to avoid children becoming discouraged and to help them see that short-term failure is no bad thing. Sometimes a teacher will need to be able to model a creative process with which they are not familiar: bravery is required here, as well as honesty to sometimes admit that *we* are doing things for the first time as well. In fact this is a valuable piece of creative modelling, but it can be an uncomfortable one. Furthermore, we must beware of the commercialization of creativity with many companies jumping on the creativity bandwagon, offering ideas and materials which lack real creative potential. They are more do than design; more craft than create.

The attributes of creative people

So now we have looked at what creativity is, and why it is a valuable characteristic to develop, we should look at what helps people to be creative. One way to do this is to identify the characteristics of creative people and then see what enables them to act in this way. Csikszentmihalyi studied a selection of particularly creative individuals in a wide range of fields and noted the qualities of their characters and ways of working. One major characteristic he noticed was these people's ability to get lost 'in the flow' of the process and be almost unaware of time or their surroundings. Circumstances likely to create this condition are hard to provide in the distracting and time-cramped sur-roundings of the average classroom. However, as teachers, we need to be aware of the need for pupils to become absorbed in creative work and, without letting pupils drift aimlessly to no purpose, sometimes allow them to drift with their ideas, make several trials of an idea, play with ideas, experiment and make real discoveries rather than those we have planned for them to make. Giving advance notice of tasks, whether the day before, or just a lunch-time before can allow mulling over time. Not many adults can write, paint, invent or create to order with no advance warning.

Many experts in creativity research such as Csikszentmihalyi (1996a), Spendlove (2005), and Craft (2001) have compiled lists of the characteristic of creative people. The following attributes are common to most lists:

1　strong sense of self, self-control and self-confidence;
2　intellectual curiosity;
3　original in thought and action;
4　independent with the courage to be different and take risks;
5　open to experience and enjoy experimenting;
6　persistent and capable of strong intrinsic motivation;
7　passionate and committed;
8　attracted to complexity and obscurity;

9   sensitive and emotionally involved in their work;
10   sense of humour/playfulness.

> ### Creative Challenge!
> Consider these characteristics of creative people. Which apply to you? How might you be able to develop some of these characteristics in the learners you teach?

How can creative characteristics be developed?

It would appear that personal characteristics play a fundamental part in determining the creativity of an individual. Therefore teachers need to be able to do more than provide inspiring lessons and learning opportunities: developing characters who are able to respond creatively to life's challenges has to be a high priority. Many of the fundamental characteristics needed to develop these attributes are probably innate: sensitivity, courage, a sense of playfulness and humour, even an attraction to complexity and obscurity are basic qualities present in pupils well before school age. These and others such as intellectual curiosity can be stimulated, and a sense of self-confidence, originality and persistence can be cultivated, given the right conditions such as freedom from fear of failure and adequate time in which to develop ideas.

Csikszentmihalyi (1996a) noted that factors which enable creatives to get 'in the flow', a state which promotes creative activity, include:

- clear goals;
- immediate feedback;
- a balance between challenge and skills;
- the elimination of distractions.

In contrast, Fisher (Fisher and Williams 2004) says that the keys to individual creativity in a supportive environment are:

- motivation fed by passion as well as internal and external encouragement;
- inspiration which thrives on curiosity fed by fresh input both inside and outside the classroom which results in involvement in engaging activities;
- gestation time for ideas to emerge;
- collaboration whether with peers, teachers or professional creative partners.

Fisher reminds us that it is not possible to be creative in all areas and at all times: we need to be focussed and work on areas in which we feel we can make a difference. So if a school or a single class teacher feels that developing the creativity of their science lessons is the area in which they can make most difference: that is the area in which to start.

Claxton (2003) outlines eight 'sections of the learning orchestra' that contribute to creativity:

1   *Immersion*: learning by steeping yourself in experiences; creative people are good at noticing.

2   *Inquisitiveness*: to be creative, you need a questioning disposition.
3   *Investigation*: you need research skills to find what you need to know.
4   *Interaction*: with others to develop ideas.
5   *Imagination*: to seek other possibilities.
6   *Intuition*: to be aware of other possibilities.
7   *Intellect*: to use intelligence to work things out.
8   *Imitation*: we need good examples to copy.

Claxton (2003) talks about fostering creativity in small everyday activities such as improving a sentence or adapting a recipe. I suggest it could also be modelled in the way that a teacher organizes a room effectively, provides interactive displays, discusses ideas about a picture or poem with a class or helps pupils to invent their own playground games.

Strategies for developing a more creative class

In this next section we will look at some strategies that can help develop a more creative class:

- Teacher as a role model
- Effective time management
- Planning for individual provision
- Making the most of the learning environment
- What blocks or enables the creative process?

Teacher as role model

The first way teachers develop any quality (for good or ill) in their pupils is to model it themselves. So combining the qualities of creative people with the skills and processes we need to be creative, gives us the following list of skills, attitudes and activities (Table 2.1) we should demonstrate as adults so as to inspire our pupils to imitate us. Albert Einstein said, 'The only serious method of education is to be an example,' and adds ruefully, 'If you can't help it, be a warning example'. Claxton says: 'Like all coaches, a creative coach has to walk the talk.'

Looking at the five characteristics to creativity as outlined by the *Creativity: Find it, Promote it* materials (QCA 2004), let's see which personal attitudes are needed for each one, for these are what we need to model in our activities as teachers (Table 2.1). For some ways to do this, see Chapter 4, 'Developing Teacher Creativity', for if we do not recognize and develop our own creative potential, how can we expect our children to do this?

This may seem an almost impossible list of qualities and activities to display on a daily basis, but some could be seen as weekly or even termly challenges. On a daily basis, all teachers can be modelling an 'I wonder' and 'What if' approach which demonstrates their willingness to act as learners themselves. If we expect pupils to be keen to see things in new ways and explore ideas and come up with original outcomes, we need to be modelling the creative process ourselves in the ways we teach and what we share of ourselves

Table 2.1 Creative skills attitudes and activities to model

Creative skills to model	Creative attitudes and activities to model *(Note: several could be placed in more than one section)*
❓ The ability to frame questions	Curiosity Independent thought Willingness to share lack of knowledge Inquisitiveness
The ability to make connections with prior learning both in and out of school	Take time to think things over and recall past events Share anecdotes Courage to suggest connections between ideas Interaction with others to share ideas
The ability to see things in new ways	Openness to new ideas Initiative Originality Sense of humour Sensitivity Flexibility Imagination
The ability to explore ideas	Investigation skills Confidence Persistence Willingness to take a risk Enjoyment in experimentation Playfulness Imitation: building on others' good examples The ability to live with uncertainty
The ability to reflect critically on ideas, actions and events.	Openness to new ideas Ability to analyse ideas, and actions Look at problems and solutions from different angles, weighing up the pros and cons Using intuition and intellect to reflect synthesize and evaluate ideas

with our classes. It is unrealistic to expect most busy teachers to be working on major creative projects outside their teaching life, though many may well be engaged in activities with creative potential such as cooking, home decorating, gardening or sport. For most of us, the way we run our classrooms may have to be the way we model creativity and problem-solving. We can discuss with pupils the ways to improve the organization and resourcing of the room, and ways to adapt areas of the school such as corridors and outside play areas to make the most of them. (See Chapter 3 for more ideas on this.)

Suggestions for practice

We can

- Model activities such as writing, solving a maths problem, demonstrating a technique in science, art or DT. This is what we are probably most familiar with doing. Talk about the process and your thinking as you do it so the children can understand the often conflicting ideas we have as we create. For example: 'I need to show that John is frightened at this point in the story. I could just say he is scared, but I think it would have more impact if I wrote "His hand trembled as he turned the heavy key."'
- Write or paint with the class for short periods while they are trying out new techniques and share our attempts, however rough they may feel to us.
- Share anecdotes and examples of problem-solving such as mending a toy or how one entertained oneself on a journey.
- Share our questions about life, the universe and things which make us wonder.
- Tell them about occasions when we have had to take a risk which was scary but worked out well.
- Share what we find interesting in a TV programme about wildlife or an item in the news.
- Plan for good quality home time for yourself so you can go in and share your excitement about the sculpture exhibition/walk/football match you took your family to at the weekend. Find ways to build on this experience with them so they can develop similar sculptures, take their family on a local walk/town trail, practice some deft moves with a ball.
- Even say at the end of a frustrating day, 'I'm sorry if I have been a bit sharp with you today. It's probably not all your fault, but I have been worried about my dog/the lack of time we have to finish this work', or whatever has made you feel ratty, helps to model reflection, sensitivity and the way that even teachers don't get it all right all of the time.

Effective time management

The report *Excellence and Enjoyment* (DfES 2003) considered ways teachers could promote pupils' creativity across all National Curriculum subjects at Key Stages 1, 2 and 3 and concluded that 'making only small changes to their existing planning and practice, teachers can promote pupils' creativity through the National Curriculum and existing teaching frameworks'.

In many instances, this will just be an adjustment of emphasis, for example, in helping pupils to ask their own questions at the start of a new topic, rather than telling them what they will learn; helping them create their own scenarios for drama; allowing them to suggest their own ideas for experiments in science, rather than doing the standard ones. Sometimes it is a case of using spare minutes such as lining up time or registration to better effect. Giving open-ended challenges for homework which build on work done in class allows children to have a more personal education which is motivating as well as creativity building. Telling pupils in advance, even the day before, about a task gives them time to mull it over and develop ideas. Allocating enough time to experiment in all subjects, not just science, and try ideas which may not work out as expected, is essential if children are to make real connections and really explore ideas and see things in new ways. Devoting adequate plenary time to reflective evaluation of learning, identifying what has been learned by all individuals rather than a few could enable a thoughtful and personal analysis of experience and provide a starting point for further creative learning.

Time management is a key skill for the teacher to ensure that in all parts of the day pupils are making best use of their time and not wasting it in activities which are better done by the teacher or a machine. Too often pupils are required to draw rather than complete tables, colour rather than interpret graphs, copy old writing into best when it could have been word-processed in the first place. Moyles (1992) suggests that teachers can find themselves with less work than usual if they organize the children in helping to manage the room.

Planning for individual provision

The *Excellence and Enjoyment* report (DfES 2003) found that when teachers actively planned for and responded to pupils' creative ideas and actions, pupils became more curious to discover things for themselves, were open to new ideas and keen to explore those ideas with the teacher and others so that 'promoting creativity is a powerful way of engaging pupils with their learning'. For ideas on how to do this, see Chapter 4. One way to do this is to set homework projects on topics which can be adapted to individual interests. Each week the class is taught a technique, such as making labelled diagrams, quiz construction or riddle writing, which could be applied to their particular subject. Over several weeks this can build into a project of which each is justifiably proud and where creative thoughts and outcomes are valued. Short one-evening tasks can be based on individual interests, puzzles and challenges as well.

Making the most of the learning environment

As Beetlestone (1998b) noted, the learning environment can extend beyond the classroom, into the school grounds and beyond. In schools with well-organized rooms and accessible resources, where stimulating displays are frequently switched, and ICT facilities are regularly used, pupil creativity flourishes.

As a university lecturer visiting trainees on placement, I regularly see learning environments ready for work. Many of these are quite superb, with indoor and outside areas exhibiting interactive, up-to-date displays and a variety of well-organized resources, including laptops and stand-alone computers for regular use by every pupil. Some are less organized, with faded displays, piles of untidy books or unsorted work and computers seldom turned on and rarely used. Unsurprisingly, the more creative pupil output and higher academic standards come from the former schools.

What blocks or enables the creative process?

To enable pupils to develop their creative potential, certain environmental conditions need to be met. Investigations into the circumstances which enable or hinder or even block creative development have revealed many impediments to pupils' creative development. The lack of time to develop ideas, over-emphasis on a rewards system for recognizably acceptable work, the discouragement of failure, a learning environment aligned to rigid subject teaching, poor resources or over-supervision, competition between individuals rather than groups or restricted choices in terms of approach or working materials, as well as pressure from external evaluation can all reduce the creativity of the individual (Amabile 1988, reported in Craft 2001).

Lack of time for the incubation and implementation of creative development has been identified by most researchers and by me when asking my own classes about what makes it hard or easy to be creative. It is difficult to be creative on demand. Few teachers can do it, but we expect our classes to produce creative writing, artistic work, ideas for investigations and designs for inventions with almost no notice at all. Time to consider a challenge in advance, mull over possibilities, find the information needed to inform the work; time to try out ideas and make mistakes; time to create, reflect, test, revise and reflect once again is essential for most projects. Therefore, advance notice of a task or the opportunity sometimes to finish it out of school, or to plan ideas with a friend or as a team, can significantly increase the availability of thinking as well as creating time. Of course, it is sometimes exciting and enjoyable to have a challenge at short notice, but not all the time. You might tell them the subject of an investigation, poem or story which will be tackled the following day, but not the exact nature. Even those pupils who do not think about it consciously overnight may well give it some unconscious consideration which will make work the following day easier and more enjoyable. Cohen and Ferrari (2010) found that time for indecision can be beneficial in the creative process. They concluded that reflective rumination significantly predicted creativity. My own classes have confirmed this.

Craft (2003) found that the four main obstacles to the development of creativity in schools are:

- limitations of the terminology;
- conflicts in policy and practice;
- limitations of curriculum organization;
- limitations from centrally defined pedagogical practice.

Not only do educationalists not agree on what creativity involves, the conflicts between what policies tell us we should do, and what politicians tell us we must achieve in a crowded curriculum with prescribed teaching pedagogies, do not make it easy for teachers to adapt their practice to the changing demands of official advice.

Research by Amabile (1988) found the following factors either enabled or blocked creativity (Table 2.2).

Beetlestone (1998a) recommended timetable reorganization to allow time for creative development across subject boundaries. Enthusiastic teachers who are responsive to the pupils' mood or even the weather and who use the outdoors as a learning

Table 2.2   Enablers and blockers for creativity

Enablers	Blockers
Adequate time	Time pressure
Having appropriate skills for the job	Fear of evaluation and failure
Intrinsic task motivation (work which is interesting, involving, exciting, satisfying, or personally challenging)	Too much surveillance
	Competition with individual peers
	Working for an external reward rather than the reward of satisfaction from the task itself
Adequate resources	
Adequate challenge	The perception of an activity as a means to an extrinsic goal can undermine intrinsic motivation
Internal criteria for determining success or failure	External criteria for determining success or failure

environment, not just somewhere to play, are extending the resources available for crea-tive development. Involving parents was seen as another way to extend creative oppor-tunity so that carers are able to build on their children's creative development at home.

Expecting the Unexpected (OFSTED 2003: 17) listed effective school leadership as a key factor in developing a creative school. The use of particularly skilled experts such as advanced skills teachers (ASTs) or creative practitioners for INSET training was recom-mended. They recognized that a stimulating physical environment which included not just displays of excellent work, but also displays used to show 'untidy' creative processes such as first drafts along with a finished article, and photographic records of work in progress which would be especially encouraging in design technology projects. What they noted as problematic was often the teacher's inability to recognize, 'the creative moment' such as when a child's doodling went unrecognized as creative exploration. Inspectors found many teachers reluctant to let go of standard calculations and allow pupils to find their own methods when appropriate, while for others, the inability to balance test requirements with creative opportunities made real creative development unlikely. Sometimes rigid timetabling reduced the capacity of teachers to forge the pro-ductive curricular links often associated with high-quality creative work, while some schools still had limited extra-curricular opportunities to develop creative skills.

From my own small-scale classroom research asking pupils what they find helps or hinders their creativity the following information emerged (Table 2.3).

Table 2.3   What helps or hinders creativity

What helps creativity	What hinders creativity
Working with people who have lots of different ideas/complementary skills, (not just friends)	Working with people who distract and waste time. (Oddly, this was often from those most likely to be distracting!)
Help and encouragement from the teacher	Not having enough ideas/not knowing how to start
Adequate resources in good condition	Not enough time or help
Hearing/seeing my ideas when I work with them	Too little/too much challenge

> **Creative Challenge!**
> Ask your class what helps or hinders their creativity and try to respond to what they say. An anonymous survey for pupils can let you know what they really feel. I certainly made adjustments to the way I taught when I received this type of feedback.

Intrinsic and extrinsic motivation

In 1988, Amabile identified the fact that people work better when doing a task for its own sake (intrinsic motivation) rather than for a reward (extrinsic motivation). She also found that competition between individuals could reduce the numbers and quality of creative ideas although competition between groups seemed to enhance it. Too much surveillance during an activity, and fear of failure were other key factors which could block creative development. In 1994, Atkinson noted that creativity was not always encouraged in schools where the need to do well at public exams was felt to be more important: exams fail to reward creativity. Two years later, Hennessey identified five sure-fire killers of creativity and intrinsic motivation: expected reward, expected evaluation, surveillance, time limits and competition. Sadly these are often features of primary education.

Research by Yeh and Wu (2006) showed that having internal motivation to solve a problem and an attitude which welcomes challenges are crucial to pupils' technological creativity. They found that most pupils have positive emotional traits which contribute to their technological creativity, but that the older pupils are, the less optimistic and the less creative, they become.

> **Creative Challenge!**
> Bearing in mind the issues listed above, discuss with colleagues what helps and hinders your creativity and find three ways to unblock it.

Stages in the creative process and creative cycles

Since adequate time and instruction have been identified as crucial to the development of creative ideas, we will now scrutinize the creative process to see where more time, or different forms of help might be required. Many experts in this field have tried to identify the phases we go though in order to create something new and of value. Wallas (1926) was one of the first to outline the steps involved in the creative process. His model has four stages and looks at creativity in a problem-solving context (Figure 2.1):

1   *preparation*: preparatory work on a specific problem which explores issues around it.
2   *incubation*: also described by Claxton as 'soft thinking time', where the problem is in the unconscious mind and externally nothing appears to be happening. This could also be described as mulling it over time and rarely is much time devoted to this in schools.

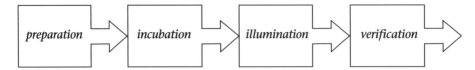

Figure 2.1 Wallas' four-stage creative process model

3   *illumination* or *insight*: the 'Ah ha!' moment when a solution is found.
4   *verification*: where the idea is consciously verified, elaborated, and then applied.

In schools, we rarely have enough time for stage 2. Even stages 1 and 4 tend to be rushed as we urge pupils on to produce a solution or end product of some sort.

Shneiderman (2000) suggests the following four stages for adults involved in creative problem-solving, although he emphasizes they are not a linear path as creative work may require returning to earlier phases (Figure 2.2):

1   *Collect*: learn from previous works stored in libraries and the Web because new knowledge is built on previous knowledge.
2   *Relate*: consult with peers and mentors who can support creativity.
3   *Create*: explore ideas, devise and evaluate possible solutions.
4   *Donate*: share the results and contribute to the libraries.

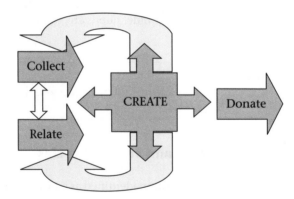

Figure 2.2   Shneiderman's non-linear creative process model as interpreted by the author

This has relevance for schools as it emphasizes the social context of creativity where solutions build on others' discoveries and ideas, where ideas are explored with peers and mentors as part of the social refinement process and are then disseminated for others to build on in turn. Shneiderman's approach also values the appropriate use of ICT for searching, consulting, creating and disseminating at each stage of the process. Perhaps we could make more use of ICT in schools, especially at the second and fourth stages?

Craft (2000) also suggests a model of the creative process which is progressive but may also be cyclical (Figure 2.3).

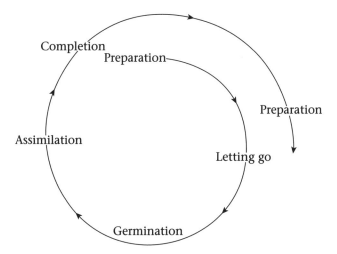

Figure 2.3 Craft's (2000) model of a creative process

None of these models is strictly linear or even strictly cyclical, as we track backwards and forwards and revisit parts of the process in order to refine our ideas (Figure 2.4). What is important about recognizing the stages of the creative process is that we understand that it is not a one-step reaction to a stimulus. If we recognize the need for soft thinking time, even if it is just a time to doodle with pen and pencil, or three minutes with eyes closed in personal reflection or a group exercise in brainstorming and making a concept map, then we can build this vital step into our lessons. All models of creative cycles recognize the stage of finding out information, though too often in schools this involves unfocussed wandering on the Internet in a way we would never encourage in a library. Modelling the way we decide what we want to find out as well as useful ways to do this are vital skills many teachers have not had the opportunity to develop for themselves as they were brought up in a less digital or less research-based era.

Group creativity and personal creativity

Although this is dealt with in more detail in Chapter 3, I would like to draw the reader's attention here to the notion that there are differences the teacher needs to consider when planning for the identification and promotion of creative skills in both groups and individuals. This is an area where there seems to be little tradition of research, with especial relevance to the primary school, and yet, nationwide, the busy teacher is charged with developing the creativity of every individual while having to plan for and teach groups of children. Although ideally we talk about personalized learning, too often this just means identifying which pupils can be helped to show they have achieved the next NC level and then targeting them with booster classes and extra homework. This may be dispiriting and pressurizing for them, while those pupils deemed to be already above, or too far below the desired levels to catch up, are given less personalized attention and inadequate levels of challenge.

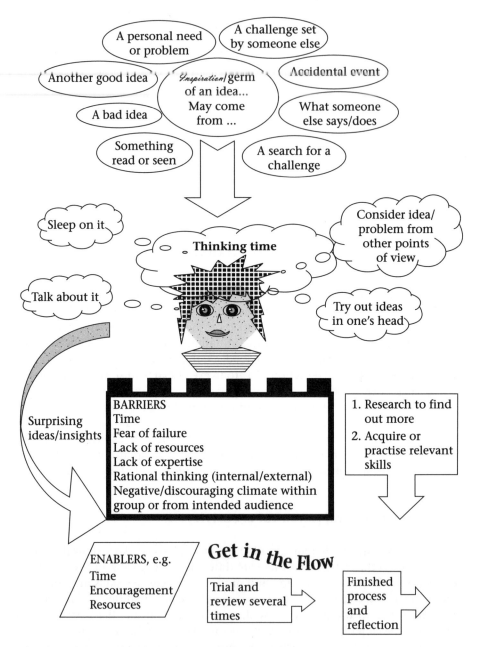

Figure 2.4 The creative process as envisaged by the author

The more able pupils are especially unlikely to be given extra attention. OFSTED's report, *Gifted and Talented Pupils in School* (2009: 5) in schools found that 'in 20 of the 26 schools visited, pupils said their views were either not sought or not taken sufficiently into account in planning tasks and curriculum provision to meet their interests'. This report made no mention of creativity at primary level at all. In *Expecting the Unexpected*, a report into developing creativity in schools (OFSTED 2003c), there is only one brief mention of creativity in connection with gifted and talented pupils.

> ### Creative Challenge!
> In what ways do you currently make provision for developing the *creativity* rather than the academic ability of the most and least able in your class?

Six Areas of Creative Endeavour (ACE)

It has already been established by NACCCE (1999), QCA (2004) and many others, that 'creativity can be developed in all areas of the school curriculum: including the sciences as well as the expressive arts' (SEED 2006). In all areas of human achievement, individuals and groups have shown both small-scale ingenuity and larger-scale originality, both of which may be termed creative. We have made astounding progress in technology, and emotional and intellectual development in art. Mathematics has gone beyond counting to complex theoretical calculations, while language has evolved to express emotions and ideas as well as demands. Physical development is highly refined in both groups and individuals, either as an art form or in trials of strategy and strength. We have gone beyond asking where is the next meal coming from, to 'Why are we here?', 'How do things work?' and 'How should we behave?'

Creativity is not domain-specific although it requires a context with domain-related skills in which it can flourish. In this way it is similar to intelligence. Although for many years intelligence was discussed and assessed as if it were a single entity, more recently researchers and educationalists, such as Gardner (1983), have suggested there may be multiple forms of intelligence, and that people who excel in one or two intellectual areas, may not excel in them all. Thus, someone with a poor grasp of logic may have excellent inter-personal or artistic intelligence. A brilliant mathematician might have poor intra-personal intelligence or a poor understanding of artistic interpretation. This unproven but popular theory can help us to see pupils' potential in a wider range of areas than those measured by the traditional IQ test.

While I agree with NACCCE (1999) that creative endeavour crosses all subject barriers, some aspects of creative outcome do appear to be domain-specific. The type of originality developed in choreography and the innovative moves developed by a premiership footballer have something in common in that they both require the performer to imagine the effect of particular bodily movements and to evaluate their effect. Both require an expertise in understanding how the body works and what its limits are. Both require a degree of understanding about how the movements will be seen by others either for artistic or tactical effect. These forms of creative bodily manipulation are very different from the thought processes required to draw or describe a scene or to explain a mathematical solution. Just as Gardner (1983) has pointed out that intelligence is likely to be a plural rather than a singular concept, perhaps there are also different types of creativity. Gardner suggests that a person can be word-, shape-, or sound-smart and suggests that the intelligence of a wordsmith is different from the type of intelligence possessed by an engineer or a musician. He proposes that there are eight domains of intelligence differentially distributed among and within individuals: linguistic, musical, logical-mathematical, spatial, bodily-kinaesthetic, and naturalistic, as well as the personal and inter-personal, intelligences which deal with perceptions of self and others. In the same way, although there is no direct correlation between intelligence type and creative outcome, it could be useful to look at the different areas of creative endeavour common in our society and in a smaller way in the microcosm of the school.

I would like to propose that there are different types of creativity, each of which uses different thought processes and domain-related skills. Some use thought processes which are essentially logical, others an equally productive but more intuitive or even emotional approach. While not suggesting that skills in different creative areas parallel Gardner's multiple intelligences, I think that if we look at the different areas in which creative development is not only possible, but flourishing, then we could give our pupils a broader and more balanced view of what creativity entails and make wider provision for this development than we do at present. Therefore, I propose, in this book, to look at creative education in six Areas of Creative Endeavour (ACE), so as to identify the skills each requires and ways to develop them.

There is some research-based evidence for this identification of these areas. Yeh and Wu (2006) have looked at *technological creativity* which they define as the way in which individuals apply science to accomplish tasks more quickly and effectively to improve the quality of their lives. Chan and Zhao (2010) refer to *artistic creativity*. There is debate among mathematicians as to whether new maths is created or discovered, but in that the maths does not exist formally until someone describes it, I suggest that *mathematical creativity* is a form of creative exploration and expression. It is certainly an area in which questions can be asked, connections made, ideas explored and looked at in new ways and all solutions benefit from reflection. Creative writing is a well-documented genre, while the term *linguistic creativity* is developed in a paper by Bhatia and Ritchie (2008) which looks at facets of bilingual creativity through language mixing as evidenced in the verbal behaviour of bilingual speakers and in global advertising. The article argues that 'language mixing is essentially an "optimizing" strategy which renders a wide variety of new meanings which the separate linguistic systems are incapable of rendering by themselves'. Zawada reviews the many definitions of linguistic creativity in the twentieth century and then proposes the definition that it is 'the activity of making new meaning by a speaker . . . and the recreation and reinterpretation of the meaning(s) by a receiver' (2009: 77). *Physical creativity* as defined by Sheridan (2010: 1) is 'the ability to innovate through action. It goes beyond memorizing a procedure and differs significantly from mimicking movement in that physical creativity focuses on the movement of the body as self-expression, improvisation and imaginative play'. Simonton (2003) has studied scientific creativity. Until the eighteenth century, science was termed natural philosophy and encompassed religious, ethical and philosophical questioning and exploration of ideas as well as what we would term today purely scientific ones, therefore in this book these areas are grouped together.

In each of these identified Areas of Creative Endeavour (ACE), there are specific domain-related skills. In each area there is the potential for outcomes which are original and of value. In each area it is possible to ask questions related specifically to that area, make connections with prior knowledge, explore ideas, look at current ideas in a new way and reflect on the ideas and experience gained.

Areas of Creative Endeavour (ACE)

1   Technological creativity
2   Artistic creativity
3   Mathematical creativity
4   Linguistic creativity
5   Physical creativity
6   Natural Philosophical creativity

I will now look at each ACE and some pupil outcomes which may be recognized in school (Table 2.4).

Table 2.4   Areas of Creative Endeavour (ACE)

Areas of Creative Endeavour (ACE)	Little 'c' outcomes at KS1 and KS2
1 Technological	Ways of exploring ideas and solving problems through practical means: engineering, cookery, craft making such as sewing, wood and metalwork. New products, new systems, new techniques and methods of working. Just perfecting a technique such as using a tool with accuracy is *not* likely to involve creativity. A technological response is only creative if someone responds to a stimulus in a novel way. Innovative questions and ideas may have a technological basis
2 Artistic	Ways of exploring ideas and solving problems through visual and aural media, e.g. painting, sculpture, music: Several areas of artistic endeavour may be involved in one act of creativity. For example, in the creation of a play, other ACEs might be involved in the creation of dialogue, scenery, and special effects
3 Mathematical	Ways of exploring ideas and solving problems through personal methods of calculation, logical procedures and identification of mathematical patterns. Raising new questions, creating definitions and puzzles may have a mathematical basis
4 Linguistic	Ways of exploring ideas, or solving problems through the use of words in any language both spoken and written to entertain or inform. Includes both poetry and prose and may involve electronic communication
5 Physical	Ways of exploring ideas and solving problems through outcomes which involve body control in response to a stimulus such as in judo, football and dance. New tactics, compositions and interpretations are possible outcomes
6 Natural philosophical	Ways of exploring ideas and solving problems through debating, developing and testing theories which may be scientific or social and ideas which may be philosophical, ethical or religious. New ideas, theories, questions and paradigms may result

Each of these Areas of Creative Endeavour (ACE) can be noted by the skills required to do them as well as the resulting outcomes. Identifying each ACE is intended as a way of appreciating creative achievement in a broader range of activities and skills areas than is sometimes recognized by either pupils or teachers. There is some overlap of skills required for each area, so that a landscape designer will need technological creative skills as well as artistic skills to be creative in their field. Each area requires its own domain-related knowledge and skills, plus a "What if . . .?" approach (Table 2.5). Each ACE requires:

- practical domain-related skills;
- domain-related knowledge.

and involves the ability to do the following:

1 ask questions;

2 make connections;

3 explore ideas;

4 see things in new ways;

5 reflect on outcomes.

Table 2.5 Skills required for ACE

ACE	Skills required
Technological	manual dexterity spatial skills hand–eye coordination information processing skills
Artistic	visualization skills hand–eye coordination interpretative skills
Mathematical	good memory ability to reason logically and analytically work methodically information processing skills
Linguistic	communication skills verbal ability organizational ability ability to explain ideas information processing skills
Physical	physical strength/fitness physical coordination visualization skills accurate spatial ability interpretative skills

ACE	Skills required
Natural philosophical	ability to think logically and analytically
	ability to deal with abstract ideas
	organizational ability
	ability to explain ideas
	reasoning and enquiry skills
	information processing skills

Creative Challenge!
What other skills would you identify as crucial to each ACE?
Which skills are common to all areas?

I have listed *technological creative endeavour* first because it may be the first way that a young child creatively explores the world and the objects around them. To be creative, this must be more than mere random fumbling – there must be some intent to discover what works and what does not, and to create a novel outcome of value. The results of such exploration may be artefacts, more efficient systems for doing things, novel ways to gain attention or just amuse the individual. As with any creative endeavour, for it to be truly creative, some degree of reflection should also be involved so that the efficacy of the outcome is assessed and valued by its creator, even if the result of an exploration is almost accidental. Architects, engineers, and craftspeople in many areas as well as children in school are able to demonstrate small c capability in the area.

Artistic creative endeavour involves the many ways we try to represent or interpret what we see and think both visually and aurally. It could be argued that dance would fit in here as it is usually dependent on music, and often categorized as one of the arts, but in this context I feel it fits better with the bodily response of Physical endeavour, since at the stage of creation or interpretation it is more of an ethereal experience than a tangible outcome. If someone is just perfecting a technique such as a wet into wet wash for a painting, or practising musical scale or playing a piece of music composed by someone else, this would not be identified as a creative response to a stimulus.

Mathematical creative endeavour involves a search for patterns in numbers and shapes as well as ways to create new patterns, calculations and solve problems in a mathematical context. This may involve spatial as well as mental agility.

Linguistic creative endeavour is more than the ability to speak or write proficiently. It must involve originality of ideas and expression, but certainly involves prose and poetry, fiction and non-fiction. Sometimes only poetry and fiction are seen as creative writing. All writing can be creative if the intended audience is matched to the way the ideas are expressed and presented. It may be as frivolous as Edward Lear or as serious as Kant.

Physical creative endeavour involves an activity where those involved have to make a novel and effective response to what they see or hear. This could be another person's serve in a game of tennis or a novel manoeuvre in a game of football. Of course, not all games of football are necessarily creative. If there is little creativity, the game will be dull, mechanical and without event. Individuals such as David Beckham and Tim Henman are more creative than others when devising and implementing tactics. Not all dances are creative: they may be just joyous, traditional celebrations of standard dance forms, or original bopping of no more value than a way to pass the time in a noisy night-club.

Here the term *Natural philosophical creative endeavour* covers the study of the physical universe which we now call science, as well as ideas about religious philosophy and ethics which were also debated by the Greeks under this term. The word *science* itself is simply the Latin word for knowledge, *scientia*, and until the 1840s what we now call science was *natural philosophy*, so even Isaac Newton's book on motion and gravity *The Mathematical Principles of Natural Philosophy*, published in 1687, used the term Natural Philosophy. Of course, skills required in the area of Linguistic creative endeavour may be needed as well to explain ideas, but if the achievement is more theoretical than linguistic then it should be recognized as such. Creativity in this area would focus on the construction of theory from experience, albeit at a child's level. Through inductive reasoning, building an agreed theory through first-hand experience and given explanations. If a pupil is not doing this for themselves, then they are just a technician, following a prescribed set of instructions for carrying out a test. In science lessons we need to help them come up with new theories and work towards a paradigm shift in their own experience. In later chapters in this book there will be ideas for stimulating creativity in each of these areas for teachers, groups and individuals.

3 Teachers' personal and professional creativity

> Teachers cannot develop the creative abilities of their pupils if their own creative abilities are suppressed.
>
> (NACCCE 1999: 90)

If we agree with NACCCE (1999: 30) that everyone has 'creative capacities', then we each have the responsibility to recognize and develop creativity in our own lives. If it is not developed, then it is suppressed. I suspect that few teachers or trainee teachers would think of themselves as creatively suppressed individuals, and yet every year, for each of the last six years, when I asked initial teacher trainees if they consider themselves to be creative, less than half answer affirmatively. By way of explanation most say they are not artistic, and many say they find it hard to think of new ideas. Despite all the publicity about creativity, all the books and articles written about various aspects of the subject, the majority of my trainees and even many of the teachers I speak to in my work, still seem to equate creativity with artistic ability and assume that if they cannot draw or produce artistic artefacts, they are not creative. On the positive side, all but two wished they were more creative. Further discussion revealed a narrow view of what creativity entails and that few trainees saw jobs such as architecture, engineering, or even teaching as having creative potential.

In this chapter we first consider the type of creativity that is needed by teachers in schools, both personally and professionally, and look at some areas of class organization where there may be room for experiment and innovation. The characteristics of creative teachers are discussed to help teachers identify the creative qualities they already have, as well as those they would like to develop, before looking at issues which may affect individual teacher creativity. Later in this chapter there is an audit to help teachers assess their current creative potential. There are also suggestions for activities to develop personal creativity in the six Areas of Creative Endeavour (ACE) identified in Chapter 2. We will consider the creative possibilities available to all, by the developing digital technologies. Finally, we look at ways of helping all the members of a school staff develop their creative potential as a team. The ideas in this chapter are not a list to be worked through and tried by everyone, but just examples of where developing teacher creativity can make the work more effective and more enjoyable.

Before you read the rest of this section, try this creative challenge.

Creative Challenge!
- Identify and list ways you feel you are currently creative.
- List areas in which you would like to be creative, even if you have never tried them before.
- Choose three areas in which to develop your creative potential.
- Once you have read this chapter, review and update your lists.

What sort of creativity is needed by teachers?

> Prospective teachers who are trained in thinking and teaching creatively and in creative problem-solving will be better prepared to value and nurture the same creative characteristics in their classrooms.
>
> (Abdallah 1996: 52)

The following kinds of creativity are needed by teachers:

- personal creativity;
- professional creativity.

Personal creativity

Teachers need both personal and professional creative skills. They need a personally creative base so that as role models and fulfilled individuals they are in a position to inspire a love of learning and exploration in their pupils. A person who is aware of their own creativity and uses it daily to solve problems, to find out more about their interests, to develop new skills and areas of expertise, is likely to be positive, passionate and involved with people. This does not mean they are necessarily euphoric extroverts, but those who are involved with developing aspects of their own creative potential are in a good position to be able to advise and inspire pupils who are doing the same. Being creative is a powerful feeling because it gives control over your problems and a direction for study or skills development whether in sport, science, art or any other area. Developing personal creativity can develop confidence as well as a fascination for a particular area of interest. All this makes life more fulfilling. Ideas are suggested at the end of this chapter to help to develop both the personal *and* professional creativity of the reader.

Professional creativity

Teachers need the same creative skills or abilities as those they are trying to develop in their pupils: the ability to ask questions, make connections, look at things in new ways, explore ideas and reflect on what they have learned.

The ability to ask questions ?

If they are not discouraged, young children ask questions all the time. This is a skill we should continue to develop in adult life. If we are always looking for new ways to do things and even pondering on questions such as the meaning of life, we can have an intellectually rich life of wondering, and wondering is the start to finding out. This style of thinking is characterized as 'possibility thinking' by Craft (2000). She sees it as the way to develop new ideas and creative thinking. Asking questions can involve analysis, synthesis and evaluation which are the higher-order thinking skills identified by Bloom et al. (1956). Consider the following questions in your current professional context. What further questions or answers do they suggest?

- What contributes to my most successful lessons?
- What systems would make the marking of children's work more efficient?
- If I allow the class to choose their own lines of enquiry in our next topic, how will I know this has been effective?
- How could I make more time for (you choose an idea)?

The ability to ask questions is a skill which requires curiosity. A creative person is always looking for new ways to do things and enjoys this exploration of ideas so that it is not a chore. A questioning stance helps us to move forward in understanding all we see and are challenged by. Having effective questioning skills is not just the ability to construct an interesting question, it involves suiting the question to the child at their intellectual stage of development to develop their thinking and questioning expertise. It is an essential competence to move pupils from lower- to higher-order thinking which is not only useful but intellectually satisfying. To do this with others, we need to be practising it daily for ourselves. It is an enjoyable and stimulating way of life, which requires drawing on relevant pedagogy, subject knowledge and thinking skills. By modelling effective questioning, we empower pupils to construct and then answer their own questions.

The ability to make connections

To make the most of the time in school, links should be made between teaching skills in one subject and using them in another. Learning to write or calculate or analyse in one project should be followed by developing these skills in a new venture. We should help them make connections, not only with prior learning in school but with skills, knowledge and ideas fostered in their home lives.

To develop a creative and cross-curricular style of teaching which motivates pupils, it is useful for a teacher to be able to spot connections between pupils' areas of interest and their curriculum needs. For example, presenting a science experiment in a Harry Potter context or creating a football themed dance in PE. When teaching on a Harry Potter or a detective theme, I found that pupils were easily involved and more likely to devise explanations for their ideas and come up with new questions to investigate when this approach was used. When we gave Year 6 a PowerPoint presentation showing plans for a theme park to be built in the grounds of Whitby Abbey as part of their residential locality study, they were required to discover the views of the residents, tourists, shop keepers and guardians of the abbey about the proposed development as well as consider historical, geographical and ecological issues. This lent relevance to the work and involved a wide range of pupil interests from those who were most interested in collecting fossils to those who were concerned about the lack of play space if the scheme went ahead. The consequent presentations and debate not only mirrored local government formalities, but developed speaking and listening and IT skills as well.

The creative teacher models the learning process as well as the teaching process in the classroom. We are spontaneous in responding to events such as a windy or snowy day or a distant earthquake. We build on the unexpected and things of immediate interest to the class. Although we won't disrupt plans to teach about the Tudors because Katy has brought in her new kitten to show the class, we can make the most of the event for a few minutes to build up their understanding about the characteristics of mammals and the way we should care for our pets. Many schools are now relaxing the subject boundaries in cross-curricular projects and enterprise activities in ways which build on skills learned in a several subject areas. Developing pupil autonomy is essential to help children develop control over their lives. Some schools allow classes to create their own curriculum through the questions they ask in areas of interest identified by the pupils. This calls for a great flexibility of approach while maintaining the development of a framework of key skills and knowledge.

The ability to look at things in new ways 👓

A key skill in being a successful teacher is the ability to organize. Looking at new ways to organize a class and its teaching is always useful. Consider the following areas with a creative eye to maximize learning and efficiency:

- Time
- Resources
- Making marking manageable
- Getting their attention
- Using computers
- Revitalizing topics.

Be creative with time!
With my own class, I felt that much time could be wasted with activities such as lining up or even taking the register. If you feel the same, use lining up time to practise alphabetical order, both forwards and backwards, by first and second name. Lining up by height or age can add interest to a dull activity. Once in line there was often time to listen to a favourite poem. Carole, a teacher colleague, improved the children's general knowledge by using registration time to teach geography. Each child was allocated a European country and a capital city. The teacher called out the country instead of the pupil's name and child responded with the capital city. After a week everyone moved to the next country on the register. By the end of half a term every child knew all the capitals in Europe and started on American or African capitals. For two minutes a day after registration children were invited to use a world map and tell the class three things they knew about 'their country'. It might be about the food, the clothes worn or just which other countries it bordered or which were south or west of it. By the end of the year they knew most of the capitals of the world as well as many facts about them. They particularly enjoyed astounding their parents with their extensive general knowledge. Carole adapted this idea to teach history facts as well. How might you adapt it?

Allocating story time for pupils to practise an art technique or illustrate the story being read can aid concentration and provide a more restful atmosphere than sitting on an overcrowded carpet and practising hair plaiting. Some craft techniques such as sewing can be practised in this way, and though it was always voluntary most of my pupils chose to do this for their story times. This is not to over-associate art and craft with creativity, but to suggest how time made be used imaginatively to aid concentration, reduce fidgeting and multi-task. Varying the activities chosen for the first few minutes after entering school or after a playtime can help to develop new ideas, e.g. discussing the artist of the week poster displayed on the IWB, or through collaborative puzzling over a maths challenge.

Creative Challenge!

Take a look at the unproductive or dull moments of time in your school and see how they can be made more engaging and useful.

Be creative with resources!

Look at different forms of waste and see if they might be useful as a school resource. The advice I give my trainees includes the brief to be mean with resources. By this I really intend that they should teach classes to use as little as they can, work from the edge of sheet materials and recycle all they can. If pupils do this, they will have a more extensive set of usable resources than any class in school. It will include pulled crackers, recycled wool, ribbons, jewellery and much more, stored in transparent (recycled, free) sweet jars to which pupils can help themselves as they need. Recycled wrapping paper has many uses. One person's waste is another's resource (Figure 3.1). In some

Figure 3.1 Flight display using recycled packaging and feathers and dead insects

areas, recycling centres exist just to pass on waste materials to schools and nurseries. Wood off-cuts, card, paper and other forms of waste can often be obtained from local manufacturers.

A collection of dead insects, shells, examples of lichen, feather, bone and stone, can be turned into a wonderful resource. Mount specimens on coloured paper or card and store them in transparent plastic boxes. Empty chocolate or cotton bud containers look like museum cases and can protect fragile specimens from exploring fingers. This means they can be used year after year. If one of these is put out in a small space with a magnifying glass, a relevant book or card with questions or added information you have an instant display which can be changed every few days. This habit has started many children making collection of their own or sparked an interest in natural history. Historical objects of interest collected from jumble sales or junk shops can provide a similar historical source of interest.

Be creative with marking!

It is not possible to mark 30 literacy and 30 numeracy books every day in worthwhile detail and have a home life as well. So plan to be creative with the marking! You might have one day a week when pupils mark their own work, one day when it can be peer marked, one day when what is done does not need marking and two days when it does. Marking can involve self- and peer assessment and target setting, as well as recording correct/incorrect answers and encouraging comments about achievement and progress. When this is not possible, try skim marking all 30 books looking for common problems to give general feedback before the next lesson, while giving quality advice and feedback to six pupils a day so that everyone gets useful rather than superficial comments and targets setting at least once a week. If they get less but more detailed feedback, it can make more of an impression, than a series of ticks and a stamped comment. If pupils put finished work in boxes labelled 'I can do this', or 'I need more help' then you will know where to put most of your attention. I have rarely found this system abused and knew who to double-check anyway.

Be creative in getting the attention of the class!

This is a basic competence which is a concern of many trainees. Try adapting the following strategies which have worked for me.

A bell or wind chime has a note higher than the human voice, but is friendlier than a shout. I gave my classes the choice between using a wind-chime or a loud voice to attract their attention and they invariably chose the chime. Since they had chosen the method, they responded to it better than a loud voice. If they became slow to respond, I counted the seconds it took for a response, marked this on the board and challenged them to improve their score next time. Trainees also find this works very well.

Another strategy is to give pupils something to do as a way to get their attention. 'Show me your pencil or pen' has the advantage that they all have to stop what they are doing and respond and you can see who has the equipment needed. I always model the behaviour I require such as holding up a pen, or protractor myself. If no equipment is required, then in any lesson, though especially in numeracy, getting the class to respond to the following commands with just their hands and fingers develops their mathematical knowledge as well as focusses their attention on a task seen as a game. For each task there is more than one possible response and other correct demonstrations are praised:

- Show me 6 fingers (or any number up to 10).
- Make me a finger triangle/circle/oval/semicircle.
- Show me your hands vertical/horizontal/diagonal.
- Show me your hands at right angles to/parallel to/above/below/beside each other.
- Make me a symmetrical/asymmetrical shape with your hands.

Now invent your own!

Be creative using computers!

In most lessons there is some form of recording done by pupils to embed and utilize recent learning. Whatever the majority of the class are doing by hand, see how the task can be adapted to computer use so that learners can make the most of the redrafting and editing features which IT affords. Such features along with templates, word banks and access to graphs and charts can release pupils from some of the tedium of the recording process so that creative ideas have space to flourish. Computers can allow original forms of recording through mind maps, diagrams and multimodal texts.

For many teachers, as well as trainees, becoming familiar with all the facilities afforded by a range of computer programs is a daunting challenge. These days, most pupils have a computer with a basic office suite either at home or in the local library, so get them to teach you and the rest of the class what they know. Better still, depending on what is being studied for the term, give pairs of pupils IT tasks to research. You can get ideas for suitable tasks using the help available on every machine. (Press F1 or the help button to see them.) Pupils can use this facility to find out what they need to know. Each day one child can demonstrate what they have learned for others to practise at home or in the next task set. In a word processing program, examples of useful tasks might be how to:

- colour the text;
- change the size or font of some text;
- move text;
- insert and colour a table;
- sort a list alphabetically;
- use the thesaurus;
- check spelling;
- alter spacing or layouts;
- insert and alter charts.

There are many other possibilities. Make your own list for spreadsheets, graphics, and presentation programs. Once you have been ingenious in helping them to learn these skills, they can make connections with other tasks to produce more original layouts and develop their ideas.

For programs available only in school, use these challenges, in a school computer club where you teach them the delights of a graphics or film-making package. It can stimulate their creativity if we show pupils that we teachers don't know everything and that this is nothing to be ashamed of as we still enjoy learning.

Be creative with revitalizing topics!

Many topics are taught year after year because the content is interesting for pupils and appropriate skills teaching can be integrated. Planning new topics from scratch is expensive and time-consuming. However, teachers may become bored with the same topics. Not every trip with Barnaby Bear is fascinating. The Tudors, mountains, designing picture frames, local studies, or any topic, however valuable, can lose vitality unless given a new slant. For any topic which could do with a new lease of life, consider how to update it:

- Could it start with a puzzle such as a mystery bag of objects with the connections between them to be found during the work?
- Could it begin with a letter from someone who requests a particular output such as a DVD of text, graphics and video summarizing the work? This might be sent to another school, possibly abroad, if it is a local study.
- Could it be run based on the pupils' enquiries, with pupils choosing questions to explore?
- Could it end in a competition between groups (not individuals) in a Dragons' Den type presentation?
- Could it result in a presentation – live/videoed? Or a radio broadcast?
- Could it be summarized in an exhibition for parents/other classes which would require interactive displays, models, electronic presentations, and live guided tours for other classes?

By taking a new angle on a familiar subject, you as a teacher are likely to be more enthused and this excitement will be transferred to the class. A new angle can also involve teaching more up-to-date skills involving ICT or improved research, drama or investigation skills.

The ability to explore ideas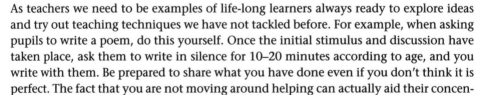

As teachers we need to be examples of life-long learners always ready to explore ideas and try out teaching techniques we have not tackled before. For example, when asking pupils to write a poem, do this yourself. Once the initial stimulus and discussion have taken place, ask them to write in silence for 10–20 minutes according to age, and you write with them. Be prepared to share what you have done even if you don't think it is perfect. The fact that you are not moving around helping can actually aid their concentration as no one sits there waiting for help.

Consider altering the focus of a subject such as Henry VIII and his wives into a persuasive competition for each wife (represented by a group of pupils) to show why each one should have been his one and only wife. Boys can be difficult to inspire in dance lessons, but if the project is styled as a Britain's Got Talent project, they are quite likely to want to learn new steps and build up an exciting routine. Look at all problem-atical areas in school and try to see them as creative challenges. For example, problems with wet playtimes and how pupils can entertain themselves without becoming too noisy or even aggressive? Solutions might be:

- class rules for behaviour written and monitored by pupils;
- children go to other classes for a change of scene in rooms designated for board games or drawing or reading or learning magic tricks or simple science activities;
- dancing in the hall;
- older children reading to younger ones.

Whatever the problem, we need to model the creative process from the identification of the problem, through looking at possible solutions, utilizing thinking time and evaluating ideas. Talking through problem-solving from our home lives, if appropriate, can also help to model a creative approach to life.

I have always tried to get my pupils to identify ways to improve the running of the class and its facilities. As a result, different classes have found ways to put the anti-glare nets on strings and rollers for ease of use; made wooden shelving and containers for woodwork and sewing tools. One group of boys noticed that the computers were becoming dusty and used a sewing machine to make covers for keyboard, monitor and printer. Every class organized its own tidying rota so that the cleaners had as little to do in my room as possible at the end of each day. With this approach to problem-solving, one of my Year 4 classes surprised me. Wood off-cuts and tools were always available for use and pupils were trained in construction techniques and we had had several wet playtimes, well supervised by lunchtime staff. I am not very tall, and my blackboard was sited high on the wall so I could not reach the top. One afternoon I returned to the class to be presented with a very solid, step-up so that I could reach the top of the board. It had been drilled, screwed, sanded and varnished to a high standard. The whole class seemed to have been involved with different aspects of its design and construction and I used it for many years.

The ability to reflect

One aspect of practice which many teachers do regularly is reflecting on their work. Sadly this is too often done in a negative way, aided by OFSTED evaluations and government reports which tell us we are not up to scratch and should be doing more of this and less of that. It is right that we should always be looking for ways to improve and develop our practice, just as I hope my doctor, dentist and MP are doing. I also think we should try to do it in the same way as we would with a class of children: see what they are doing well and build on it, as well as identifying ways to do things differently. I suggest that at the end of each week teachers ask themselves the following questions:

- What went really well and why?
- In what ways did I enable pupils to develop their creativity or initiative, or encourage problem-solving?

- What aspects of their creativity were developed?
- What opportunities for original ideas did I give them in maths/science/the humanities?
- How can I build on this next week/term?
- What was the most creative outcome of the week for a group/an individual?

Sharing such evaluations with colleagues informally over a cup of coffee can be an encouraging way to end a week. Involving yourself with classroom-based action research projects, possibly as part of a master's course, is another way to develop teaching skills. I have found that communicating my ideas and results of small-scale research projects to my classes inspires them to investigate ideas of their own. They have always seemed pleased to know they were helping a university-based project, something wider than their current world.

We should also remember to model the reflective process for pupils so they do not think it is something just to be done in school which identifies what they are doing wrong. If we talk about the ways we are trying to improve our performance out of school, whether in a sporting, culinary or choral, context, they will see this is an adult process.

The characteristics of creative teachers

Teresa Cremin, cited in Wilson (2007), reports that a study by Creative Partnerships in Kent noted that the *teachers' personal characteristics*, their *pedagogy* and *the class or school ethos* were the three interrelated factors which most affected teacher creativity. Cremin looks at the characteristics of creative teachers as identified by Grainger et al. in 2006. which noted that such teachers exhibit the following attributes:

- curiosity and a questioning stance;
- the ability to make connections;
- autonomy and ownership of their teaching;
- originality both in themselves and others;
- ability to use their creative capacity in a classroom context.

Considering each of these features in the light of a teacher's personal qualities, the pedagogy employed and the ethos of the class or school, Cremin instructs teachers to develop their own creativity so they are able to identify and reward creativity in others. To do this, some practical starting points are suggested below.

The personal characteristics of teachers are central to the way they work, and their ability to model creative development and inspire it in their pupils. If you feel you do not have as much curiosity as you'd like, or wish to pursue a wider range of interests, take a look at what already interests you and in what new directions you might look. An interest in travel, an aspect of natural history or the arts might be inspired by a friend, or watching a TV programme or just the need to find out about a subject in order to teach it well. There are so many things to be excited by and involved with in life, whether it is making things, growing plants, computing, reading or discussing ideas with friends. Enthusiasm is infectious and pupils readily respond to the inspirations of their teachers. My classes often developed enthusiasms for collecting rocks, identifying plants or creating their own toys and games because those were some of my interests which I shared with them. On residential trips children clamoured to identify every lump of rock, brick, and even concrete on the beach! In my colleagues' classes they would be more inclined to take up a new sport, try out a musical instrument or become interested in collecting something else. It didn't matter what we involved them in as long as we communicated enthusiasms for subjects and ideas outside ourselves. As a result, pupils were exposed to a wide range of ideas from which to choose their own interests and passions. It is sad but true that as Susan Ertz commented in the 1920s, 'Millions dream of immortality, who do not know what to do with a rainy Sunday afternoon.'

Creative teachers are good at making connections between learning in one subject and ways it may be applied in another. They try to personalize the learning situation for the interests of classes or even individuals and bring their personal experiences, anecdotes and ideas to share with their classes. Children enjoy hearing about the books their teacher read as a child and seeing photos of their younger selves. They are more likely to be inspired by a teacher fresh from a weekend trip to a local sculpture park enthusiastically talking about an exhibition there and inviting ways to make similar constructions, than being given a standard lesson on sculpture which is no longer fresh. Ideally the class should be taken to the same venue.

The most difficult connection may be for pupils with EAL who have little idea of the content of some parts of a lesson. A recent trainee of mine, faced with two pupils recently arrived from Poland who had almost no understanding of English, went further than my initial suggestion to use an Internet translation site to procure a few phrases to help them on a regular basis. I suggested teaching the whole class some basic Polish phrases such as daily greetings, instructions to line up, and praise for involvement. Sarah decided to translate all basic instructions and information on her whiteboard presentations as well. The new pupils came on in leaps and bounds and other pupils developed a greater understanding of their friends' linguistic isolation as well as an enjoyment of starting to learn a new language.

A teacher who is creative will takes risks, be open to new ideas, share the success or development of these ideas with a class and model a curious and creative approach to life, often wondering aloud about an idea or a new way to try something. Cremin suggests that 'Although good teachers recognise the importance of inventiveness, creative teachers see the development of creativity and originality as the distinguishing mark of their teaching' (2007: 3).

The pedagogy of a teacher will be dictated to some extent by the culture of the school which may determine the organization of pupils, the structure of the day, or even of lessons. Particular teaching strategies such as using the TASC wheel (see p. 77) or Thinking Hats skills (see p. 86) or Enterprise activities (see p. 135) may be required as part of a whole school strategy, or introduced by teachers keen to explore a new approach. In lessons, teachers should use questioning strategies to help pupils explore their ideas and develop new suggestions and questions of their own. Brainstorming, talking partners, using metaphors and analogy and encouraging higher-order thinking with 'what if?' and 'how can?' questions can help the class do this.

Which personal characteristics do you see as instrumental in developing the creativity of a class? My list would include:

- *imagination* to visualize other possibilities;
- *willingness* to foster an atmosphere where risk taking and things not working out as expected are not regarded as failure but as a part of the learning experience. Ask pupils about ways to improve your teaching and what they most enjoy. Anonymous, half-term surveys are useful for this. Class discussions in circle time may produce useful results as well.
- *honesty* which does not confuse teacher creativity with that of the children so that they end up merely following instructions to do something or decorating her designs;
- *tenacity*: we exercise muscles to keep them fit and we need to exercise and develop our creative skills and train our brains to adopt a creative way of life, so we are constantly asking questions, and looking at others' ideas with a positive but critically evaluative eye.

Creative Challenge!
Make your own list of characteristics you feel the creative teacher needs to have.
Which do you have?
Which would you like to develop?

Recognizing individual teacher creativity

To help you act as a creative role model, we need to identify the creative abilities you already have and those you wish to develop. It is a problem that many teachers do not see themselves as creative individuals because they perceive creativity to be a feature of arts and crafts-based skills rather than an enquiring, exploratory, reflective and problem-solving approach to life.

Research by Bronte (1997) and by Kastenbaum (1997) into creativity in later life, reported in Kerka (1999), suggests there is no reason why the creative development of healthy adults should not continue throughout their lives. In fact, creative activity has been found to improve mental health and happiness. Kerka also reports on gender differences in creative output, as men and women may have different constraints on their creativity. This is sometimes due to lack of education and training or to parenting roles. She notes that some people attain creative peaks at later ages or that a secondary peak often occurs after the late sixties.

Assess your potential

So now that you know that it is never too late to start or to continue your creative development and that this can be beneficial to your health and well-being, let us look at ways to take this development forward. First consider your interests. Which have creative potential in the classroom and which could you develop further in your personal life?

If you are interested in popular culture, IT, sport, travel, national heritage, or some other activity, then you already have something you can build on. Don't underestimate the creative skills, talents and thinking processes, in which you are already experienced, whether it is being able to adapt a recipe, re-design a garden, or organize your own working/living areas. Maybe you have an interest in photography or like to exhibit original tactics in competitive sports? Each of these is an area on which you can build and in which you can inspire others.

Creative skills audit

In this creative skills audit, you first need to list your personal interests and then take a look at some of the skills and attitudes below which are useful in developing a creative outlook and lifestyle (Table 3.1). Which of these do you do well? Which do you need to develop? Rate yourself from 1 to 5, with 1 being the lowest score. Which of these characteristics would you like to develop? Put a star * beside them.

Table 3.1 Creative skills audit

	Assess and score 1–5	
Find it hard to think of questions about a subject		Constantly curious and questioning
Find it hard to apply what you have learned to new situations		Making connections
Like to be told what to do		Prefer to plan own work and be autonomous
Find it hard to think of new ideas; not very imaginative		Enjoy devising original ideas, imaginative
Prefer strong organization		Flexible in style, pace and approach
Lack confidence in your ideas		Confident in judgement
Not very intuitive		Use intuition
Prefer to play it safe		Enjoy risk taking
Find it hard to concentrate on a task		Easily become preoccupied with a task
Easily discouraged		Very persistent
Prefer to conform		Like to be different
Little excites you		Enthusiastic and passionate
Do not feel very creative		See yourself as a creative being
See failure as a negative experience		Perceive failure as a learning opportunity
Have grown out of play		Enjoy play and exploration of new materials games, equipment
Like all class experiences to be well planned		Enjoy spontaneity alongside planning
Not resourceful		Resourceful
Have just a few interests		Have a wide range of interest and passions
Feel stupid if you do not know all the answers		Share the fact that you don't know all the answers
Never use analogy or metaphor		Enjoy analogy and metaphor
TOTAL score out of a possible 100		

- What *positive* message does this give you? Do you already have many creative skills or do you have plenty of scope for developing more?
- In which areas do you score highest? These are your most creative skills.
- Which three areas would you most like to develop?
- How might you do this?
- What help would you need to do this?

Creative Challenge!

What areas, skills, interests have you never had time to develop, but would like to take further? Aim to take up something new and then decide how to go about it. Perhaps:
- Join a club, e.g. sports or knitting, etc.
- Go on a course, e.g. night school, residential holiday or master's module.
- Start something new with a friend.
- Read something new.
- Reorganize one or more areas of your life.

Join other members of your school staff to develop as a group. It can be difficult to rise above uncreative traditions in a school without the support of like-minded professionals.

Whatever you decide, it will be easier and more enjoyable if you can involve your family and perhaps your friends in what you are doing in some way. In the case of people with children, this is an excellent way to help bring them up in a creative way of life.

4 Developing teacher creativity

Developing teacher creativity in each Area of Creative Endeavour

To develop teacher creativity, we first need to develop personal creativity. Here are some suggestions for ways to develop your personal creativity in six Areas of Creative Endeavour (ACE). Creativity is a way of life. It requires habit, effort, time, thought and review, knowledge, a willingness to take risks as well as domain-related skills. Bear in mind that all Areas of Creative Endeavour require some knowledge and skills on which to base development. Each ACE requires its own skills, so that logical deduction skills which might be required for creativity in the Mathematical or Natural Philosophical domains might be less useful for artistic or physical creativity. If you lack knowledge and skills in mathematics, music or physical activities, it may be necessary to acquire the domain-related knowledge on which to build your creative exploration. Remember that it is the process which is as valuable, if not more valuable than the final draft, because with the process you are building yourself, but the product is merely evidence of a stage in that development which may be out of date within minutes of its creation due to further reflection and evaluation. As Leonardo da Vinci said, 'A work of art is rarely finished, it is merely abandoned.'

Now we turn to some creative ideas for developing personal creativity in each ACE.

Technological

1   Re-plan your personal workspace to include at least one interesting artefact/picture you have not had there before. This could be a piece of old machinery, an arrangement of shells or stones, a piece of driftwood – whatever is pleasing to you artistically and might stimulate new ideas. Reorganize your bookshelves according to their subject matter, writer/some other way to find what you need.

2   Design a new road sign to deal with something you find annoying while in a car.

3   Design your ideal car. Don't worry about the mechanics of this – a labelled diagram of your personal motoring wish-list is the goal. Share this with your class and ask for their versions.

4   Create a new soup or salad from a basic recipe using at least two new ingredients you have never used before, e.g. fruit, vegetables, herbs or spices.

5   Invent a board game for your class/family/friends to play which involves either a subject you teach or a personal interest of yours/the group.

6   Model your ideal garden either using ICT tools or with plasticine or waste recyclable materials.

7   Create a system for organizing your holiday information which includes sections on what to take, insurance, proposed destinations, and bookings. This could be a hard copy or IT file.

Artistic

1   Make a model of a creative person, using just card, pipe-cleaners, a modelling medium such as plasticine or Blutac, and other materials to hand. This will not show their actual appearance, but will exemplify their creative characteristics such as tenacity, the ability to come up with novel ideas and perhaps features of the subject area in which they are creative. This is an exercise I have done regularly at the start of a creativity course (Figure 4.1), and once the students

Figure 4.1   A model of a creative person showing aspects of their personality

understand they should model an idea rather than a person, their own creativity as well as their ideas of what creativity entails develop in unexpected ways. They start to recognize some of the different facets of creativity; that some of their friends and relatives exhibit creative flair; that creativity involves trial and error, domain-related skills, persistence and ingenuity.

2   Create a cartoon character to represent yourself. You do not have to be a good artist to do this as you are not trying to make someone who looks exactly like yourself, but rather a symbolic character along the lines of the Mr Men series which could be reproduced quickly with the addition of a speech bubble to show what you are saying or thinking. This could be done by hand or on a computer. If done on a computer, the results could be saved and used when sending messages to friends or to lighten up an instruction to the class. It might even be an animal or animated shape. For years I have used a simple cat face, usually hand-drawn, to do this (Figure 4.2).

3   Create a computer cartoon of yourself. Figure 4.3 is my attempt to create my character using draw tools. It does not look like me apart from the unruly hair-do, but can be used to show pupils how to create a cartoon character which might be used to record their ideas about learning in different subjects.

4   Use your phone or digital camera to take photos of familiar places and objects from new angles: above/below/inside, looking up or down on them/zooming in to see details often ignored. Can your family/class guess what they are?

Figure 4.2 My cartoon cat

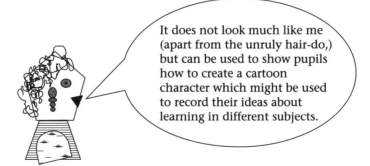

Figure 4.3 My cartoon self

5   Take digital photos of yourself or a friend which shows their personality. What different aspects of their personality could you show in the way? (This would make a very personal present.)

6   Cut parts of pictures from magazines to create a fantasy collage of a place you would like to visit, or better still hate to visit! (More imagination is probably required for the latter.)

7   Create a still-life arrangement for a place in your home or garden of objects from natural materials such as cones/shells/plant/stones/metal items which interest you.

8   Learn three chords which you can play on a guitar or keyboard, or using musical software. Add other notes which complement them. This does not have to be a repeatable composition, just an experience which will improve with practice. Type *on line musical software* into Google to see what you can find.

Mathematical

1   List all the ways you can find to add or multiply two numbers, e.g. 35 + 68 . . . You could count on, add the tens and units separately, start with the larger number, round up and adjust the numbers and so on. With 65 × 45, how might rounding, doubling, dividing or other operations help?

2   Consider the problem described by Debbie Robinson and Valsa Koshy in their chapter 'Creative mathematics: allowing caged birds to fly' in Fisher and Williams' *Unlocking Creativity* (2004), when a group of children were asked whether they would prefer to be a decimal or a fraction. What would your response be and why? Discuss your ideas with a friend. Your answers could help you to see some of the problems children have in understanding the relationships between the two types of fraction and their comprehension of number families and calculations.

3   List as many ways as you can to solve a problem about household budgeting. For instance, you could use a spreadsheet, keep manual accounts, use a calculator and what else? Decide which is most appropriate for you and plan a holiday or gift-list budget.

4   Use a multimedia programme such as PowerPoint to make a short presentation showing the relationship between different fractions such as halves, eighths and quarters. Use the animation features to make it dynamic and use when teaching equivalent fractions to a class. If you do not know how to do this, open the program you want to use, Press F1 or the Help button on your computer and type 'create animation' into the dialogue box. This will bring up advice to help you to do this.

5   Devise a mnemonic or rhyme to help remember a mathematical formulae or calculation method. For instance, 'To read a grid of reference squares, go along the hall and up the stairs' (i.e. use horizontal axis number before vertical axis number).

6   Invent a mathematical game which uses dice or playing cards and particular types of mathematical calculation. See if the children you teach can improve the game in some way.

Linguistic

1   Invent some new words to describe how you feel or things around you, e.g. chillaxation is what you might want to do on holiday after you've had a spell of excitomania or museofatigue. An estanphidelphia is a type of plant I invented during my 11+ examination English paper, and have transplanted it for different purposes several times since then!

2   Take a popular poem such as 'The Owl and the Pussycat' and rewrite it in another context replacing one word at a time, but maintaining the original rhythm and rhyme scheme. Write it with a friend or particular audience in mind, even if you do not read it to them, e.g.

> The cat and the kangaroo went for a trip
> On a bicycle made for two.
> They took some meats and plenty of sweets
> Wrapped up with paper and glue.
> The cat looked up to the moon above
> And sang to a small banjo
> How we love to ride and cycle beside,
> The hills and the valleys below, you know
> While singing sad songs as we go.

> It can be fun to do this with limericks as well.

3   Read a poem such as: Jenny Joseph's popular 'When I am old I shall wear purple', or 'How to paint a perfect Christmas' by Miroslav Holub (both easily found on-line) and write your own version. Don't try to make it rhyme, just use the fewest number of words you can to convey what you want to say. Avoid words which end in 'ing' to keep the writing immediate and vivid. Use precise nouns such as oak or sparrow if required, rather than vague ones such as tree or bird.

4   Practise writing a short story or a 'Thank you' letter to a travel company in no more than 300 words using 6 nouns or adjectives found at random in a dictionary/other book to hand. We often ask pupils to write imaginatively at short notice on topics we have selected. It can be quite daunting to take up a similar challenge oneself, and a useful exercise in developing imaginative ideas and connections.

5   Compose a poem or acrostic about yourself which refers to your past, present and future fears, pleasures and aspirations. Try to start some lines with prepositions to give a sense of direction and movement. Edit words which are inessential to the sense of the finished work.

6   Start a loose-leaf or electronic reflective diary on developing your own creativity. Start by looking at where you feel you are and assessing your current creative skills. Identify areas you would like to develop, and reflect daily or weekly on your actions and progress in each area.

7   There are many excellent books on the market which give guidance and direction to anyone wanting to develop their creative writing. I have found those by

Sandy Brownjohn especially effective and each exercise is worth trying out in a personal context by the teacher, before trying them with a class of pupils not only to appreciate the problems and possibilities involved, but to develop their own creative writing as well. For those who would like to take their writing further, there are many excellent writing courses in all genres, such as those run by the Arvon Foundation.

Physical

1   Find some music you like and develop a keep-fit routine to develop your own strength, stamina and flexibility.
2   If you go to a gym, devise your own circuit training routine. If not, work out an outdoor exercise routine of jogging or walking combined with stretching exercises at specific points.
3   Find out about simple orienteering activities and devise an orienteering exercise for your school grounds or a local park or woodland. Try it out with a class, cubs group or a group of friends.
4   Take up yoga or Pilates or another form of exercise by going to a class and then building your own daily routine from the basic exercises and positions. If you belong to a sports club, try to develop innovative tactics to improve your individual score or the team score for the sport.
5   Look at your current lifestyle and see how many ways you can improve your current strength, stamina and suppleness with small adjustments to your routines, e.g. taking the stairs, not the lift, getting off the bus one stop early, taking a lunch hour walk, devising stretching exercises for every hour spent at your desk, starting all PE lessons with a warm-up routine where pupils follow your actions.
6   Devise a new set of indoor/outdoor games activities which you could use with your current class and currently available resources in your school. You could use this as a basis for asking pupils to attempt a similar challenge.

Natural philosophical

1   List questions to which you would like answers about this world/universe and list ways you might find some of the answers. Follow up your ideas.
2   Devise an experiment to find the crunchiest crisp or the longest lasting mint sweet.
3   Find out about the factors which affect how long sun-tan lotion remains effective on the skin, or which hand cream is most efficacious. Devise a test to find which lotion is most suitable for you.
4   Investigate a moral issue such as factory farming, chocolate production or recycling and work out your rationale on the issue from different viewpoints such as a producer, a consumer or those involved in any stage of production.

5   Read up about the current knowledge on the size of the universe and work out a scale to try to explain this to children.

6   Whatever your religious or philosophical belief, list reasons both to believe and not to believe in a deity, an afterlife, a spirit world or another controversial area of belief.

Developing the creativity of all school staff

It is easier for individual members of staff to develop their creativity if this is part of a whole school ethos which recognizes the creative potential of every staff member, including the caretaker, dinner and kitchen staff, secretary, governors, teachers and head teacher. Each of these is likely to have skills and interests which can be shared and developed for the benefit of the whole school. In some schools the caretaker or a talented parent leads on making resources for the school or the kitchen staff advise and help with food technology sessions. This does not just result an individual's skill being recognized, but provides a whole school resource and example and helps to show that all members of staff are valued by pupils and colleagues. There may be INSET sessions which can be run by a non-teaching member of staff, or a session where they would feel valued and able to develop themselves if they were able to attend: a session on digital photography or creative cookery, for example.

It is becoming common practice to work in year groups or Key Stage teams. To improve group creativity, Mauzy (2006) advocates improving the creative abilities of individuals within an organization. He defines creativity as the ability of an individual to create new, relevant ideas and perspectives and has worked with corporate groups to develop the creativity of individuals using a range of techniques. He identifies four stages in the creative development process.

1   Understand the processes involved in creative thinking. (A visual model may help here.)

2   Identify an individual's blocks to creative thinking.

3   Practise techniques to develop new ideas.

4   Foster an atmosphere where an individual's ideas are valued and people feel they can achieve goals, both personal and professional.

Metacognition is thinking about our thinking processes and knowing about when and how to use particular strategies for learning or for problem-solving. Mauzy (2006) believes that the metacognition in understanding the creative process is essential to developing the process further. He advocates creating visual models such as diagrams or flowcharts to help people work out their own creative cycles and the factors which affect them. Craft (2001) suggests that adults who act as role models by providing learners with an apprenticeship approach to developing creativity are a powerful aid to fostering pupil creativity. We must lead by example, and the mentor may be not just the teacher but another adult or even another pupil. Every class is likely to have pupils or parents with interests and expertise they can share.

Developing the professional creativity of individual teachers

Ideas to further develop your professional creativity

Table 4.1 presents some ideas for furthering your professional creativity. Try them all.

Table 4.1 Developing your creativity

	Suggestion
? Ask questions	Develop a small-scale piece of research in your school which aims to find out about the best way to develop the creativity of the children
Make connections	Apply to your local university to work as a university link tutor, visiting other schools to support trainees on placement. This will help develop your own creative practice as well as theirs as you discover new ways to teach and learn Find out about local CPD in this field and experiment with what you learn in your own school
See things in new ways	Ask your classes about ways they like to learn and follow these suggestions when appropriate Ask your friends and colleagues, or even the class, how they think writers, scientists, artists as well as people in business and the media might teach similar subjects
Explore ideas	Develop at least one new IT technique every term Try out new teaching techniques regularly to see which are most effective
Reflect	Reflect regularly. If this is done in diary form, it could provide the basis for reflective reviews as part of CPD which can lead to higher qualifications Look critically at all aspects of your classroom organization to see how it can be altered to make the time, space, resources and displays work more effectively

Developing the professional creativity of a staff team

- Find out what areas of expertise there are among the school staff or among parents and learn from them. Check with the secretary, caretaker, teaching assistants and others to see who has interests or talents they are willing to share.
- See what resources can be acquired locally for free, e.g. wood from a local manufacturer, or other local recycling centre: think of new ways to use them.
- Link with another school/cluster to share best practice ideas.

- Encourage CPD/staff INSET sessions with feedback to the rest of the staff.
- Learn from teacher trainees who will often bring new ideas and skills to a school.

Suggestions for head teachers to encourage their staff

- Lead by example and try out some new ideas for running the school from a suggestions box with contributions from staff and pupils.
- Encourage staff to continue their learning through CPD opportunities.
- Invest in INSET days where all members of staff are able to learn about the nature of creative practice.
- Hold INSET days where the staff try out new skills at their level such as creative writing, sculpting or digital photography.
- Praise staff when they do something risky and creative.
- Give opportunities to try out new media, with a teaching and follow-up task required.
- Give weekly/termly time, e.g. 2 hours a month, to experiment without pressure to produce visible outcomes . . . a verbal report might suffice.
- Take it in turn for different staff to lead meetings, or to bring in an idea which works in a staff show and tell session.
- All change is risky. In a creative direction it may seem even more risky. Encourage a climate where it is OK to take risks and OK not to succeed every time.
- Encourage staff to work with the local university on teacher training. This can help to keep people up-to-date, gives them influence in the selection of teacher recruits, and may enable them to help supervise trainees on placement which is a good way to learn from others' professional practice, by sharing ideas.
- One of the most enjoyable and rewarding CPD opportunities I have had was during an Advanced Skills Teacher (AST) creativity development course run by CAPE UK. In groups of five or six, we were asked to explore Leeds and create a presentation. We were given a digital camera, an audio recorder, a movie camera and £10. One group explored by going alternatively right, left, right, left from the hotel door recording visual and oral items of interest to be used in a presentation. The money bought an assortment of souvenirs to represent the many places of interest found in this random exploration. Another group navigated the city using a large dice which they threw at each road junction to determine if they should go on/right/left/take a picture/interview someone or buy something. One group worked on the theme of circles and others on different cultural or problematic aspects of the city. We each discovered fascinating details about Leeds which a normal guide-book or city walk could have not given us. The presentations were diverse and eye-opening. Perhaps your staff would enjoy a similar challenge or one where an unusual object has to be included into another type of activity such as a drama, radio broadcast or exhibition in such a way that it is not out of place?

A whole school approach to developing creativity

> For school leaders the first step in developing a creative school is the fostering of a whole-school approach. Creativity is not an add-on and it cannot be imposed by the head teacher. There needs to be discussion, involvement and ownership.
>
> (http://www.teachingexpertise.com/articles/creativity-in-the-curriculum-156, accessed October 2011)

For school leaders, the first step in developing a creative school is the fostering of a whole-school approach. Creativity is a foundation stone not an add-on and it cannot be imposed by the head teacher. There needs to be discussion, involvement and ownership. The staff needs to feel that they have ownership of the curriculum they teach and the curriculum needs to be one where creativity is recognized as a central element of learning for every pupil and in all subjects. Ways to motivate both staff and pupils to develop their creative potential need to be found and put into practice. Parents and governors should be involved so they understand that some of the practices their children describe do more than achieve academic results. Creativity should be a part of the staff development programme, and the professional development of all the staff, both teaching and non-teaching should be regularly updated so they can make the most of new technologies and share creative practice.

How does your school deal with creativity?

- Does your school improvement planning framework (SIPF) refer to the creative development of staff, pedagogy or pupil development?
- How involved are pupils in organizing the curriculum and in a creative approach to learning and teaching?
- Does your school plan visits to galleries and plan projects in school involving artists, technologists, sportspeople and craftspeople?
- Does your school celebrate and promote creativity to a wider audience such as families and the community?

Managing creativity

Head teachers who use intrinsic motivation and create the right climate for developing adult as well as pupil creativity in their schools will find that this is the most effective way to improve results. To do this, they need to ensure that the people they manage have the right amount of challenge and the freedom to meet it in their own way. Adequate resources which include time as well as money are essential to develop creative practices. The adults in a school must work as a team, and changing the composition of the teams to include people with diverse talents can help spark new ideas as well as share expertise. Organizational support which includes regular encouragement should acknowledge effort as well as results. Research by Rasulzada and Dackert (2009) showed that enhancing the conditions for creativity and innovation in an organization is beneficial for the individual in terms of improved psychological well-being. The happier the members of staff are, the happier and more effective the whole staff is likely to be. In her article, 'Doing what you love and loving what you do', Amabile (1997) suggests that to enable creativity in our work, we need two conditions: first, we must maintain our intrinsic motivation by finding work which matches our expertise, interests and creative thinking skills; second, we must find a work environment that will support an exploration of new ideas.

Conclusion

Teachers need both personal and professional creativity if they are to be successful in inspiring their pupils' creative development. They also need creativity in organizing their classes and workspaces effectively. They need to develop the same creative five behaviours in themselves which they promote in those they teach. When trying to develop the skill of looking at things in new ways, a useful starting point is to see how the *time* spent on routine tasks can be reorganized for the benefit of all. Using computers to save time and communicate effectively may mean teachers updating their skills. Not only the pupils, but administrative staff or parents may be able to help with this. The characteristics of creative teachers are not those of professional artists and often go unrecognized as creative attributes by those who possess them. We all have the potential to be creative and can develop the necessary attitudes and attributes as well as new skills if we are willing to do so. With the right frame of mind, context-related skills as well as intrinsic motivation, anyone can expand their creative capability. It is much easier to do this, when working in an organization which has a whole school approach to creativity and where managers lead by example in an encouraging and supportive way. Creativity is a way of life, a set of skills to practise daily where we are always looking for new questions and interesting ways to answer them. As Robert J. Sternberg and Wendy Williams (1996) note: 'The most powerful way to develop creativity in your students is to be a role model. Children develop creativity not when you tell them to, but when you show them.'

5 Group creativity

This chapter looks at the differences between group, individual and personal creativity, their features and how each has been defined by experts and targeted in research. The ways in which groups behave and interact and how people within these groups may perform both as individuals and group members deserve consideration in the context of primary education as children strive to develop both a personal identity and their place within their peer group. Pupils are under pressure to develop personal excellence as well as peer-cooperation skills. These can raise conflicting demands so that the development of personal creativity may be hindered by issues both inside and outside the classroom. A number of strategies are suggested to develop creative thinking, questioning skills, and ways to help groups of learners make connections, see things in new ways, explore ideas and reflect on their creative development. Throughout there are practical suggestions for developing group creativity in the six areas of creative endeavour and ways to use ICT for creative development.

Factors affecting individual and group creativity

Although groups are composed of individuals, groups may think and behave very differently from the individuals of which they are formed. Consider the actions of football crowds, armies, governments or businesses that act as groups in ways they might not as individuals. In a school, groups can be more daring, vocal, and excitable than single pupils while individuals may be more cautious or adventurous with their ideas. Groups may be quicker to start ideas, but find it harder to focus on them: they are less likely to dry up but less reflective as well. There is more ownership of ideas for individuals or a small group, while there is a wider range of skills and ideas to draw on from within a larger group. In a group, an individual's ideas can be validated at once, rather than waiting for teacher feedback so this can reduce dithering time. However, good ideas may get lost to more vocal, but less useful contributions. Group members can share skills and imitate best performers, thus increasing group productivity. Pupils in a group can feel a shared responsibility for plans but may lose individual ownership of particular ideas or be unwilling to share very personal ones. Ultimately the success of a group depends on the skill of the individuals in it, so we must make provision for the development of both groups and individuals.

A study by Galton et al. in 1999 concluded that the pattern of classroom interactions in the primary school had made little progress in the past 20 years. The survey found that whole class teaching was dominated by low-level questioning and that although children were ostensibly organized into small groups, most children still worked individually. Research by Hardiman et al. (2003) found that, rather than promoting higher levels of discussion and interaction, teachers rarely extended or even encouraged children's contributions in group work. For group work to be valuable, the classroom climate must enable all learners to feel part of a learning community to which they can contribute and in which problems can be solved by group effort. Real group work is more than a seating plan arrangement of children who are sharing resources. Real group work might involve pupils working in cooperative groups on separate tasks to achieve a class objective or in collaborative groups as they work on similar tasks to achieve a group objective. They might be working on discussions, at a problem solving or production-type challenge. For a discussion-type task there could be a controversial or interpretive activity based on a poem, story or article resulting in a group decision or the development of individual social skills and personal ideas. With a problem solving task or investigative challenge, each group might approach the work in a different way which would give scope for differentiated activities. With a production-type task, each group might be involved in a different part of the production according to their interests or abilities.

The ideal group size will vary with context, but it needs to be large enough to build on the differing skills of its members, while being small enough for every member to feel valued and able to contribute. The best group size may be just three pupils in science with one to test, one to observe and measure, and one to record. With a multimedia project, or a local study, the optimum group size will depend on the number of tasks to do or the resources available. For recording learning in some contexts, pairs might be sufficient and easiest to help. Studies by Björkman (2004) and Wiltermuth (2008) have shown that a team benefits from a range of skills and interests and that the composition of the groups should be changed regularly. The latter notes that in adult contexts, individuals tend to produce fewer ideas and ideas of lower quality when in groups than they do individually.

We regularly teach classes as whole groups but ask pupils to respond individually. Try asking yourself for each task you set, 'Would it be more appropriate to require a group or an individual response?' It may be quicker to answer group queries and give group feedback, so all individuals benefit from this. On the other hand, some members of a group may freeload or distract. Individual marking of work requires considerable time and may not elicit an immediate response from a pupil, even if it is read. Time saved on individual marking can be put into a detailed response for a group effort which could give all members of a group more extensive and effective feedback to be discussed and responded to by the group. Reflection is a key creative skill and pupils can be more willing to reflect and learn from critical feedback if they feel it is not an attack on them personally. Frequently in school the outcome seems to be of prime importance, while the process is downplayed. Too often, the final mark rather than the development of ideas measures a learner's success. For a group response individuals in that group can try out, model and share ideas, a process from which all members can learn. Teaching groups is a means to an end: the end being the education of the individual.

Some learners prefer to work on an individual basis either because they do not want to have their ideas diluted, or they prefer to keep the credit and ownership of them, or they do not want to be distracted by group dynamics. These individuals are more likely to take risks and try out unusual ideas to which a group may not subscribe.

Although there are times when everyone should have to work both individually or in groups, at other times it can be beneficial to let classes choose how they will organize their learning so that some work in groups, while others work on their own if they wish. A mix of methods can develop different creative responses. A one-minute think time for individuals, followed by a short time with paired development of ideas before sharing with the rest of the group, may aid personal inspiration as well as group creativity.

While teachers must educate the whole class, simultaneously they have the responsibility to nurture the needs and talents of every pupil. In the context of creativity, the needs of the class, small groups and individuals may be very different, depending on the experience, skills and reflective capabilities each has developed. Acceptable noise levels, complexity of challenge, and time allowed for the job will vary for group and individual projects. The teacher may have to act as mediator, advisor, encourager, or facilitator in different ways for group and individual tasks. The creativity of individuals can flourish or be stifled within groups. Björkman (2004) reports that in groups, individuals sometimes limit their contributions and rely on others to accomplish the task because either they feel their ideas are of less value than those of their peers, or the shared responsibility for action reduces their motivation. Ideas may be lost if only one person talks at a time. For individuals, 'being unable to express ideas as they occur impairs productivity because ideas become irrelevant, people forget their ideas and people rehearse ideas to avoid forgetting ideas, which may prevent them from generating new ideas' (Pinsonneault et al., cited in Björkman 2004).

To overcome this, encourage pupils to jot down notes or diagrams as and when ideas occur to them so that ideas are not lost. The pressure to conform may limit the expression of original ideas. This groupthink may be addressed through challenging questions from a supporting adult. Amabile (1996) showed us that intrinsic motivation is more powerful than extrinsic motivation, so to perform well, children must be really engaged with the task in hand and feel personal involvement with it. She also noted that group productivity tends to be high when tasks are divided into sub-tasks which are each given strict time limits. It helps if participants are clear about the rules for each stage of a project.

Wiltermuth (2008), working with adults in a business context, found that people who dominated a group, even through well-meaning expertise and enthusiasm for a task, were likely to elicit submissive responses from some group members who then contributed fewer ideas, thus reducing both the quantity and diversity of creative ideas produced. It seems likely that a similar effect may be found with primary pupils so that group composition needs careful management as well as teaching about cooperative working to ensure that creative potential is not lost. Wiltermuth reports on other research which found that groups with individualistic orientations are more creative than those with communal orientations, and that groups in which people feel a sense of personal autonomy, or intrinsic motivation are more creative than others. Group cohesiveness is affected by group size as well as group diversity, both of which have been shown to influence creativity. In any group a social hierarchy will tend to emerge, so it is beneficial to change the composition and size of groups regularly so as to maximize the chances of everyone to contribute. Dominant members are likely to be louder and take up more body space than submissive peers. Reducing these characteristics can encourage submissive group members to contribute. Groups function most effectively when the following conditions are met:

1   Group composition is changed regularly.
2   Speaking time is shared fairly.
3   No one takes up more body space than others.
4   No one is seated or standing higher than others.
5   No ideas are ridiculed.
6   Positive and constructive language rather than negative or critical language is used.
7   Loud voices are not used.
8   Highly original individuals are distributed among groups to model creative originality.
9   Groups are praised for coming up with original ideas and encouraged to identify those of most value.

Personal creativity

Engaging pupils personally goes one step further than engaging them individually. Individuals may work alone on a group task, contribute skills and even volunteer safe suggestions, but not engage on a personal level with their own ideas which is a more risky and revealing experience. Look at the following list of the characteristics of group and personal creativity (Table 5.1). Consider how they might apply to your class and how you might need to build on these to help both groups and individuals develop their creative potential.

Table 5.1   Comparison of group and personal creativity

Group creativity	Personal creativity
Builds on skills of several people	Builds on personal skills
May be externally initiated by problems/challenge	May be internally initiated in response to a question/personal interest/problem
Requires cooperative working	Requires independent motivation, initiative, effort and perseverance
May need external leader to initiate and organize	May need adult encouragement, permission and validation
Low status members of a group may not contribute, so good ideas are lost. Others may freeload. Individual ideas may be lost while waiting turn to speak	Can be inhibited by problems with dominance/ submission or social interaction

(continued)

Table 5.1 *(continued)*

Group creativity	Personal creativity
Requires supportive atmosphere between group members. May benefit from individuals disagreeing/negotiating and sometimes working away from the group for a while	Characterized by flow (periods of intense concentration)
Pressure to conform may result in low-level creativity and little risk taking	May be quirky/highly individual and involve risk taking
Group members can distract or compensate for an individual's time out	May involve problems with concentration when thinking
Lack of autonomy can demotivate	Sense of autonomy can motivate
May be enhanced by competition with other groups	May be reduced if in competition with other individuals
Benefits from group support for ideas	May need adult support for ideas
Groups with diverse ideas and skills have greater opportunity to make unusual mental connections between ideas than groups with similar ideas	Some people prefer to work on their own and are more reflective than individuals in a group

Creativity in a social context

In NACCCE's view of creativity that everyone has the capacity, and the right, to be creative, creativity was considered to be a 'function of education' (1999: 6) rather than a specific subject. It was stated that the term should apply to both teachers' teaching and pupils' learning and that creativity was something which could be taught. The report defined creativity as 'imaginative activity fashioned so as to produce outcomes that are both original and of value' (1999: 30). Bandura (1986) and Vygotsky (1978) also recognized the social component of learning.

Loveless, in Wilson (2009) points out that although there is a tradition of lone artists and inventors working away in garrets on their own, very often their ultimate creations have emerged as the result of discussions and cooperation with others at some point. There is the potential within a group to share ideas, get feedback, improve and put them into action. There is the opportunity to learn from others as they model their creative processes. There is also the danger that some pupils will dominate others, rejecting good ideas without proper scrutiny and that less confident learners will not dare to contribute. A pupil's personal creativity can bloom or wilt in a group. Care should be taken when allocating learners to groups so there is a balance of skills and personalities who will cooperate, support and learn from each other. Sometimes putting good friends together will work well: at other times this may not work well. The most and least able should not *always* be teamed up in ability groups, although sometimes this has its benefits as well. For every subject and class and mix of pupils, there will be different groupings which work well or less well. It is useful to change the composition of groups regularly before some pupils always think of themselves as the scribe, or the person in charge. Group creativity will be affected by the personality of the teacher, the pedagogy used as well as the ethos of the school (Cremin, in Wilson 2009).

Who decides what is creative?

Feldman, Csikszentmihalyi and Gardner (1994) suggested that creativity arises from interaction between an individual's intelligence and an area of human endeavour and the specialists in that area, who they suggest act as gate-keepers and sit in judgement over that field deciding which ideas are of worth and which are not (Figure 5.1). This of course means that the accolade that something is creative may be a very subjective judgement. It also means that the label 'creative' may change with the passing of years and the changes of taste and perception which come with time and distance. Many artists who were not perceived as particularly creative in their own lives have been feted

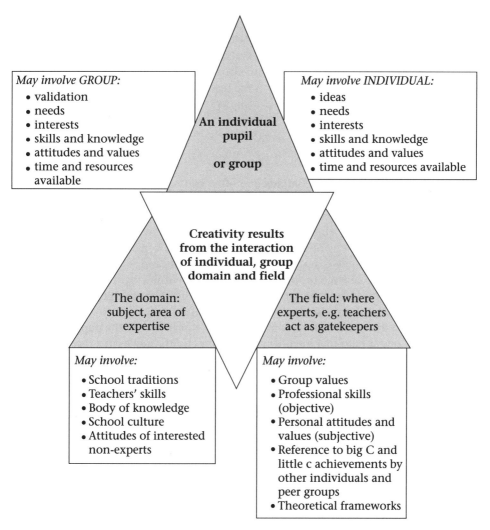

May involve GROUP:
- validation
- needs
- interests
- skills and knowledge
- attitudes and values
- time and resources available

An individual pupil

or group

May involve INDIVIDUAL:
- ideas
- needs
- interests
- skills and knowledge
- attitudes and values
- time and resources available

Creativity results from the interaction of individual, group domain and field

The domain: subject, area of expertise

The field: where experts, e.g. teachers act as gatekeepers

May involve:
- School traditions
- Teachers' skills
- Body of knowledge
- School culture
- Attitudes of interested non-experts

May involve:
- Group values
- Professional skills (objective)
- Personal attitudes and values (subjective)
- Reference to big C and little c achievements by other individuals and peer groups
- Theoretical frameworks

Figure 5.1   An adaptation of Csikzentmihalyi's (1996) systems model showing some of the influences on group and individual creativity in school

posthumously. Items in music, literature, fashion, art, architecture, even particular people associated with each, come in and out of fashion, gaining and losing the status of creative. Here of course we are talking about high level creativity of the historic rather than personal scale. In school, we must be aware that as teachers we are also gatekeepers with the power to approve or discourage a child's effort. We are the ones who will award the accolade of 'creative' to a particular idea or outcome so we must take care that our taste or personal feelings about a child do not cloud our judgement. Craft, Claxton and Gardner (2008) pointed out that creativity needs to be enriched with wisdom and trust for it to provide a suitable foundation for work which is excellent and ethical.

There may be tensions between individual teachers, or between schools with agendas to appear particularly creative and, or to produce quotas of pupils who are identified as gifted and talented in creative work. Once a school becomes known for its creative output, there may be considerable pressure for a teacher to appear to be doing exemplary creative work with a class, while also raising the academic grades of the pupils. If the teacher does not have the appropriate skills for this, a Blue Peter approach where everyone produces similar work based on the teacher's creativity rather than their own may result.

Assessing creativity

The assessment of creativity is complex and often controversial, with the experts disagreeing as to what makes an idea, process or outcome creative due to the subjective nature of the quality. What one person regards as of value, another may reject. Teachers routinely judge results or behaviours rather than processes: the child who works quietly and neatly is praised. The child who is apparently day-dreaming or fiddling may be asked to stop wasting time or resources when the thinking and experimental time is an essential part of the creative process. Few of us get anything right first time without thought, trial and error. Teachers whose own creative side is not well developed or who are uninformed about a technological or mathematical process may not recognize a good idea when it is presented. They may even feel threatened by the pupil's creativity. As a child, I found it hard to remember all the names for the angles in a theorem which I had to recite correctly, explaining how the angles ABC+ BAC were somehow equal to something else. I understood the process, but got confused with all the letters so I suggested that if I called the interior angles little a, b and c and the exterior ones big ABC I could do it easily, but this was not allowed. Today that would be encouraged as a personal solution to aid understanding.

There are several problems with assessing classroom creativity:

- Is it even possible to assess creativity?
- Why and when should creativity be assessed?
- Who should assess?
- What should be assessed?
- What should be done with the assessments?

Is it even possible to assess creativity?

Many people claim to have found ways to assess creativity. Some are looking at the process, others at the result of a creative process. In order to choose an assessment procedure, it must be clear why one is trying to assess such a nebulous and subjective quality which is hard to define, let alone, grade. I find that some trainees, and even teachers, say that creativity cannot be assessed at all since it is a personal matter of taste so that anything a child says is creative is just that and should not be judged otherwise. This is particularly true of art activities, though they are less sure about areas such as creative writing. (They are usually against creative spelling!) If we follow this argument, there will be little support for creative development in school as we just give uncritical praise for all efforts. The multitude of creativity tests would suggest that it is possible to judge and even measure some aspects of creativity, but the reasons for doing so need to be clear.

I have tried grading my own lessons to see if they give a lot, some or no potential to exhibit creative behaviour. (This is a useful exercise to check just how controlling, and sometimes insecure we are as teachers.) When the results were compared with the creativity exhibited by the class, I found that the lessons where the pupils exhibited the most creative outcomes were not the ones where they were given almost free rein to write or create a piece of art or move in any way they liked in PE, but ones where they were given guidance within a set of options, where each option had been taught previously and where perhaps several key words, techniques or movements had to be incorporated in some way. I graded the children's outcomes on a simple scale of my own (Table 5.2). Doing this helped me to extend the creative opportunities I gave my pupils, allowing both them and myself to take more risks and require more innovation as well as constructive reflection for tasks in all subjects.

I was once teaching a class of Year 5 about sight. After my instruction and some experimental activity by the class, I set them to work to record what they had learned in a range of ways. At once, Sam, a very bright boy, came to see me. 'I know all that stuff we've been doing,' he said, 'and I don't think it will help me to write it all down, but I'm not too sure just how my eye lets me see things. Can I make a model to help me work it out?' I had to consider if I said yes, that there would be no evidence that he did actually

Table 5.2 Assessing creative work

	Process involved	Assessment
1	Copies	Replicates given ideas. Does a conventional write-up in science, hardly alters the modelling of a story in literacy, and copies the work of other children in PE. No reflection
2	Develops	Uses given ideas and adds some of their own, and those of others. Little reflection
3	Extends	Working with a given starting point, adds many ideas of their own. Work shows some reflection
4	Innovates	Using no more than the basic requirements does something completely unexpected and different from everyone else. High degree of reflection

Figure 5.2 Sam's eyeballs

know what he claimed and that perhaps everyone else would want to start making models and I had not much modelling material to hand. 'I just need some paper and glue,' said Sam, so I agreed. A few minutes later he was back with crumpled ball of paper onto which he had pasted a white cornea, a green iris and a black pupil. We talked about the problem of the pupil being a hole and he went off to modify the design. By the end of the lesson, after much trial and error, and research about sight, there were six eyeballs on my desk demonstrating varying stages of his understanding (Figure 5.2). The final model had eyelids, eyelashes, an optic nerve, and a tear duct, and Sam knew the part each one played in helping him to see. No one else had asked to do the same thing but all were interested in Sam's explanation about how his eyes worked. The models were not particularly beautiful or perfect biologically but they were an accurate and interesting record of the process Sam had gone through to understand his sight. Sadly my tick sheet did not have a creative column at that stage, but Sam had taught me to take more risks.

Who should assess?

Since self-assessment is a life skill, children should be helped to assess different aspects of their work so that it become part of their way of life to look with an appropriate degree of criticality at whatever they do, say or believe. They should be helped to see the positive aspects of any piece or work, whether it is the conception of an idea or the quality of a finished product. Just attempting a new task deserves credit, as does diverging from a brief in a purposeful and constructive way. Children may need encouragement to see that the most valuable work is not the longest or the neatest or that done with most speed. Teachers should assess their planning to ensure engaging presentation and motivating challenges are involved as well as gauging the creative response of their classes. If the latter is poor, then it is the teacher who needs to consider what is restricting the children's natural inclination to experiment and should increase the potential for creative development and expression in class.

Why and when should creativity be assessed?

As with all assessment, this may be diagnostic, formative, or summative. Perhaps the first reason to attempt the assessment of pupil creativity is to see if the children are in fact being creative at all or are they just following instructions and following their teacher's creative suggestions? It is easy for an experienced and creative teacher to instruct pupils in a way which makes their work look exciting and original, when all they are doing is following a given formula. A quick look at the display boards, or pupils' books in a school, will often find just limited variation on a given theme. A second reason is to be able to see at what level they are working and how best to encourage their individual creative development. Reflection which involves a level of assessment is a feature of creativity in itself. Another justification for assessment is to see if it is taking place in a range of curricula area, and not only in the traditionally artistic ones. The process should not just examine outcomes, but be a consideration of the creative process at all stages. It may be done daily by the creator, but perhaps formally, just once a term by the teacher.

What should be assessed?

We need to be clear what it is we are assessing. Is it originality of ideas, bravery in attempting something new, tenacity, the quality of reflection or something else? Are we assessing a product or a process? There may even be no easily assessable outcome if the result of a challenge to improve the running of the class produces a new system for lining up or rules for keeping the place tidy rather than a pupil-made tidy box for each table. Whatever it is, we must remember that judgements in this area are likely to be very subjective. Excellent technique should not be confused with originality.

Several systems for assessing creativity have been devised, most notable the Torrence test of Creative Thinking (1966), which aims to measure divergent thinking and other problem-solving skills. These are scored on the following measure:

- *Fluency*: the total number of interpretable, meaningful and relevant ideas generated in response to the stimulus.
- *Flexibility*: the number of different categories of relevant responses.
- *Originality*: the statistical rarity of the responses among the test subjects.
- *Elaboration*: the amount of detail in the responses.

The Creativity Classification System (CCS) by Kirschenbaum (1998) looks at nine dimensions of the creative process including contact, conscience, interest, fantasy, incubation, creative contact, inspiration, production, and verification. More recently, Ellis et al. reported in *Assessing Learning in Creative Contexts* (2007) on assembling and trialling an assessment package which consisted of:

- *a creative learning observation framework* for use with individuals or groups;
- *a template for an assessment portfolio*, to be compiled for individuals, groups or a whole class;
- *a creative learning five-point scale*, based on the National Curriculum attainment targets in arts subjects.

The project established that it was both possible and practical for teachers to assess children's learning in creative arts subjects, if supported by professional development.

Although the teachers involved were appreciative of the assessment materials they were given, most felt it was only possible to make such detailed assessments with a couple of case study children but felt that 'focusing on a few children informs your observation of all'. They did, however, feel that the assessment materials could have value in subjects other than the creative arts.

What should be done with the assessments?

There is no point in assessing a child's creativity unless the assessment is used to improve teaching or learning. It may be to show pupils how well they are doing and what to work on next. Evidence of such progress should be put with the record of achievement for the subject concerned. Those who do not show evidence of these characteristics or who do so at lower levels (see Bloom's taxonomy on p. 70), or in only a few subjects, should be helped to move on through questioning, modelling and scaffolding by the teacher.

Suggestions for practice

What most teachers do not need is another or set of tick sheets for a whole class. Creativity is not another subject but an integral characteristic of the way we can tackle *every* subject. An awareness of the characteristics of creativity should be in the back of every teacher's mind so that credit can be given when assessing any subject for pupils who do the following:

- Ask interesting questions involving 'what if' and 'should'.
- Make connections with prior learning whether through home or school experience.
- Take risks, try out new ways of working.
- Innovate in their planning or recording.
- Reflect on their process or outcome at any stage of the work.

Pupils should be congratulated when they show these characteristics and be invited to try them out when they don't. Summative assessment can be done through portfolios, but formative assessment needs to be ongoing and consider the process as much as the product, with remedial action being taken as necessary. Teachers might find it useful to look for particular aspects of creativity in particular subjects and assess these before encouraging pupils to apply them elsewhere. For example, looking for evidence of the children's abilities to propose alternatives linked directly to the needs of the user in DT and then placing an emphasis on this skill when teaching writing for an audience or communicating through ICT.

Must, should, could

Many schools now use the 'must, should, could' approach to target setting and self-assessment. At the start of a task the children choose their own target from a given set prepared by the teacher to scaffold their progression. In a science context at KS1, it might look like this:

- All pupils *must* describe what they did in the test and what they learned.
- Some *should* also suggest how the test might be improved.
- Some *could* also suggest other explanations for the results.

In a KS2 literacy context it might look like this:

- All pupils *must* discuss the text and say what they thought of it.
- Some *should* also explain characters' motives.
- Some *could* also look at characterization, how it was done and how it affected the reader.

When children choose their own target level, it helps them to be in control of their progress and ownership of the assessment.

Developing creative thinking

What is creative thinking?

You might argue that all thinking is creative thinking in that all thinking requires some degree of analysis, synthesis and evaluation, if only on the mundane level of 'What do I want to eat?'Alternatively, one could argue that factual thinking about events and observations and conceptual thinking about beliefs and issues involve different processes, with the latter being more abstract and theoretical and leading to the development of ideas rather than just the recall of facts.

The National Curriculum (DfEE 1999) listed the following thinking skills:

- Information-processing
- Enquiry
- Reasoning
- Creative thinking
- Evaluation.

However, it could be argued that creative thinking involves all the elements in this list. The term 'creative thinking' implies not only ideas and reflection but also an element of novelty and the exploration of possibilities. Several ways to promote creative thinking in children have been proposed. Some, such as the Head Start programme in the USA (see http://www.nhsa.org/ for details) favour improving the quality of the questions we ask pupils so as to develop their thinking. For example, asking:

- What will happen next?
- What would something be like if . . .?
- Suppose this was changed, what might the results be?
- What does this remind you of?
- What are the connections between these things?
- What could be done differently in a given situation?

Many of these are variations of the 'What if?' possibility thinking identified by Craft (2002) as a valuable tool for creative development. Wegerif (2010) believes that a dialogic approach where people share and explore ideas verbally is the best way to develop creative thinking. He and his colleagues favour what they term 'Exploratory Talk' to develop children's thinking skills and have put together a Thinking Skills Program of activities to promote investigative discussion and develop thinking skills. Lipman (1991) proposed that even young children could be taught philosophy (see Chapter 6) while Robert Fisher is a proponent of *Communities of Enquiry* (Fisher 2007; see Chapter 6) which can help children develop their thinking skills in the context of moral education. De Bono (1999) has developed a range of ways to promote original thinking while experts on science and maths education have devised their own cognitive acceleration programs. Another way to help pupils organize their thinking in a work-related context is the TASC wheel (Wallace 2010). These and other methods of developing thinking skills are outlined in Chapter 6, but first let's look at a way of classifying different types of thinking based on the complexity of the thought processes used and the practice of metacognition.

Using Bloom's taxonomy of thinking skills

Bloom's taxonomy was devised in 1956 and revised by Anderson and Krathwohl in 2001, and it classifies types of questioning, thinking and learning into six levels, starting with the simplest of recall and understand, which many teachers tend to prioritize, through apply and analyse up to evaluate and create. It can be used to develop thinking skills at all ages.

Table 5.3 shows some of the activities at each level. Considering this progression can help teachers extend the creative thinking and learning they require of different groups in a class.

Table 5.3   Using Bloom's taxonomy to extend learning

	Level	Words involved	Pupil action
Lower-order thinking skills	**1. Knowledge** Recall of information but without change, use or understanding	Describe, identify, name, list, collect, define, retell, tell, examine, match, record, label, copy, quote, who, what, where, when, how	Talk about what they have learned, write and draw about the things they have seen and done
	2. Comprehension Understanding knowledge acquired without applying it	Compare, describe, predict, group, discuss, summarize, estimate, contrast, interpret, order, convert, explain	Explain events, actions and observations both from real life and in stories
	3. Application Using concepts learned to solve a problem appropriately	Classify, apply, change, solve, illustrate, experiment, demonstrate, show, use, calculate, teach, relate, discover, develop, report	Use information in new situations. Solve problems, continue a story, make a model or plan a test

	Level	Words involved	Pupil action
Higher-order thinking skills	**4. Analysis** Taking apart, sorting and seeing how the components of what has been learned fit together	Analyse, classify, arrange, connect, infer, compare, contrast, explain, order, break down, discriminate, prioritize, illustrate a point, select, infer	Identify factors affecting a situation, motives, create flow charts, role plays, interviews and surveys. Recognize and explain patterns and meanings
	5. Evaluation Looking at the value of items, information or methods involved in the whole	Assess, compare, decide, discriminate, rank, test, convince, conclude, explain, judge, summarize, appraise, critique, persuade, justify, defend, grade	Make judgements about information and situations. Evaluate the actions and opinions of characters in a story, check the fairness of a test, assess value, make choices and defend an opinion
	6. Creation Generating something new from what has been learned	Compose, invent, plan, design, substitute, combine, adapt, modify, rewrite, generalize, reorganize, negotiate, rearrange	Design or create a new item, system, question article, poem, story, or plan. Create new information and solutions

Creative Challenge!
Choose a text or topic you are planning to work on with your class. Use Bloom's taxonomy to create a set of questions and tasks to challenge individual pupils at different levels. List questions for each of Bloom's six categories. Figure 5.3 presents an example of using Bloom's taxonomy in a literacy context.

Metacognition

Metacognition is thinking about our thinking. It involves looking at what one knows, what has been learned and evaluating the thinking process so as to improve it. It is a skill which needs practice and support to develop. We need to reflect at all stages of a challenge and evaluate both practical progress as well as the development of our cognition. The implication for doing this in school is that sufficient time has to be allocated to make the process worthwhile. Too often our plenaries deal with little more than the recall of facts. To develop thinking skills, we must help children to reflect on their progression in thinking so as to make them aware of the process as well as the outcome. Learning diaries for reflection are now used in some schools to help with this.

Fisher (2006), who defines thinking skills as 'the human capacity to think in conscious ways to achieve certain purposes', builds on Bloom's taxonomy because we do

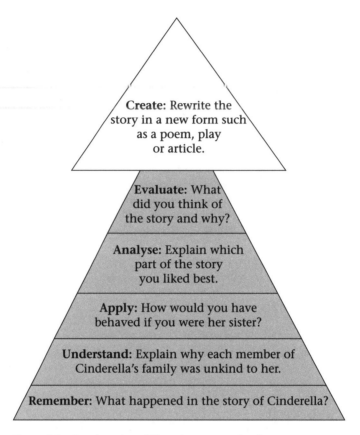

Figure 5.3   An adaptation of Bloom's taxonomy in a literacy context

not teach pupils all they will need to know in their lives, and learners will 'require trans-ferable skills to enable them to address different problems in different contexts at differ-ent times throughout their lives'. He suggests (cited in Arthur et al. 2006) that to develop creative thinking, children need:

- *cognitive challenge*: challenging children's thinking from the earliest years;
- *collaborative learning*: extending thinking through working with others;
- *metacognitive discussion*: reviewing what they think and how they learn.

McGuinness (1999) evaluated research into thinking skills and found that:

- Pupils benefitted from being coached in thinking.
- Not one model, but many approaches proved effective.
- Success was due to pedagogy (teaching strategies) not specific materials.
- Strategies were needed to enable pupils to transfer thinking to other contexts.
- Teachers needed professional support and coaching to sustain success.

6   Developing group creativity

Developing questioning and thinking skills

Several methods for developing creative and critical thinking are outlined below. For each of these there are studies to show they can be efficacious if applied consistently. There is not enough space to evaluate each in detail here.

Philosophy for Children (P4C)

Matthew Lipman, a philosopher and educator, was the creator of the Philosophy for Children Program. During the Vietnam War in the 1960s he was dismayed at how many Americans were unable to reason and express their views about the conflict. Fearing that it was too late for adults to develop these skills, he responded with the radical idea of teaching philosophy to children. His goal was to foster critical thinking which he defined as 'thinking that (1) facilitates judgment because it (2) relies on criteria, (3) is self-correcting, and (4) is sensitive to context' (Lipman 1991: 116).

Lipman's method involves children sitting in a circle and taking turns to read aloud from a work of fiction which is used to stimulate a philosophical conversation on something arising from the text. Initially, the teacher directs the discussion but soon children learn to ask their own questions such as 'What is happiness?', or 'Is it ever right to take something which belongs to someone else?' or and with the help of their peers to answer them. Lipman called this approach a 'community of inquiry' and trials met with success. Teachers found that children often ask the same fundamental questions which puzzle us all such as, 'What happens when we die?', 'Where did the world come from?' or 'How can I know the right thing to do?' Educationalists like Jean Piaget believed children were not capable of critical thinking before the age of 11 or 12, but those who have tried this approach have found that it can help children to grow their ideas, develop their sense of morality and respect the views of others. While some teachers are reluctant to cram another subject into a packed timetable, others have found that the children's resulting behaviour and understanding in many curriculum areas are so improved, that the time taken is well worth it. Lipman justified his approach on the grounds that children work best on what interests them, and so working from stories about children similar to themselves, and then choosing what to debate motivate involvement. He believed that helping them discuss controversial issues not only developed their critical thinking and their values but their creativity with ideas as well. P4C recognizes that thinking can be exciting and emotional, and it provides ways in which children can talk about and analyse those emotions as they deal truthfully with what they find problematic or puzzling. This method of teaching children to think stresses the concept of a shared enquiry which develops empathy and compassion for others. Traditionally teachers have taught and helped pupils to practise many practical skills, but perhaps hoped they would pick up thinking skills along the way. Judging by the way many adults behave and express themselves, this does not always happen. With P4C, pupils learn to develop their opinions into considered judgements, through conversations and the practice of finding good reasons for their judgements.

Teachers using this method have found that children enjoy P4C sessions because they are stimulated to think for themselves, explore their ideas and help each other become aware of the implications of their beliefs and actions. Children find them valuable as the skills learned can help to solve playground conflict and not to take everything said to them personally. Although this is not a quick fix solution for uncreative or fractious classes, as it takes at least a term to make a difference, many find that collaborative skills are increased through this practice. The logic which they learn through P4C sessions to explore moral issues can also be applied to problems in maths and science. By learning to think in small steps they can apply similar small steps to the processes of invention and problem-solving. They get better at the creative skill of asking questions and deciding if they can be answered, and identifying the best methods to answer them. They get better at making connections with previous ideas, previous learning and situations with which they are familiar. They are able to explore ideas verbally and theoretically and refine them with the help of their peers and their teacher. They look at situations and others' ideas from different perspectives than their own, and learn to reflect critically on their ideas and the events they see around them. You might argue that this is creativity with ideas and opinions.

To teach P4C well, a teacher needs to have training in how to conduct a P4C discussion, how to use the exercises and discussion plans that are provided in the many books on the subject. Further information about P4C can be found online at http://www. philosophy4children.co.uk/.

Community of Enquiry

This is a UK-based approach to P4C, which goes beyond teaching P4C in the classroom and extends the method to parents and community groups who are involved with education for citizenship (Philosophy for Communities). It is an adaptation which sometimes uses Stories for Thinking (Fisher 1996). Further information can be found at www. sapere.org.uk (SAPERE is the Society for Advancing Philosophical Enquiry and Reflection in Education).

This website outlines the key principles or elements of a *Community of Enquiry* where participants develop the 4Cs: creative, critical, caring and collaborative thinking skills. Elements of this approach include learning to question, to create hypotheses, to construct reasons for ideas, and to make connections with others' ideas. Participants are encouraged to look at the implications of any assumptions which are aired and to be consistent in their conclusions. Moral issues may be used to help children work through problematical ideas. For example:

- Should everyone share a fraction of their income/pocket money?
- Should animals have the right to live free from pain and fear?
- How could we make this school/this country a fairer place?
- Is it right to steal medicine to save a sick child? Why? How about a sick criminal?
- Should the rights of the individual or the community come first?

Cognitive Acceleration (CA)

The two main programmes of cognitive acceleration are CASE (Cognitive Acceleration through Science Education) and CAME (Cognitive Acceleration through Math Education). CA uses challenging activities, group work and metacognition to develop ideas and creative solutions to problems. In CA lessons, learners are given practical problems to solve and argue with each other as they work on their solutions and conclusions. They are encouraged to see themselves as thinkers who can develop and justify new ideas. Initially this technique was developed in the contexts of science (CASE) and math (CAME). At first, CA activities were restricted to secondary education but later they were adapted for primary use, starting with materials for Year 1, in the 'Let's Think' project. See http://www.cognitiveacceleration.co.uk for details. It is an approach which builds on the research of Piaget and Vygotsky. Proponents claim that all school subjects can be used as a vehicle for cognitive challenge. Let's Think sessions are mainly oral and help children to reflect on and understand their learning processes. Students are challenged to see how they can use their learning from one context in other situations. Using constructivist theory in this way, learners build their own understanding of ideas, rather than just remembering what they have been told. Sessions focus on how children arrive at their answers rather than whether the answer is the expected 'correct' one.

TASC (Thinking Actively in a Social Context)

The TASC framework is an eight-stage tool to help learners organize their work and develop creative thinking skills through practical problem-solving activities. It was devised by Belle Wallace who believes that children need to be taught to use their brains effectively (Wallace 2010). She sees learning as an adventure where we learn best from our failures. The TASC wheel lists skills which an expert thinker will use (Figure 6.1). These skills can be used and revisited in any order as required. The TASC wheel can support inclusion and personalized learning and be used for learning in all subject areas and with children of all ages. It is an approach which maximizes thinking in a problem-solving context while minimizing recording.

This way of working incorporates ideas for developing each of the five creative behaviours: asking questions, making connections, seeing things in new ways, exploring ideas and reflecting, and many schools now use this approach to help pupils plan group topic work and individual investigations. See http://www.tascwheel.com/ for further details.

Figure 6.1 The TASC wheel. Source: © Belle Wallace 2010

Helping groups to make connections ⚬⚬⚬

Lateral thinking

Lateral thinking is a term invented by Edward de Bono (1967) to describe the ability to think creatively, to use inspiration and imagination to solve problems by looking at them from unexpected perspectives. It involves discarding the obvious, leaving behind traditional modes of thought, and discarding preconceptions. De Bono sees creative thinking as a skill which anyone can acquire with some training and effort. He divides thinking into two types: (1) 'vertical thinking', or traditional thinking which is the kind we are normally trained to do; and (2) 'lateral thinking' which involves looking at problems in different ways, and finding solutions from new angles. Both types may be forms of logical thinking, but arrive at their solutions in different ways. To him, this term is interchangeable with the term creativity.

Lateral thinking, is also sometimes known as thinking 'outside the box'. It is the sort of thinking that computers cannot do, because it requires perception and comprehension rather than data handling. The process covers a variety of methods to avoid our usual lines of thought and involves willingness to do the following:

- Look at things in new ways.
- Challenge assumptions and traditional ways of thinking and working.
- Generate alternatives, sometimes in unorthodox ways or using seemingly unconnected input to develop new lines of thinking.
- Try new ideas to see where they lead.
- Find new ideas from a creative thinking session and move forward with them.

Practical lateral thinking activities

These challenges could be done by pairs, small groups or even a whole class so that less confident children can have the activities scaffolded by those who are more willing to take risks and propose ideas. Answers could be oral or scribed, and might be enjoyable and challenging activities to start or end the school day.

- List as many uses as you can for a brick/plastic cup/other item suggested by class.
- How many ways can you find to move a brick? (One of my classes found over 30!)
- List all the things you can think of which are blue.
- What could you use an empty box for?
- What could you use a 2-metre piece of string for?

Help pupils to understand that a problem may have a number of possible answers and that problems rarely have perfect solutions.

Random input association

Our thinking often follows similar lines so to create new ideas we should use new starting points. This way of generating new ideas uses random words as a prompt to solve problems or create new ideas. By using an unusual starting point, one is likely to arrive at an unusual solution to a problem. To use this you need to prevent yourself from thinking that the ideas produced are just silly and to try several associations between the words to find ideas of value. This simple idea is often used in business to create new products. Random inputs can be words, objects or images.

Practical techniques for generating random words

- Have bag of words written on small pieces of paper or card. Select one at random to apply to a problem or two words to invent ideas for products or items to be included in a text.
- Make a collection of pictures or small objects which can be used as random ideas to be pulled from a bag.
- Open a dictionary, at random and choose a word.

It is important to use the first word you find or one is likely to follow old ways of thinking.

Once you have chosen a word, object or image, list its attributes. Then consider each attribute on the list and see how it applies to the problem or how it can be associated with another word to create a new product. This technique works because the brain is very good at making connections and is an effective way to generate ideas for new products.

Odd one out

This is a simple strategy for looking at the properties of objects, seeing them in new ways and making unusual connections. It can be a quick filler activity, a challenge at the start or end of the day. It can be done orally or as an interactive sorting challenge with actual objects.

Take any three objects you have to hand or those in a special collection and challenge the class to spot the odd one out. There may be reasons for any one or even all of the objects being the odd one regarding its shape, colour, material, construction, name, or some other quality suggested by the class. There can be no wrong answers if a justification can be made for an answer. This exercise teaches sorting and classification, while also developing creative and critical thinking skills. A useful bank of objects might include man-made and natural objects made of a range of materials, in many colours and with different shapes.

Practical subject challenges for odd one out

Table 6.1   Odd one out

Subject	Choice
Numeracy	Put three numbers on the board, such as 3, 15 and 20
Science	Three materials or three pieces of equipment
English	Three characters from stories
History	Three monarchs
Geography	Three countries/continents
MFL	Same rules in the MFL concerned.

This strategy can reveal gaps in pupils' knowledge, vocabulary and understanding of key concepts. Pupils enjoy making up similar challenges for the rest of the class. This approach encourages creative thinking and reasoning (Higgins et al. 2001).

An extension might be to link the objects in a given set with a chain of connections as below.

leaf/seed	(both from a plant)
seed/fur	(both brown)
fur/feather	(both from something alive)
feather/short ruler	(similar shape)
ruler/spoon	(both plastic)
spoon/piece of string	(both could be used to lift something)

A further challenge could be to order a whole set of objects according to a criteria set by the pupils, such as from oldest to newest or from dearest to cheapest or from hardest to softest.

The Creative Problem Solving process (CPS)

This is also known as the Osborn-Parnes CPS process, and was developed by Alex Osborn and Sidney Parnes in a business context in the 1950s. It is a structured method for finding novel and useful solutions to problems. CPS follows set stages, involving both divergent and convergent thinking at each stage.

Each step begins with divergent thinking in a search for many alternatives. This is followed by convergent thinking, to evaluate what has been found and eliminate less useful options. Divergent techniques include applying the Five Ws and H (Who, Why, What, When, Where and How) to a situation and brainstorming to a problem. Convergent techniques include highlighting and then short-listing the most useful ideas at that stage.

The steps in the Creative Problem Solving process are:

1   *Objective finding*: identify the goal, wish or challenge.
2   *Fact finding*: gather the relevant data.
3   *Problem finding*: clarify the problems that need to be solved in order to achieve the goal.
4   *Idea finding*: generate ideas to solve the identified problem.
5   *Solution finding*: move from idea to implementable solution.
6   *Acceptance finding*: plan for action.

The steps may be used in a linear fashion, but it is not always necessary to use all the steps, if some part of the process has already been covered. In a school context, pupils might use the stages to decide how to plan a project. If challenged by their teacher to show families what they have learned in a history topic, for example, the CPS method could be used to identify how they are going to demonstrate their learning:

1   *Objective finding*: Decide how to present their learning, as a live presentation, a DVD of information, a website or other publication. They would then need to identify what data they will have to collect.
2   *Fact finding*: Decide on what would need to be done to create the presentation.
3   *Problem finding*: Next, work on the content of each part of the presentation.
4   *Idea finding*: Decide on evaluation criteria and strategies.
5   *Solution finding*: Decide how the work will be allocated.
6   *Acceptance finding*: Create an action plan for carrying out the work.

Teaching pupils to use these steps gives pupils greater ownership in the organization of their work while teaching them a structured way how to organize it.

ACTS (Activating Children's Thinking Skills)

Instead of teaching subject-specific thinking in single subjects such as the CASE or CAME projects, the ACTS methodology adopts what is termed an 'infusion approach'. Here teachers start by constructing a taxonomy of thinking skills which are required by each curriculum context, such as causal reasoning in science, classification in maths and decision making in geography, and then teach them in tandem with relevant curriculum topics. It is reported by McGuiness (2000) that this approach can lead to a deeper understanding of their use which facilitates transfer and reinforcement of learning. She describes a successful project which drew on Swartz and Parks' (1994) taxonomy of thinking skills. Teachers first developed a vocabulary for talking about thinking, used diagrams to clarify the steps or components in a thinking process and then tried to make pupils' thinking more explicit through discussion, reflection and collaborative enquiry.

The ACTS thinking framework involves:

- Searching for meaning.
- Critical thinking.
- Creative thinking.
- Problem-solving.
- Metacognition.
- Decision making.

Brainstorming

Brainstorming is a technique for groups who want to find a solution to a specific problem by collecting ideas. The term was popularized by Alex Osborn (Osborn 1953) who also suggested guidelines for the process. Working in advertising, he noticed that individual employees found it hard to come up with new ideas but through group think sessions the quality and quantity of their creative ideas increased. Independent research has not verified this, although the technique is widely used today. Care needs to be taken that all members of a group participate fairly without blocking each other's ideas.

Osborn's rules for brainstorming are:

1 *Focus on quantity:* as the greater the number of ideas suggested, the greater the chance of producing a solution.
2 *Withhold criticism*: so that participants will feel free to come up with unusual ideas.
3 *Welcome unusual ideas*: as seeing things in new ways can often provide new solutions.
4 *Combine and improve ideas*: to form a single better good idea.

Variations on this technique involve *anonymous brainstorming* where each member of a group writes an idea on a piece of paper and passes it to another group member. Each person adds their thoughts to the idea suggested until all have commented and then the ideas are evaluated. *Electronic brainstorming* is a computerized version of the technique which may be done using e-mail or an electronic meeting system (EMS). *Individual brainstorming* is done by someone on their own writing as many ideas as they can without censoring them for value until the end of the list. *Question brainstorming* involves brainstorming the *questions*, rather than trying to find short-term solutions. *Tin-opener brainstorming* is useful for project work when wondering what to discover. This involves writing the words who, where, why, when, what and how on a page and then adding questions about the topic which start with these words (Figure 6.2). It could also be used to design new products or select ideas for story writing.

what?
who?
where?
why?
when?
how?

Figure 6.2   Tin-opener brainstorming

Concept mapping

Concept mapping was developed by Joseph D. Novak at Cornell University in the 1960s and is based on the theories of David Ausubel, who wrote about the importance of prior knowledge when learning new concepts. A concept map is a diagram used to organize ideas and show thinking processes stemming from a key word, often placed at the top of a hierarchy of ideas. The relationship between ideas, images or words on the map is shown by arrows and phrases to explain the relationships between key concepts. Creating a concept map helps a learner to reflect on what is known and what is not. Concepts are usually shown by a single word in a rectangular box, with lines linked to other concept boxes to show a network of ideas. A concept map is best constructed through first brainstorming ideas onto Post-it notes and then organizing these into a consistent structure of groups and subgroups, addling arrows and words to show the relationships (Figure 6.3). A final version can be created either on paper or a computer using colour and changes of font to add interest. Some computer programs such as Kidspiration are dedicated programs for creating concept maps. This method of idea organization can help to clarify thinking and develop new connections and ideas.

Mind maps

Mind mapping is a similar technique, devised by Tony Buzan who developed the concept map into a mind map to help people organize their ideas about a subject (Buzan 1991). A mind map is formed from a central word or concept, around which are drawn five to ten sub-ideas that relate to that word. From these are drawn further key words relating to the sub-ideas. The difference between concept maps and mind maps is that a mind map has only one main concept, while a concept map may have several. A mind map can be represented as a tree diagram, while a concept map is more of a network. A mind map often uses colour and diagrams to make the subject material memorable (Figure 6.4). It can be a very personal style of recording.

This mind map of guidelines is intended to be more memorable and quicker to scan than either a prose description or a list of instructions. By representing ideas in a graphical, non-linear manner, both concept maps and mind maps use a brainstorming

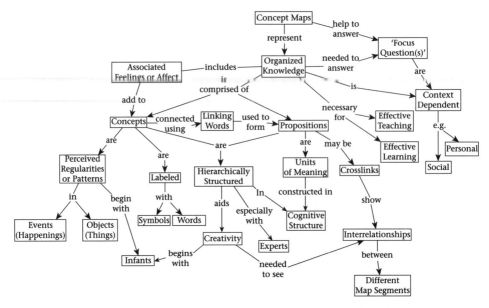

Figure 6.3 Concept map summarizing the use of concept maps. Source: Joseph D. Novak and Alberto J. Cañas

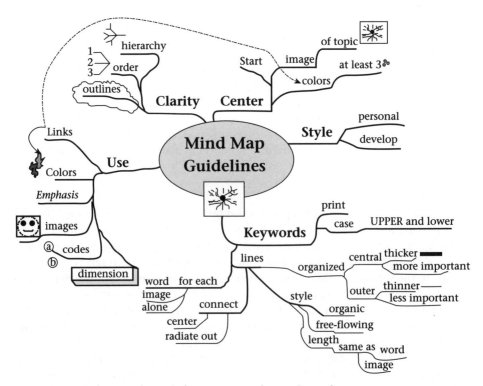

Figure 6.4 Mind map to show mind map structure. Source: Danny Stevens

approach to plan and organize information which shows the connections between concepts. Both techniques can be used to show the relationships between characters in a story. They can record what is known at the start of a project and be completed to show what has been learned by the end. They are useful for recording information in a way that makes it memorable, especially to those who use visual cues and images and those who are less confident with writing and linear recording. Both techniques help to map knowledge in a way which develops understanding and recall. I have used them to help classes summarize the main points of a project as a whole class or by pairs of pupils or even individuals working on personal projects. It can be an original form of recording and used creatively by both groups and individuals to good effect.

Both concept mapping and mind mapping can aid:

- creative personal or group recording of ideas;
- idea generation as part of the brainstorming process;
- making connections and seeing information in new ways;
- exploring and explaining relationships in complex ideas;
- classification of ideas or information;
- assessment of learning and misunderstanding;
- planning a complex information structure such as a hyperlinked text;
- reflection on learning.

Helping groups to see things in new ways

Synectics

This technique for increasing creativity was developed by George Prince and William J. J. Gordon in the 1950s (Fryer 2003). The word 'synectics' means bringing arbitrarily selected things together to create a useful connection which can involve a humorous and playful approach to problem-solving. The process uses several techniques to move people from fixed mind-sets into new ways of thinking. For this method to work well in a school, a whole staff approach is required with training for all staff including the head teacher and teaching assistants. Those who use synectics say it encourages new insights, divergent thinking and stimulates creative ideas.

Starting with a problem, a range of practices are used to throw new light on it by changing its situation or the perspective of those involved. Free association with random objects is used to generate fresh ideas. Metaphor and analogy are sometimes used. Emotional or unlikely aspects of a situation may be emphasized rather than obvious and rational aspects. For example, when considering how to improve a playground, pupils might be challenged to look at the problem as if they were an alien, a bird, an old person or someone who was blind or deaf. They might consider how the situation might change if it was an indoor playground or use random words such as 'banana', 'rabbit' or 'CD' to generate new ideas. The latter might suggest looking at waste disposal, provision of playtime snacks, developing areas where they could hide or take shelter from cold weather, or ways to introduce mobiles or music into the playground. Using metaphors, a playground might be looked at as if it were a business, a classroom or an art exhibition. Using analogies such as 'a playground is like a country . . .', or 'A playground is like a circus because . . . .' could lead to new playground rules or ideas for fresh equipment, its organization and distribution. Synectics allows new and surprising solutions to emerge and is designed to result in *action* not just *ideas*. Some analogies may be pure fantasy such as imagining a playground made of sweets or just paper, but participants are asked to play with the ideas and make connections until they have a new perspective on the subject.

Synectics recognizes the importance of reducing inhibitions to release creative ideas so no suggestion is ever ridiculed. These techniques can be used for problem-solving, or conflict resolution as well as creating new ideas, products and systems. Originally developed for use in business, the education world is now trying them out with some success in primary schools, even with pupils in Key Stage 1. Other tools used include brainstorming (see p. 80), spring-boarding where phrases such as 'I wish' and 'How can?' are used to preface ideas, and excursions, where seemingly unrelated ideas and activities are also introduced to look at the problem in new ways. In a playground context, someone might say, 'I wish there was a way to keep warm here in winter' or 'How can we make the ground more interesting?' An excursion might be to play an indoor game or sing a song with the class to spark off new ideas. A report on 'Excellence, creativity and innovation in teaching and education' by Faulkner in 2006, looked at whether synectics, normally applied in a business context, could be transferred successfully to the education sector. He concluded that in classes using Synectics regularly and consistently, there was clear whole class engagement without the issues of the most able, or the most confident dominating the class (2006: 31). He recommended this approach as valuable, but noted that a whole school approach was required to obtain the most benefit in supporting group problem-solving and creative team work. The Faulkner Report found that Synectics techniques could be used to support individual and group learning across the curriculum, including in the Literacy hour, with both KS1 and KS2 children, to support work with SEN pupils, in PSHE lessons and to extend ICT projects.

Six thinking hats

De Bono (1999) claims that people tend to think in limited ways and from their own particular perspective which is not always the most appropriate one. To develop more useful ways he recommends teaching children to think through his 'thinking hats' approach where the same problem is considered from a number of different angles in turn (Table 6.2). With young children, he advocates actually using coloured hats to help identify the type of thinking practised. Each 'thinking hat' represents a different way to look at a problem and children are encouraged to try different 'hats' (approaches) to look at a problem from different points of view.

This technique can help both teachers and their classes to think creatively about any topic and shows learners there are different ways of looking at a problem as well as different viewpoints. It helps to focus ideas and lead to creative ways of tackling problems. Using six thinking hats can promote higher-order thinking skills, including analysis, synthesis and evaluation (Figure 6.5). Simultaneously it improves group communication skills, individual thinking and decision making.

Table 6.2 The six thinking hats

Hat	Title	Questions to ask
White hat	Neutral objective thinking deals with factual information	*What do we know about the problem?* *What information do we have which might help us to solve it.*
Red hat	Emotional thinking deals with feelings, hunches, intuition	*What do we feel about the problem?* *What are out gut feelings?*
Purple/ Black hat	Critical thinking, analyses problems from a logical and even negative view and looks at the drawbacks of an idea	*What are the problems here?* *What are the drawbacks with any proposed solution?*
Yellow hat	Optimistic thinking is logical and positive, looks at the good points of an idea	*What are the benefits of any proposed solution?*
Green hat	Creative thinking looks at possibilities and new ideas	*What ideas have we got?* *How could we look at the problem in a new way?* *What are the possible solutions?*
Blue hat	Overview thinking deal with organizing and making decisions. Thinking about thinking	*What are our aims?* *What will we do?*

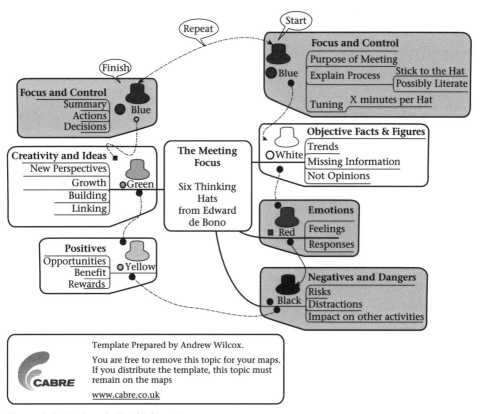

Figure 6.5 De Bono's Six Thinking Hats

Steps in the six thinking hats process are:

1 Present the facts (white hat).
2 Generate ideas on how the problem could be tackled (green hat.)
3 Evaluate the merits of each idea, listing benefits (yellow hat) and drawbacks (black hat).
4 Ask people for their feelings about the problem (red hat).
5 Summarize, and make decision (blue hat).

Training in using the six thinking hats method along lines envisaged by its creator can be accessed from http://www.debonothinkingsystems.com/tools/6hats.htm.

Treasure chests

Another way to help learners see things in new ways is to use groups of objects which may be linked in some way. This involves teacher ingenuity to develop pupils' creativity. Treasure chests can be anything from a painted cardboard box to jewelled caskets either bought or home-made, which contain items to stimulate ideas and help make connections (Figure 6.6). One of mine is a small gift box which contains just four tiny glass frogs and the word GAME on a piece of card. With this I challenge students to see how many ideas they can create which link the two in a school context. They usually suggest at least a dozen such as:

• Use frogs as counters in a board game.
• Design a lily pad and frog game to teach maths concepts.

Figure 6.6 Examples of treasure chests

- Teach life cycles through a drama game.
- Use leapfrog/jumping like frogs in a PE game.

A wooden chest holds items relating to the Derbyshire village of Eyam, which isolated itself during the seventeenth-century plague: a bottle of vinegar, old coins too battered to identify, photos of the village, a piece of cloth, a felt rat, name cards of village locations and local families, the fraction 83/350 (approximate number who survived), a nursery rhyme, a peg doll in historical costume, and a model well. These can be used to introduce the story of the plague in Eyam, to see what is already known and what needs to be taught. It can be used by groups of pupils selecting an item as a focus for their research or a story or poem, or the objects may be used as the starting point for a museum about the plague.

A folder contains copies of my mother's birth and death certificates, a photo collage showing different aspects of her life, and a medal citation for bravery in the Second World War. Some of the photocopies are aged with tea, and each set (I made several) can be used by groups of learners to see what can be deduced from original documents. I am always surprised by just how many deductions can be made from so few items. She would be delighted to be the focus of interest for so many young people.

A friend gave me a cardboard treasure chest which she had covered with beads and sequins. This now contains items to help stimulate questions when starting a topic on India, and has been used to stimulate story-writing and poetry as well.

Helping groups to explore ideas

Thought experiments

A thought experiment is a mental exercise which explores the consequences of an imaginary situation in order to understand the way things are. Often the experiment is one which could not be performed in reality, but is useful to explore mentally in order to comprehend the possible consequences of a decision and the principles behind it. This is a technique which goes back to the days of the Ancient Greeks, and which was used by Galileo and Einstein to work out some of their theories. Galileo developed his ideas about falling bodies in this way; Einstein imagined what it would be like to ride across the universe on a photon beam of light and this thought experiment enabled him to come up with his Theory of Relativity and ideas about black holes.

Thought experiments can be used to develop creative ideas and critical thinking. They are conducted in areas such as philosophy, science and maths, not just because they are interesting or entertaining, but to clarify understanding. Hypothetical situations can be devised to clarify moral decisions, e.g. a thought experiment might present a situation in which someone intentionally kills one innocent person in order to save many other people. Here, the question is not just whether this particular action is moral or not, but whether morality is determined just by the consequences of an action. Thought experiments may challenge, refute or confirm a prevailing idea but generally challenge the status quo. Practising this kind of mental or discursive argument can result in people developing different outlooks. They may help to solve problems, explain the past or generate new ideas. Children enjoy not just discussing given ideas, but inventing imaginary scenarios of their own and may come up with more challenging ideas than adults. In this way they can consider issues from the past, present and even the future:

- What might have happened in the past if . . .?
- What could happen now if . . .?
- What will happen in the future if . . .?

Craft (2001) maintains that Possibility Thinking is at the heart of little c creativity, and that children even in the Early Years, should be encouraged to ask 'What if ?' questions in connection with anything which engages them in order to develop both problem-finding and problem-solving skills. In order to do this, children need to be able to ask questions, make connections, be imaginative, take risks, play with ideas, connect with other's ideas and work with them (Craft 2005).

What-iffing is a form of thought experiment devised by Robert Harris (2010) who feels that many people's creativity is blocked by 'the mind's fierce grasp on reality'. He says that What-iffing involves describing an imagined action or solution and then examining the probable associated facts, consequences, or events without criticizing the idea as unrealistic or impossible, but considering how it might be made to work or why it might be useful. What-iffing allows us to explore other realities so as to see novel situations in a new light. Harris proposes What-iffing as a skill to be developed playfully as an aid to creative development, problem-solving and idea invention.

Some scenario suggestions
- What if animals could talk?
- What if we could see smells?
- What if there were no exams?
- What if we never had to sleep?

Further thought experiments
- What might have happened if the allies had lost the Second World War?
- How would our lives be different if plastic had not been invented?
- What might happen if all the TVs in the world stopped working?
- What will happen if the world population goes on growing?
- What will the world be like in 100/1000 years time?
- If you could remember everything you read and saw, how would it affect you?
- What if we could read each other's minds?
- How would the planet be different if there was no money in the world?
- Would you rather travel back in time, or into the future? Why? Where and when would you go?

Don't forget to let children challenge each other (and you) with thought experiments of their own. Thought experiments can also explore scenarios with moral issues. 'How should we?', and 'How could you?' are the questions to be debated rather than the less personal 'What if?'

SCAMPER

The principles of the SCAMPER technique were first suggested by Alex Osborn and later arranged by Bob Eberle as a mnemonic in 1991 to increase interest in the perceptive, imaginative, and creative abilities of children. The technique suggests seven alterations which may be made to an existing product or process in order to create a new one. The technique may also be applied in a problem-solving context, e.g. How can we improve indoor playtimes? Use it to help with product development or ways to make their stories and poems more exciting. SCAMPER is an acronym which can be used as follows (Table 6.3).

Table 6.3 SCAMPER

	Element	Action	General examples	Class examples
S	Substitute	Substituting one part of the product/process for something else	Change one ingredient for another in a recipe	Use symbols instead of words when note-taking
C	Combine	Combining the two products to create a different product/process	Combine boat and plane as sea-plane	Combine PE warm-ups and pop music to create dance routines at playtime
A	Adapt	Adapt part of the product/process to change the nature of the product/process	Adapt a story to make a film	Write instructions as spells
M	Modify	Change part or all of the current situation, or to alter it in an unusual way	Eliminate the dust bag so that collected dirt can be seen in a vacuum cleaner	Use dinner queue time to learn facts about food
P	Put to new use	Use the product/process in a new way	Use reflectors as cat's eyes on road	Recycle waste to make new products
E	Eliminate	Eliminate parts of the product/process	Eliminate a keyboard and mouse and use touch screen	Ask pupils to create without first designing on paper
R	Rearrange	Rearrange part of the product/process so that it works in a different order	Put the engine in the boot or the centre of a car	Put a school trip at different stage of the topic

Practical activity
Challenge children to apply each element to a well-known story such as Goldilocks to see how the plot could be updated.

Build it better

Find ways to redesign familiar products both practically and fantastically. Sometimes the fantastic can be translated into the practical and possible. Look at an object such as a pen, a brush or a comic. Consider how it could be improved or made relevant for different users, the young, the old, the eccentric, the very rich, or a particular personality or even an animal or mythical figure:

- First SCAMPER it.
- Then personalize it.
- Resize, add extra functions, magical properties, consider how ICT might improve it.
- Talk about how a system or institution might use it.

Exploring design

In Science and DT sessions there are almost limitless possibilities for exploring ideas and keeping options open as variables are altered in a science test or different designs are trailed in a DT context. Pupils should be scaffolded to progress from following teacher-led investigations to designing their own. They should be helped to ask as well as answer their own questions about the world around them, to explore the implications of advances in science and technology for themselves, their families and the wider world.

Giving children an open-ended challenge such as how to drop a raw egg from the second story of a building without breaking it or to make a vehicle which will travel across a room without being touched, allows them to make connections with the skills and knowledge they have and apply them in a new context. The design in DT should mean real design not decoration of someone else's design. It is a context where we teach skills and then give a challenge in which they can be applied.

Helping groups to develop reflective skills 🖋

Many people, including adults, find it hard to reflect, let alone record their contemplation effectively. It is a process which involves a personal response to an experience with the aim of improving learning and developing new ideas and although often suggested as a final part of the creative cycle or required at the end of a task, reflection can be used to illuminate and improve every stage of a project. Reflection can be as creative as any other stage of learning and is sometimes described as a processing phase where thinking and learning take place. The very term process suggests that several aspects or stages may be involved and teachers can help learners to identify these for particular contexts. Reflection can be built around each stage in the skills hierarchy identified by Bloom's taxonomy of thinking skills, from simple recall of facts through understanding, apply-ing, analysis, and synthesis to evaluation. Moon (1999) suggests that we reflect for several reasons:

- to build theory from observations;
- to engage in personal development;
- to make decisions;
- to empower ourselves as individuals.

Reflection can be used to work out how to improve a situation or to learn from any experience. To develop the necessary skills, learners are sometimes required to produce written accounts of their reflection although this is not the only way of recording ideas and may not suit everyone. The tools used to reflect or record can affect the process itself as some people prefer a visual or discursive approach. The use of objects to aid comparison can engender new trains of thought depending on the object chosen. Reflective outcomes and conclusions will also be influenced by the purpose of the reflection and the mental state of the person concerned. When a written reflection is composed, the inexperienced may need prompts and scaffolds to learn the technique. Sometimes a discussion, diagram or chart will be more effective to develop reflective ideas. Many techniques are just visible forms of a mental process, which is the actual reflection and it can be useful to employ a range of reflective techniques to tease out and sometimes record our ideas. If this process is taught from an early age, it can help crea-tive development and social skills. The suggestions below are starting points and teach-ers and learners need to find their own ways to developing reflective skills. Whatever technique is chosen, reflection may be done individually, in pairs or groups. Each tool suggested should be adapted by the user to suit their needs and circumstances. Encouraging pupils to devise their own aids to critical reflection is a further way to develop their creativity. However, teachers should consider what amount of critical reflection is suitable for a task and not insist on in-depth analysis for every one as this might be disheartening. Sometimes a quick oral evaluation will be quite enough.

Some tools to aid reflection are:

- A helping hand.
- Object analogy.
- IT prompt.

A helping hand

This is a list of five areas to consider when learning how to reflect. Written on a hand shape, they can be remembered as a handful of ideas to aid reflection (Figure 6.7). For each question, encourage explanations to help further analysis.

For more experienced reflectors the questions might be altered to read:

1 What was the most useful part of this task?
2 What was the hardest part?
3 What was the easiest part?

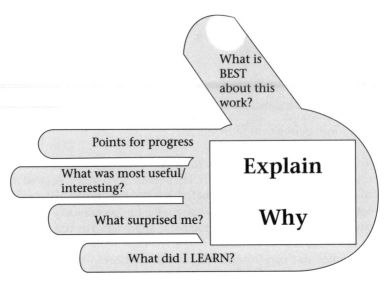

Figure 6.7 A helping hand of reflective prompts

    4   If I did this again, how would I improve it?
    5   What have I learned about this process/the product?

Not all reflective evaluation needs to be written down individually. A group discussion with one person or even no one scribing may sometimes be more appropriate. These prompts are just starting points to focus the process.

Object analogy

The purpose of the analogy is to see a situation in a new way with fresh insight. If a seemingly unrelated object or a saying is chosen at random, ideas associated with it may throw fresh light on a process or product (Table 6.4):

    1   Think of an object at random: here I chose a stone/car/plant/a proverb.
    2   List the qualities of the item and see which might relate to the project in hand. In this case I am writing a book.

Reading these observations helps me consider the many aspects there are to writing; how the ideas can sometimes lead the writer rather than the other way round; that not all ideas work; that I must build on firm foundations as well as develop new ideas to be of use to people with different needs; that organizing myself to settle down to write one section at a time is vital. Not every object or saying will produce relevant ideas, but it is worth trying with what may at first seem unpromising ideas in order to develop new ones.

    A collection of carefully selected objects might be a more engaging way to do this. If the teacher has a bag with objects such as those suggested in Figure 6.8 from which

Table 6.4   Random object or idea game

Random object or idea	Qualities or features	Reflections using these ideas as starting points
Stone	Hard, old, many uses, rough/smooth	Writing this book is hard, I need to build on old ideas and develop new ways to use them. My first draft is very rough and needs work. I need to work on strong foundations
Car	Moves, takes different travellers. Needs fuel	The process of writing moves at different speeds needs plenty of ideas to be useful to different reader
Plant	Grows, may provide food, attractive	This book grows as I write, sometimes in directions I had not expected. It needs to be food for thought and attractively set out on the page
Proverb	A rolling stone gathers no moss	I need to focus and settle to the job. I must not keep flitting from one idea to another. Growth, like writing, takes time

pupils draw out one object or saying to help them reflect on their learning. This could help to develop questioning skills, the forming of connections, seeing things in new ways, exploring ideas all as part of the reflective process.

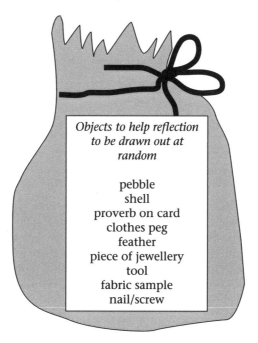

Objects to help reflection to be drawn out at random

pebble
shell
proverb on card
clothes peg
feather
piece of jewellery
tool
fabric sample
nail/screw

Figure 6.8   A bag of ideas

IT prompts

Using a template on a computer can aid reflection in two ways. First, prompts which can be altered by the teacher or pupil to suit the task or the learner can help to scaffold their thoughts. Second, the provisional nature of word processing enables instant redrafting of ideas until the writer is satisfied that they have expressed their reflections in a way which helps them to move forward, such as target setting or reworking part of a project. For young children, the template could involve faces to be coloured to show progress (Figure 6.9) or a self-awarded grade if this was felt appropriate. There could be simple questions about what was learned and enjoyed.

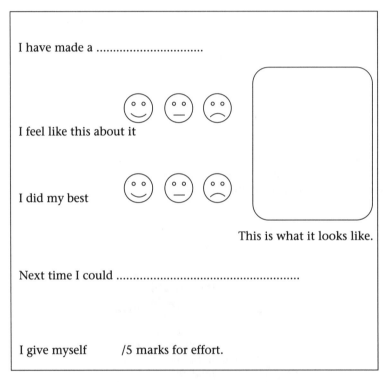

I have made a ....

I feel like this about it

I did my best

This is what it looks like.

Next time I could ....

I give myself   /5 marks for effort.

Figure 6.9 Reflective scaffold for younger children

More experienced reflectors may go on to consider other people's viewpoints and ask 'What if?' type of questions which consider alternatives. Questions might consider the process, the effort involved, cooperative working skills and other participants' reactions. Older pupils might find it useful to select from a bank of questions in order to identify progress and set targets for further development (Figure 6.10). Critical reflection considers the validity of the learner's views as well as those of others involved.

Reflective diagrams and charts

It is sometimes helpful for learners to create their own diagram as reflective aids. These could take the form of concept map or chart. It is not always easy to put ideas into

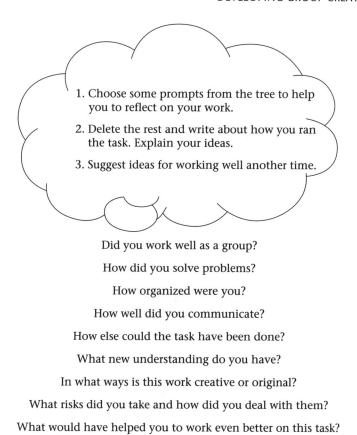

1. Choose some prompts from the tree to help you to reflect on your work.

2. Delete the rest and write about how you ran the task. Explain your ideas.

3. Suggest ideas for working well another time.

Did you work well as a group?

How did you solve problems?

How organized were you?

How well did you communicate?

How else could the task have been done?

What new understanding do you have?

In what ways is this work creative or original?

What risks did you take and how did you deal with them?

What would have helped you to work even better on this task?

What was the most surprising/interesting thing you learned?

TARGETS FOR FUTURE WORK WILL BE:

Figure 6.10   Reflective tree for older children

words. To facilitate this, some learners might create a grading system to help analyse their feelings and experience. This could simply take the form of a line with polar descriptions at each end for the learner to mark where they feel they are on a continuum (Figure 6.11). Learners would create their own categories as part of the reflective process.

Another self-evaluation aid on a computer template to make the recording quick and simple might be to award oneself marks out of 10 in self-defined categories (Figure 6.12). Charts could be kept for comparison to assess progress. These will of course be personal assessments where the values of the numbers awarded represent subjective personal evaluations. An evaluation which goes down could represent a greater understanding or more critical look at a particular skill rather than a poorer performance. The chart is in any case just an aid to identifying different aspects of a task and considering how well they have been done.

I did my best	I could have made more effort
My plan suited user needs perfectly	My plan did not consider user needs enough
I worked very cooperatively	I could have been more cooperative

Figure 6.11 Line evaluation. Note: Wording to be adapted to age and ability level

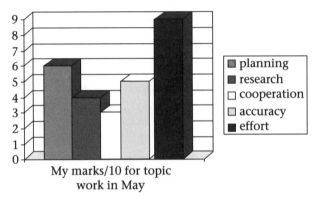

Figure 6.12 Graph to aid reflection and self-evaluation

Practice ideas: questions to stimulate creative thinking in spare moments
- What might a magician have in his pocket?
- How would a musician/artist/scientist/mathematician/author . . . dress/send a birthday present?
- Try puzzle jokes, e.g. what do you break by saying its name? (Silence)
- Create a character for a story from suggestions by class.
- Invent a machine. As each child draws part of the machine they have to explain what it does. (Decide on function first . . . could inspire with Heath-Robinson pictures first.)
- Create a sentence which includes three random words suggested by class or chosen at random from a book.
- Practise metaphorical thinking: school is like a circus because . . .
- Scribble a simple shape, and challenge the class to make it into something.

Developing group creativity in each ACE

We will look at this aspect of developing class creativity first before considering what can be done to help individual pupils, since a class teacher normally has to plan for whole classes or groups before making more individual provision. Ideally a good medium-term plan will incorporate the potential for aspects of individual creative development, but that may have to be built on what is proposed for larger groups. Today some schools let pupils have a voice in the planning of their curriculum so that teaching follows the interests of both groups and individuals. What follows are suggestions for developing creative skills in each area of creative endeavour. Further suggestions, which are more specifically topic- or subject-based appear in Chapter 7. These suggestions have been differentiated for three primary age groups of KS1, Lower KS2 and Upper KS2 (Table 6.5). Of course, depending on the interests and development of the pupils, ideas from one section may be more appropriate for another developmental level. Each idea will involve teaching some basic skills for pupils to then use in designing their own artefact or system. It should not involve pupils all making very similar outcomes. Enterprise activities (see p. 135) could provide suitable creative challenges at any age.

Note: the skills required for each of these challenges must be taught first. No one can be really creative without the requisite skills for the particular context. Most of these you are probably teaching already.

Table 6.5 ACE skills and ideas for KS1, lower KS2 and upper KS2

ACE	Ideas to develop the creativity of groups in KS1
Technological	1. Groups to design and make smoothies/breads/picnic food from a range of familiar and unfamiliar ingredients. Compare results 2. Decide how best to organize wet playtimes 3. Challenge groups to come up with their own contexts for small world play and create/assemble the parts required
Artistic	1. Teach a range of printing skills to be applied in the design of fabrics or wrapping papers. Each group to create a design suitable for a different purpose 2. Teach photographic skills so pupils can take pictures of objects or the school from unusual angles, perhaps as part of a group project on shapes, colours or pattern 3. Ask pupils to explore the different sounds which can be made from one instrument. Ask three children to use their ideas to make a sound-scape
Mathematical	1. Solve measuring problems without conventional measuring equipment. Talk about what would happen if there were no weighing scales in the world 2. How many patterns can be made by 6 bottles in a crate for 12? 3. Look at different options when budgeting for a party 4. How many numbers up to 20 can be made using the digits 1, 2, and 5?
Linguistic	1. Talk about alternative endings to well-known stories. Use SCAMPER with them to alter familiar tales such as Cinderella 2. Let children act out problematic situations such as, what to do when you find something you do not own, or someone is unkind, or someone asks for help 3. Design (and film?) an advert for a new product they have created

ACE	Ideas to develop the creativity of groups in KS1
Physical	1. In pairs help children to devise games which use bean-bags, a hoop or a rope
	2. Teach some basic dance steps which can be put together in simple disco-type dance routines
	3. Ask children to devise their own follow-my-leader routines
Natural Philosophical	1. Discuss how life might be different if animals understood what we said
	2. Ask groups to find ways to sort natural objects and explain their ideas. How many ways can one set of objects be sorted?
	3. See how many questions they can devise about a woodlouse and suggest different ways each one might be answered

	Ideas to develop the creativity of groups in lower KS2
Technological	1. Groups to design and make dips and salads from a range of familiar and unfamiliar ingredients
	2. Design and make a shadow or glove puppet to be used in a performance for parents and peers
	3. Find ways to improve the organization of the classroom so that it does not get in a mess. Groups could consider different areas
Artistic	1. Teach ICT and photographic skills for pupils to create photographic portraits of their friends to show their personalities
	2. Using an electronic keyboard, show pupils how to start composing by using a set beat and adding musical phrases. Try this on-line at http://www.bgfl.org/bgfl/custom/resources_ftp/client_ftp/ks2/music/piano/
	3. Share a painting you like. Ask groups to explain what they do/do not like about it, what they would like to ask the artist and how they would change it in some way
Mathematical	1. How many ways can each group solve a similar maths problem?
	2. Find different ways to record answers to maths problems through diagrams, cartoons, speech bubbles and posters
	3. How many maths questions can they devise (and answer) about a tube of coloured sweets?
Linguistic	1. Create magazines or e-zines on a group interest
	2. Write plays and film them
	3. Write jingle/advertisement for a new product
Physical	1. Help pupils identify basic actions used in a favourite sport such as football and to put them first into individual then paired and later group dances
	2. Groups to devise circuit training activities with small apparatus
	3. Challenge pupils to devise their own warm-up routine for a PE lesson
Natural Philosophical	1. In groups, how many questions can they devise about bubbles? Which can they answer?
	2. Do they think animals have feelings? If so, how should we treat cows and slugs?
	3. If they could invent a new material, what would its properties be and what would it be used for?

(continued)

Table 6.5   *(continued)*

	Ideas to develop the creativity of groups in upper KS2
Technological	1. Challenge pupils to design their own exhibition or museum to show parents and peers what they have learned in a particular subject or topic. The exhibition could be class-, hall- or corridor-based and involve pictures, models, videos and IT presentations constructed and displayed by pupils themselves, with some help from adults with relevant expertise in each area. An aural guide to the exhibition could be devised and recorded by groups responsible for each section 2. Groups to design and make mueslis/soups from a range of familiar and unfamiliar ingredients for specific groups of consumers 3. Groups to design and make a bridge/tower from paper or spaghetti
Artistic	1. Teach a range of sewing skills to be applied in the design of a village tapestry, banner or fabric collage which tells a story in sections such as a creation story or local history event 2. Use electronic keyboards with groups of pupils to compose jingles/ring tones/ other compositions 3. Demonstrate a range of techniques, e.g. paint/pastel/on a computer paint programme for pupils to apply in different contexts
Mathematical	1. Make an electronic presentation to show another class how to recognize equivalent fractions 2. Plan how to redecorate and furnish a den/a play area, on a given budget 3. Work out the best way to complete a holiday journey with and without using motorways and toll roads. What could be saved in terms of time and petrol, in each case?

Linguistic	1. Group writing of surreal questions by one team for another team to answer, e.g.
	  a. What is the colour of silence?
	  b. Where does fear come from?
	  c. What do owls dream of?
	  d. How do waves call?
	  e. When does the red bird sing?
	2. Create an interactive CD of information about their area for pupils in another location
	3. Devise an audio book of a story the group has written or on a factual subject for a younger class

Physical	1. Teach basic country dance steps for pupils to create their own country dance. Even boys enjoy this once it gets to the 'devise your own dance' activity 2. Pupils could plan their own potted sports day which includes a new set of challenges the school does not usually employ 3. Help groups of pupils to devise physical responses to stories/poems/musical pieces. Ideas which require a strong physical response work best, e.g. the enacting of a conflict
Natural Philosophical	1. Ask them to explain their predictions about whether time travel will one day be possible 2. Challenge them to design a model of the solar system using just themselves to represent the sun, planets and moons 3. Discuss what would happen if the sun was obscured by an ash cloud for over a year

7　Personal creativity

All children are able to develop creative ideas as soon as they can manipulate their surroundings and reflect on the consequences. Piaget did not use the term creativity when describing his developmental stages but referred, instead, to constructions. In his book entitled *To Understand Is to Invent* (1948), he suggested that personal invention, however small, showed understanding. This concurs with constructivist theory in that each person creates a personal and meaningful view of the world through interaction with it.

The theory of *personal* creativity focusses on the creative process rather than the product. Runco says, 'The definition of creativity as construction of personal meaning is also consistent with the notion that creativity is a kind of self-expression and self-actualisation' (2003: 3). This view states that since the vast majority of the population has the potential to construct meaning, they all have the ability to develop the everyday little c creativity described by Craft (2002). He continues, 'If creativity is defined in terms of objective performances and actual achievement, children . . . have a poor chance of being identified as creatively gifted.' Personal creativity is interpretative and involves the individual not only in acquiring new information, but also in accommodating new concepts by reorganizing existing understanding to include them. We acquire new information only when we are interested, so teachers should ensure that learners are given inherently interesting tasks to engage them. To do this, they need to discover what each pupil finds engaging within the subjects taught and build on that. A tall order!

Personal creativity builds on an individual's skills and knowledge and is coloured by the particular qualities of that individual. Current approaches to learning attempt to develop pupils' potential through helping them to create personal constructs, develop cognition and metacognition as well as social and practical skills. Some teachers consider aspects of their intelligence, and preferred learning styles as well. Differentiating the experience of learning takes many forms from the 'assess to improve grades' to 'intrinsic motivational' approaches.

What is involved in personal creativity?

How a child's original ideas and behaviour are treated from an early age will certainly affect whether new ideas and risk-taking behaviour are repeated. In many cases, children will have had originality and risk taking suppressed well before school either to make them easier to handle or to keep them safe. Sadly this is not always in the best interests of the individual and an aversion to doing things differently or to suggesting new ideas or to getting messy may have to be unlearned once they start school. To see how to develop personal pupil creativity, we need to consider the characteristics of the creative personality which we wish to develop and then see how this can be done in a crowded classroom.

In Chapter 3 we noted some of the characteristics of personal creativity such as its quirky nature and reliance on personal skills. Personal creative responses may be internally initiated by those who are self-starters, while other creative types respond best to external stimuli or requests. It is important to recognize both types of creative individual in a class or only the creativity of the self-starters will be recognized and promoted.

While personal creativity involves independent motivation, initiative, and perseverance, it may also, especially in children, need adult encouragement, permission and validation. A sense of autonomy can fuel creative engagement but this is decreased if the individual feels over-supervised, or in competition with other individuals. Personal creativity may be highly individual so that its value may be unrecognized by a supervising adult with different tastes and ideas. It can involve risk taking with either time or resources which can lead to class conflict with peers and adults alike. It may be characterized by 'flow', or periods of concentration, which mean that the child is so involved that they do not respond well to outside stimuli or they appear to be day-dreaming. All these factors can make organizing the development of individual pupil creativity hard to pursue.

Rego et al. (2009) summarize several studies which focus on personal characteristics associated with creative achievement, and suggest that since *creativity often involves challenging the status quo*, resilience and optimism are personal qualities to cherish. This research built on studies by Youssef and Luthans (2007) and others which found that hopeful people tend to be happier and that happier individuals are more creative, and concluded that hope is a natural predictor of creativity. While these studies involved adults rather than children, there is no reason to suppose that these findings do not also apply to pupils. Since happy people are likely to see failure as a temporary set-back caused by situational rather than personal circumstances, keeping pupils feeling happy, hopeful and positive about their work is a key to giving them the confidence to develop creative ideas.

Runco (1996) sees personal creativity characterized by the transformational capacity of the individual. A transformation occurs whenever we interpret or make sense of something in the world. He suggests that the process of transformation is a fundamental part of information processing and creativity, because all non-reflective information processing requires our interpretation and how we do this depends on our individual experience and understanding of the world. Very young children of 2 or 3 years will transform their experience and ideas through pretend play, although it might be argued that unless they are being intentionally original it is not really an example of creative thinking. Runco refers to several experts who consider intent a crucial facet of creativity (1996: 18). He also distinguishes creativity from problem solving since creativity is sometimes the result of self-expression and although it can be a challenge, it is not necessarily problematical. Some educationalists believe that younger children are more creative than older ones. Sternberg and Williams (2011) write that creativity is routinely witnessed in young children but harder to find in older children and adults. They suggest that this is because their creative potential has been suppressed by a society that encourages intellectual conformity. If this is the case, then a challenge for teachers is to help their pupils develop resilience around their creative ideas, while continuing to respond positively to assessment and evaluation. Younger children may appear more creative because they are inexperienced. They are less likely to be aware of conventional approaches, perhaps because they are poor at drawing or inexperienced in knowing what will work and so come up with fresh ideas. However, if children are not consciously creative and are not aiming for novelty, but just concerned with the present process, should this be seen as creative? Part of the educator's job is to help children reflect on what they have created and to tease out ideas about originality and value, so that with metacognition as part of the process, a truly creative outcome is recognized by both creator and assessor.

What is required to develop personal creativity?

Building personal qualities

The NACCCE report suggests that the first task in teaching for creativity is to 'encourage young people to believe in their creative potential, to engage their sense of possibility and to give them the confidence to try' (NACCCE 1999: 90). We can do this by recognizing effort, risk taking and originality and not just conformity, compliance and success. We can praise unusual questions, record especially interesting and challenging ones on a question of the day/week poster and share the task of discussing or researching answers. Sternberg and Williams (2011) agree that 'the main limitation on what students can do is what they think they can do'.

Runco (2003) believes that creativity involves the construction of new meaning at the individual's level and that it is children's creative *potential* rather than performance which educators should seek to develop. If teachers agree, they will put more emphasis in their classes on helping children to develop their ideas rather than on polishing them. He also suggests that children need to learn *discretion* – when to be original and when to conform. Claxton (2002) feels that we should develop the Resilience, Reflection, Resourcefulness and Relationships of individuals to build their learning power, and of course this will increase their creative power as well.

Cremin (cited in Wilson 2007) says that in order to be creative, children require a balance of safety, and challenge, of structure and freedom, the chance to play and be playful, stimulating physical space, as well as space in time to reflect. Successful exploration of ideas helps to develop new memes – ideas which spread from person to person within a culture (Dawkins 1976). The development of memes which take a culture forward in a beneficial way is one of the most creative outcomes possible for an individual, and although they may have been developed in association with others, can move what Margaret Boden (2004) would describe as p-creativity (personal) into the h-creativity (historical) range.

To develop the personal creativity of individual pupils, it is necessary to know them as individuals. To do this takes time to listen to their ideas, hopes and fears. Talking to small groups or individuals, perhaps while the rest of the class is engaged in a whole-school assembly of some kind, or even a playtime, can elicit crucial details about their interests and areas with which they would like more challenge or support. Just knowing that you are taking the time to see them as individuals can promote confidence in their self-worth. Building confidence, discretion, resilience, resourcefulness and worthwhile relationships as well as providing a safe, but challenging environment with time to reflect on motivating tasks, are effective ways to develop the creativity of the child.

Developing mindfulness

Mindfulness is the art of paying attention to the details of the present. It is a process which makes us aware of the context and the perspective of our actions, rather than relying on prior assumptions. Developing mindfulness can give us:

1   greater sensitivity to one's environment;
2   more openness to information;
3   the ability to create new categories for structuring perception;
4   enhanced awareness of multiple perspectives.

(Langer and Moldovenau 2000: 2)

Langer and Moldovenau claim that education is an area much involved in *mindlessness* because we often pass on mind-sets which are not always helpful. For example, we may pass on assumptions about learning the basics of a subject without questioning who decides what the basics are and if they are the most engaging facets of the subject. Groups who are asked to construct meaning rather than memorize given material recall it better. Therefore, it would be more effective to explain the story of the plague from the different perspectives of people who lived in Eyam, and then ask pupils to decide what they would have chosen to do rather than simply trying to memorize facts. Mindfulness is a vital skill to develop the creative behaviour of seeing things in new ways.

Practical ideas for developing mindfulness

1. Encourage pupils to look closely at things, perhaps using small mirrors to see under leaves or standing on chairs to get a new view of a room. When this is done with questions which encourage making connections and exploring ideas, creative ideas can be developed.
2. Introduce ideas in a conditional way, using language like *might* and *could be,* and *perhaps*, instead of the traditional absolute way of *is, always* and *can only be*. Langer and Moldovenau (2000) report on research which found that students learned better this way, even though they had to deal with more information. They conclude that it is a state of mind which increases creativity, flexibility and improves memory.
3. Explore new learning from multiple perspectives such as those of a sparrow in food chain, a character in a story or an elderly resident in a local study area.

Creative Challenge!
1. Look at your planning for the past week:
2. How often did it involve building on the personal interests of pupils?
3. When were difficult questions praised and recorded?
4. When were risk-taking and originality praised and setbacks used as opportunities to learn?
5. When was mindfulness promoted?

Approaches to learning in school

There are several approaches to learning which bear in mind different aspects of a learner's personality and which may have a bearing on the development of a creative individual. We will consider these before looking at ways to move from building group creativity to developing personal creative practices. For each approach, one on-line site for further reading is suggested, but it is best to read ideas from several sources to ensure a balanced view is obtained.

Maslow's hierarchy of needs

To make sure that pupils can reach their creative potential, we should consider Maslow's (1943) theory that we all have a hierarchy of needs. This theory states that in order for people to reach their potential, including their creative potential, more basic needs must be met first. These needs are physiological and are to do with safety, love, and self-esteem. Consider Figure 7.1 in relation to individual members of your class. Who might need provision at the lower levels in order to achieve at higher ones? What can you do to ensure the first four levels are catered for, for all learners? Several answers may involve whole-school issues.

Implications for creative development
Before we attempt any form of education or creative development, we must first ensure that pupils are neither hungry, nor dehydrated nor suffering from lack of sleep. After a playtime, it is worth considering if some children need a few minutes with relaxation techniques or to listen to a story or to practise brain gym. At the second level of need, are there class and school routines in place to give security, and are pupils, especially the more difficult ones, free from constant criticism? Is the classroom comfortable, attractive and well organized so that learners have some autonomy in selecting resources and clearing up? At the next level do they each feel cared for and approved of by class staff, with opportunities to share personal concerns and ideas? At the fourth level, is there a culture of respect between children and all classroom helpers whether they are paid or working voluntarily? Are support staffs shown the same respect as the teaching staff? Once all these needs are met, pupils will be able to think about taking sensible risks with ideas and developing their personal interests and creativity. If they do not, we need to find out what is blocking this aspect of their personality. Some will have other special needs which require consideration and these may not always be obvious. Look at the

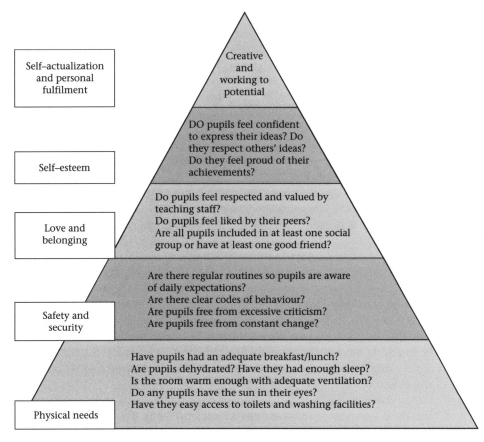

Figure 7.1   Maslow's hierarchy of needs as applied to pupils' learning needs

range of teaching methods you currently employ and see if they appeal to all learners. Consideration of intelligence type, individual interest and learning style can be catered for though open-ended activities which follow lessons on basic concepts, attitudes, skills and knowledge.

> **Creative Challenge!**
> Follow up at least one of the learning theories outlined above, preferably from several sources, and see how you might put it to use with your class in your next teaching week.

Multiple intelligences (MI) theory

> http://www.multipleintelligencetheory.co.uk/

Traditionally intelligence has been seen as a single entity, and although tests have tried to measure it in different ways, it has often been assumed that if a person was highly intelligent, it was a general ability. Multiple intelligence theory was proposed by Howard Gardner in 1983 when he suggested that there might be different types of intelligence so that a person who excelled intellectually in one domain might be less advantaged in others.

Gardner believes that there are many types of cognitive ability and that most people will have greater aptitude in some areas, than in others. The theory suggests that the ability to learn and apply a new technique quickly does not necessarily indicate a high intelligence, as the individual may have just memorized a taught technique rather than worked out a solution from first principles for themselves. Alternatively they could prefer a different approach, be interested and even excel in another subject or just want to explore a process at a deeper level.

Gardner has suggested there are at least eight types of intelligence which can be identified, and which should be considered when teaching pupils. He does not isolate a creative intelligence, but suggests that this strand runs through each of the others.

Viewing intelligence as 'the capacity to solve problems or the ability to fashion products that are valued in a cultural setting' (Gardner and Hatch 1989), it is suggested that we all have aspects of each type of intelligence to varying degree:

- *Linguistic intelligence* involves sensitivity to spoken and written language, the ability to learn languages, and the capacity to use language to learn. Those with linguistic intelligence are word smart, use language effectively to explain ideas and as a means to remember information. They enjoy reading, writing and talking about things. They think in words, like to read and write, enjoy stories and poems as well as word games.
- *Logical-mathematical intelligence* consists of the capacity to reason deductively and think logically and investigate issues scientifically. Those who are number smart are good at maths and solving problems. They see patterns easily, like abstract ideas, strategy games and logical puzzles.
- *Musical intelligence* involves skill in the performance, composition, and appreciation of musical patterns. Those who are music smart can recognize sounds and the timbre of a tone. They may sing, or hum, to themselves, can remember melodies, have a good sense of rhythm, may play an instrument and need music on when studying.
- *Bodily-kinaesthetic intelligence* involves using one's body to solve problems and express themselves. These pupils enjoy sports and may be good at dance, drama, mime, athletics, gymnastics, and other sports. They remember through bodily sensations, find it difficult to sit still for long; have excellent coordination, communicate well through gestures and learn best through physical activity, simulation and role play.
- *Visual spatial intelligence* involves the potential to recognize and use the patterns and space. Those who are picture smart are good at art and activities which involve visual images such as map reading, mazes and graphs. They think in images and pictures, remember where things have been put; enjoy drawing, designing, building, daydreaming and creating diagrams and charts.
- *Interpersonal intelligence* is concerned with the capacity to understand the intentions and desires of other people. It allows people to work effectively with

others. Those who are smart about people (people smart) learn best through group work and social games where they may be good at leading and organizing.

- *Intrapersonal intelligence* entails the capacity to understand oneself, to appreciate one's feelings, fears and motivations. Self-smart people often prefer to work alone, are self-motivated, are intuitive and are self-confident. They are aware of personal strengths and weaknesses and reflection.
- *Naturalistic intelligence* applies to those with the capacity to classify easily, make distinctions and recognize patterns in the natural world. Those who are nature smart are curious about the world around them.

Others have proposed further intelligences, including creative, moral, spiritual, and existential intelligence.

Implications for creative development

This theory, although popular with the public and with many teachers, has not had universal approval from experts in this area. The relationship between intelligence and creativity is not clear and high intelligence does not necessarily result in high levels of creativity, although some intelligence is needed for any creative output. If we accept the multiple intelligences (MI) theory, we should consider that with eight types of intelligence, individuals may benefit from learning through different intellectual approaches to create ways to develop and memorize knowledge and skills. In each subject we should give opportunities for children to work creatively from personal intellectual strengths to create a response which will develop new constructs. If, for example, a pupil has problems with writing, using music, art, or drama, to learn through musical, spatial or kinaesthetic intelligence, could improve attainment. Novelty is an acknowledged facet of creativity so when learners are able to use their personal intellectual approach to process knowledge and skills and create a novel response to their learning, they are likely to produce outcomes which are memorable and of value. We would not ignore intelligences in which children were less capable, but with success in preferred areas, they would have confidence to develop others. Differentiation for some lessons would be less in terms of easier and harder, and more in terms of creative opportunities offered to process the learning, perhaps using interpersonal intelligence in a collaborative response, or through an intrapersonal and singular view. If we group pupils with complementary intelligences they can learn from each other. Individuals with a talent for explaining ideas can help those who are good at creating diagrams to record them. Those who have a creative flair for organization may help those who have innovative ideas, but struggle to put them into practice. We might broaden the curriculum for groups to give more scope for developing different aptitudes and perhaps narrow the curriculum for individuals so that individuals can use their personal intellectual skills to focus on developing through personal creativity.

One benefit of valuing MI theory is that it can lead to valuing the skills and achievements of children in many areas rather than just the traditional academic disciplines. Some educationalists favour it as it appeals to what they already sense is true, that everyone can be smart and learn in different ways. Others complain that it implies they should be teaching in eight different ways. It should be remembered that this is not a proven theory and there has been much criticism of these ideas. Some would say that we all have the potential to do well in each field of study, but that we tend to develop in just a few with a positive feedback loop from showing excellence in a few areas on which we tend to build. It could be argued that rather than concentrate on areas in which pupils excel, it is the teacher's task to try to help develop areas in which they show less aptitude.

MI theory has few enthusiasts among those with a traditional psychological background because of the lack of experimental evidence. What evidence there is has been interpreted by some to show that there is a correlation between different abilities which would suggest the existence of an overall intelligence factor. It has been suggested that Gardner is confusing ability with intelligence. Perhaps the greatest value of MI theory is that it has helped educators to reflect on their practice, and given them a reason to widen their criteria for what should be valued in their pupils and this can lead to increased self-esteem in pupils which in turn raises confidence and creative attainment.

Learning styles theories

http://www.itslifejimbutnotasweknowit.org.uk/files/LearningStyles.pdf

There are many theories about the way we learn and one which has caught the popular imagination suggests that most learners prefer one of three learning styles: visual, auditory and kinaesthetic (VAK). This VAK theory seems to have acquired most recognition in schools, perhaps because it resonates with many teachers' personal experience as well as being relatively simple to translate into classroom practice. However, it should be remembered that it *is* just a theory which may be of value, but should be considered with caution.

- A *visual learning* style is attributed to those who benefit from pictures, diagrams, films and visually memorable material. These people may need to make their own visual versions of material given to them.
- An *auditory style of learning* works for those who prefer to learn by listening and discussing new material. They may find films and podcasts and taped recordings useful and are good at interpreting underlying meanings. They may like to hear written texts read to get the most from them.
- A *kinaesthetic learning style* is preferred by those who learn through practical, experiential methods. They enjoy hands-on scientific investigation and a tactile approach.

Implications for creative development
It is sometimes suggested that if teachers know the preferred learning style of each child in their class, they will be able to deliver sessions in ways which suit individuals. This is not to suggest that all lessons should be presented in three ways, but that over the course of a day and over a series of lessons in one subject, a variety of learning styles should be catered for.

People favour different learning styles for particular situations or subjects. Some topics seem to lend themselves more to one learning style than another. If, as the constructivist hypothesis suggests, we learn by creating personal theories and responses to the world, then we need to help learners to apply preferred visual, auditory and kinaesthetic approaches to create their own constructs. There are times when we prefer to listen to given information and other times when it helps to act it out or see a film or picture which illustrates it. To internalize it, we must use the new knowledge or skill in some way. By creating our own response either visually as we write or make a diagram, orally as we explain it to someone else, or kinaesthetically as we dramatize or model it, we build new schema. What we can take from this theory is that lessons need to involve a range of approaches and that individuals may respond better to one approach than another in different situations.

For example, when pupils have been given access to historical information, allowing them to work with it in a range of ways can be beneficial. When learning about the Fire of London, instead of writing about it and adding a picture, they might have the option of creating an electronic presentation (visual), creating a short radio broadcast (aural) or writing a short play and filming it with a group of puppets or even Lego people (kinaesthetic). None of these need take longer than a traditional write-up. Using Lego or their own hands with felt-tip faces and paper head dresses will avoid spending too much time on making props, and give most time for telling and explaining the story. Follow-up work in geography might be to create a labelled diagram, (visual) or a rhyme about what has been learned (aural), or a plasticine model with labels (kinaesthetic). Having to use particular words as part of each task can ensure that subject specific vocabulary is learned.

Experiential learning theory

David Kolb (1984) developed a theory of *experiential learning* which suggests that there are two ways to encounter experience, through *Concrete Experience* and *Abstract Conceptualization*. He claims that the ways we make sense of our experiences are through *Active Experimentation* and *Reflective Observation* and that learning should involve all four approaches for the learning to be effective. His theory suggests that, as we learn, we tend to develop strengths in one *experience-encountering* approach and one *experience-transforming* approach which results in one of the following preferred learning styles. Each style builds on one or more of the five creative behaviours:

1   *Convergent* learners enjoy creative experimental approaches to develop abstract concepts. They are good at making connections with prior learning, applying practical strategies and deductive reasoning to solve problems.
2   *Divergent* learners question assumptions and explore ideas. They require concrete experience and first-hand observation to feed reflections and generate new ideas. These learners can see things from multiple perspectives, are imaginative and good at creating novel ideas.
3   *Assimilators* are good at abstract conceptualization, seeing things in new ways and reflecting on their experiences. They use inductive reasoning to create new ideas in both theoretical and practical contexts.
4   *Accommodators* also use concrete experience and first-hand exploration to see things in new ways. They prefer to learn from practical exploration and risk taking rather than theoretical reading.

Implications for creative development

Teachers who wish to consider experiential learning styles to develop personal pupil creativity should note that three of them rely heavily on a practical approach, where experience is used to develop abstract generalizations and new concepts. It is not enough to provide just a type of learning experience: to get the most from any experience, adequate time for reflection and personal assimilation of ideas is essential. These learning styles are not rigid personality characteristics, but rather preferences which may be adapted according to circumstance. This theory suggests we can all utilize each of these styles to some extent and that learning can be improved if we identify our preferred styles and develop our underused ones. It is a theory worth considering by primary teachers as it emphasizes aspects of personality which they may wish to consider when planning learning opportunities for individuals within groups.

One benefit of considering learning styles is that teachers are likely to plan for a wider range of teaching activities than before, which can add interest and variety to the school day for all concerned. A danger is that pupils may be pigeon-holed as having just one preferred learning style for all occasions, or that activities which are not seen as suited to a particular learning style may be neglected. The UK think tank, Demos, looked at the scientific validity of learning styles and in 2005 published a report which said that the evidence for learning styles was 'highly variable' (Hargreaves et al. 2005). In 2009, Pashler et al. published a report on the scientific validity of learning styles practices and concluded that 'at present, there is no adequate evidence base to justify incorporating learning styles assessments into general educational practice'. Whether or not Learning Styles theory is proven, it makes sense to teach pupils in a variety of ways to develop their creative potential and to allow them a range of ways in which they can explore and record their own learning.

Accelerated learning and brain-based learning

http://openlearn.open.ac.uk/course/view.php?id=2477

From the above approaches has developed *accelerated learning* or *brain-based learning* which considers the research on how the brain works, using multiple intelligence theory as well as learning style theories. Accelerated learning involves consideration of learners' physical and psychological readiness to learn and employs teaching and learning techniques such as developing thinking skills, mind-mapping, and metacognitive techniques to review learning. Improving the learning environment includes using music, rhythm and rhyme to teach. Considering a child's physical and psychological needs involves brain gym, relaxation techniques and the use of motivational systems such as *RAP* (Recognition, Affirmation and Praise) or *The Three As* (Acknowledgement, Approval and Affirmation). It is claimed, though not proven, that using these techniques with others such as Building Learning Power can significantly raise personal confidence, creativity and achievement.

Implications for creative development

It is unlikely that any learner has just one way to develop their creative potential. Their preferred learning style, type of intelligence and thinking skills employed may depend on the subject, their mood, the relationship they have with the teacher, or the time of day. Using a range of teaching and learning techniques which cater for physical and psychological needs is a systematic way of building on what many teachers already know works.

Learning Power

Learning Power is a term which describes a combination of personal *capacities* (Claxton 2002) which affect our power to learn. Learning Power describes a way of behaving when faced with any new experience and strategies have been developed to help the learner develop an open mind and enjoyment of challenging situations. While intelligence is often seen as fixed, the elements of Learning Power are believed to be capable of development. Its theorists value the role of experience in developing the abilities required to enjoy and make the most of life-long learning. Several experts in this field have written about developing the intellectual skills required by older students while Claxton, Lucas and Deakin-Crick have worked to develop Learning Power in primary schools and informal settings.

Building Learning Power (BLP)

www.buildinglearningpower.co.uk

Building Learning Power is about helping people to become better learners, both in and out of school. Claxton suggested that learners need to develop the four Rs of learning, which include all five creative behaviours: Resilience, Resourcefulness, Reciprocity *and* Reflection (Figure 7.2). If these are taught systematically in schools and classes where the culture is one of 'can do', then young people can be helped to cultivate positive attitudes and habits which will help them deal with new or difficult situations with confidence and creativity. These ideas are founded on the belief that confident pupils learn faster, and with greater enjoyment. They can be more creative, independent, willing to take sensible risks and even do better in tests and exams. BLP aims to prepare young people for opportunities in a time of change, whether they need to be 'tenacious and resourceful, imaginative and logical, self-disciplined and self-aware, collaborative and inquisitive' (Claxton 2011). BLP makes use of recent educational and psychological research and is grounded in practical suggestions for classroom use which teachers are encouraged to try out in small-scale action research. It is an approach designed to help everyone, learners of all abilities and is concerned with more outcomes than literacy, numeracy and examination grades.

Claxton, Lucas and Webster (2010) differentiate between practical and academic learning and are trying to discover how people can be helped to get better at learning whatever it is they want to learn, whether this is playing the piano, kicking a ball, resolving heated arguments or joining a social networking site. They use the term *Real World Intelligence* (rL) as opposed to genetic intelligence and stress that the former type of intelligence can be learned. This social and cultural view of intelligence is geared to developing people's well-being so that they not only feel personally fulfilled, but in a national context, our creative and therefore economic potential is expanded. They

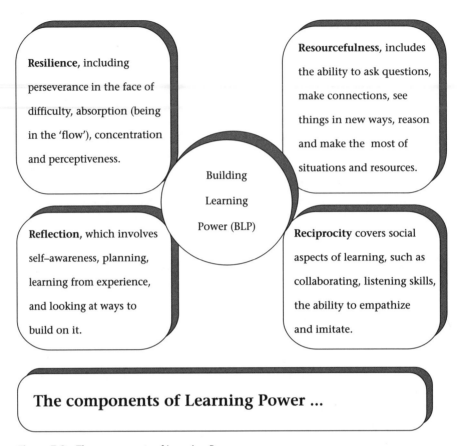

Figure 7.2   The components of Learning Power

advocate cultivating mind-sets and activities from which 'spring confidence, pride and *creativity* as well as enhanced competence in whatever area . . . is being learned' (Claxton et al. 2010).

The Effective Lifelong Learning Inventory (ELLI)

www.ellionline.co.uk/

Deakin Crick, an expert in personalized learning, has worked on a research tool designed to track a student's 'learning power' – the values, attitudes, dispositions and identity that are personal to them – in the Effective Lifelong Learning Inventory (ELLI). ELLI categorizes the features of a person's learning power into seven dimensions including creativity. By increasing awareness of these learning dimensions and by fostering them in the classroom with learners from Foundation stage to higher education, it is suggested that educators are able to help people to become better learners.

Implications for creative development

The four Rs of learning – Resilience, Resourcefulness, Reciprocity and Reflection – are terms which cover many of the characteristics of creative people as identified by Csikszentmihalyi (1996b), Spendlove (2005), and Craft (2001). BLP works on the processes of learning such as creativity, critical thinking and problem-solving. Central to these are the ability to ask questions, make connections, see things in new ways, explore ideas and reflect. The skills associated with these behaviours help us to reason and make the most of situations and resources, therefore, they are essential skills to be made explicit in learning and consciously developed by all learners.

8 Developing personal creativity

Moving from group to personal creativity

Although teachers generally have to work with groups of pupils, and most often with a whole class, one challenge is to help the individual pupil work independently and make autonomous decisions. This is essential for them to develop as people and become responsible creative members of society. When learners feel they have a shared ownership for their learning, they make more progress. When teachers model and scaffold the learning process this leads learners in the right direction. When they can personalize the curriculum to suit individual interests and abilities, this enables learners to create their own learning through exploration and trying out ideas.

We will explore here the opportunities provided by:

- Teacher scaffolding
- Personalizing the curriculum through
  - Personalized learning
  - Varying ways to record learning
  - Recording achievement
  - Personal projects
  - Differentiation
  - Using ICT for personal creative development.

But first, consider Loveless' view, outlined in Wilson (2007: 23), that creativity is 'the interaction between characteristics of people and communities, creative processes, subject domains, and wider social and cultural contexts'. This implies that it is the individual characteristics people have which need to be developed in association with the community (home or classroom) in which they operate, and that both generic and domain-related skills and knowledge are part of the process. Being creative requires a context and as teachers we provide the domain knowledge, the skills as well as opportunity. Since the *All Our Futures* report on creative and cultural education, defined creativity as 'imaginative activity fashioned so as to produce outcomes that are both original and of value' (NACCCE 1999: 29), we must give opportunities for imaginative and original work rather than just copying the imaginative ideas of others. This may seem obvious, but so often children are asked to copy Monet's water-lilies or carry out an experiment set up by the teacher, or decorate a puppet designed by someone else. Not all their ideas will be original or of value, but without multiple attempts and some set-backs, they will never produce ideas which are either of these.

So what is it that makes one pupil creative and willing to share new ideas, while others find it hard to come up with any ideas at all or are unwilling to share them? There are two problems here: idea generation and idea sharing. Idea generation comes with practice. As with any other skill, to do it well, one needs to practise regularly and risk doing it badly to get it right. As the twice Nobel Prize-winner Linus Pauling said when asked how he had so many good ideas, 'The way to get good ideas is to get lots of ideas, and throw the bad ones away.' Personal idea generation requires inspiration, time, effort and courage and may be unusual in concept, process and outcome. It may build on the ideas of other individuals or groups, but it requires internal motivation from personal interest, unlike group creativity which is more often externally motivated through a set challenge or group need: this is particularly true in school. It is the nature of personal creativity that it is likely to be more unusual group efforts which get the edges knocked off them to make them socially acceptable and less risky. Unfortunately the first evidence of a pupil being personally creative in school may be when the individual concerned seems to be doing either nothing but thinking as they gaze into the distance or doing something they have not been asked to do, or even doing something seemingly contrary to what has been requested. Soft thinking time for the mulling over and development of new ideas is essential and so little time is allocated to this in schools. Doing something differently from what the teacher has asked a pupil to do may seem like a misunderstanding of the situation or even sabotage if others try to copy so that the format of the lesson is disrupted.

Scaffolding by the teacher

First, the teacher needs to be an inspirational role model. This may not mean coming up with lots of new ideas all the time, but it does mean being willing to share the process of looking for inspiration, thinking things over, evaluating the thoughts which arise, trying out ideas and deciding which are of most value. Teachers and parents are often heard moaning that their children are interested in nothing but football and TV: sometimes these are only the interests they have modelled for them by the adults in their lives.

Ideas to develop the creativity of individuals
1. Share your own creative ideas about devising meals, exploring and fixing problems, trying new tactics in sport, collections, taking photos, visiting galleries, tackling new challenges or whatever interests you have and you can model with enthusiasm.
2. Introduce new areas of interest. I talked to my classes about plants, geology, astronomy, making things, sculpture, garden design, photography, keeping fit and many other things with which I hoped to infect them with enthusiasm.

3. Provide regular puzzles and challenges with open-ended possibilities for solutions. This might be a daily puzzle to start or end the day, subject specific challenges for early finishers or homework and holiday projects. Challenge them to find puzzles for you and the rest of the class so that learning can be seen as a shared process for all ages.

4. Teach them how to be organized, by modelling an orderly class and showing how this is done in terms of filing, having a place for everything and having daily routines to keep things tidy. If this is a problem for you, share the problem with them and ask them to help you be organized as this saves time and frustration in the long run.

5. Encourage and praise them for all their efforts to be original and creative and take sensible risks, while fostering a climate of exploration and discovery in your class. Modelling an appreciative and positive attitude is the best way to create a class supportive of new ideas.

Creative Challenge!

What was the last example of creative thinking or behaviour you modelled for your class?

Personalizing the curriculum

There are many ways to personalize a generic curriculum so that the particular needs of pupils are met through support or extension to develop their creative skills. The busy teacher needs simple strategies to help pupils record their learning in an individually engaging way so they can build on personal skills and interests. Ideas for developing personal and homework projects from generic skills and topics are outlined later but we will begin by looking at personalized learning, a term with many definitions, some more aspirational than specific.

Personalized learning

The DfEE defined personalized learning as learning where 'all children and young people, whatever their starting point, are able to fulfil their potential as learners' (2007: 8). David Hargreaves, a key architect of the idea, prefers the term 'personalizing' rather than 'personalized' learning, in order to emphasize the processes involved rather than any end product.

Personalization differs from differentiation in that it gives learners some choice about what is learned, as well as the timing and method. This 'anywhere, anytime, anyplace' learning can provide pupils with the opportunity to learn in ways that suit their individual learning styles, interests and intelligences, although targets still have to be met. While individualization means having the same objectives for all learners but achieving them by different means, personalization involves different objectives for each learner, which can seem daunting for a teacher with 30 or more individuals in a class. Here the learner is an active co-designer and manager of their learning experience. Strategies such as 'must/could/should', where pupils are given the option of choosing their objectives from a differentiated list go some way to making this manageable. This form of target setting by pupils is a good way to help individuals to challenge and monitor their own progress, as the standards for each level are explained to a whole class. Dialogue is an essential element in personalizing a curriculum and learning logs and thinking skills lessons may be used for reflection and to develop metacognition.

ICT can be a powerful tool for personalized learning as it gives learners access to a wide range of information types, and provides a mechanism for communication, discussion, and recording achievements. Personalized learning involves the learner in creating and reflecting on their own targets while working through guided opportunities to develop individual learning pathways that promote personal skills rather than just knowledge.

Encouraging personal interests

We need to know about our pupils' interests so we can build on them. It can be useful to have a regular slot for sharing ideas and achievements. Key Stage 1 teachers are often very good at this with frequent show and tell sessions. If a small space can be found for regularly changed exhibitions by the children, then they can bring in their collections, inventions, medals and certificates which can be arranged with relevant books to encourage others to develop personal interests. (This may include sports trophies which may be evidence of creative physical activity.) To find out what engaged my pupils I tried to have 10-minute chats with them individually about once a term so that I knew which personal skills and interests I might be able to encourage or build on in class sessions. I knew who preferred to create a drama, a drawing or use ICT to explore learning and who wanted to work through written methods though not necessarily in ways I had envisaged. This way I found out which children had personal interests and skills which they might use in class such as gymnastics, dance or musical experience. I discovered one Year 5 girl was a campanologist and she brought in her hand bells to demonstrate to the class. A boy who was interested in mild horror stories shared his creepy books with us, while another brought in his collection of fossils. During the year, every child found something they could share with the class, and some started new interests just so that they could do this.

With any subject taught it can be useful to get pupils to identify aspects of the topic they find most interesting and encourage them to create artwork, poems, jingles or other activities to accompany it. If they are keen on sport, craft, or fashion, challenge them to use these interests in relation to the class topic, so if the class is studying castles, sport lovers might devise a game for the castle children to play, those who like crafts could design or even make their own castles from waste materials (Figure 8.1) while fashion lovers might create up-to-date jewelry or accessories on a medieval theme. Encouraging children to build on the science and technology done in school can lead to original studies of wildlife in their gardens or pupils making their own toys at home.

For older children, personal diaries or better still journals which are not written daily are a way to record new ideas and reflections on the world around them. These

Figure 8.1   A castle made from waste materials

may be the basis for a poem, story, or invention. Poems about themselves and their world help to develop creative ideas where metaphor is part of the distillation of ideas.

Personal projects

Working on intrinsically motivating projects which pupils have chosen for themselves is not normally possible for most of the school day. One way to develop this aspect of learning is to help scaffold project work as part of homework set for the class. For example, if the overall homework project for the term was 'Animals', most pupils would be able to find at least one type of animal which interested them enough to make it the focus of an individual project. They might look at pets, dinosaurs, minibeasts or jungle animals. Each week pupils are taught one technique which can be applied to any of their projects, such as drawing a map to show some form of distribution, whether local or international, and this becomes one part of their homework for the week. Animals might be a suitable topic in a term when little biology was being studied. Other engaging subjects for personal projects might be Sport, where children focus on particular sports or sports and games in general, Travel, where they could look either at aspects of transport or types of holidays, Space, or Superheroes.

Some of the following techniques taught as part of the regular curriculum or as focussed input will help pupils create original material for their projects (Table 8.1).

Table 8.1 Techniques for personal projects

Labelled diagram	Map	Time line
Graphs and charts	Photos	Quiz
An annotated equipment list to pursue this interest	Instructions to make or do something	An illustrated alphabet of relevant words
Crossword/puzzles	Acrostic	Poem/story
'Did you know?' section	Report/article	Jokes
Treasure hunt	Maths/science trail	Newspaper-style report

See Appendix 1 for an example of a help sheet. This should be adapted to make it suitable for different topics.

As well as building on these weekly ideas, the pupils are encouraged to access and record information from different sources and in different ways, including ICT, but with limited copying and pasting. They may add drawings, poems, photos, pictures cut from magazines, quizzes, riddles and jokes and statistics. Depending on the age and ability of the class, they are helped to make notes in appropriate ways and to organize the work into sections. They may add models and films when relevant. With some school topics it might be appropriate for each child to work in more depth than is possible in class on an aspect of their history or geography work. My classes were always keen on their personal ancient Egypt project and individual local studies projects. They were encouraged to keep and present the work in a loose-leaf file with dividers, which gave a professional feel to the work and each child received a positive written response congratulating them on what was particularly interesting, what they had done well, telling them what I had learned and suggesting further ideas they might want to add if they had time. If a computer proforma is used for this, it will not be too onerous a task (see Appendix 2).

Most households now have access to a computer either at home or in the local library so pupils can write, edit and print relevant material. Hand-written work should be encouraged as well. Of course, some children are reluctant to exert themselves or receive little home support, but with the provision of just one school period a week to develop their work and the help available in some homework and after school clubs, this is one way of developing creative ideas in a chosen context for many pupils. If they decide to present the whole project as a film or multimedia presentation or scrap-book or set of models of some kind, then so much the better. Liam, who was interested in dinosaurs, presented part of his project on a large paper skeleton he had constructed which was covered with details he had researched. 'My infosauraus' he announced proudly!

Varying ways to record learning

Too often the standard ways to record individual learning are writing down what has been learned, and perhaps adding a picture or completing a worksheet. It is more engaging to get pupils familiar with the idea that there are many ways to record learning and as long as sufficient appropriate terminology is used and the work completed in a set time, then other means may be employed. Individual choice can improve motivation and lead to higher standards. If pupils invent their own ways to record, for example, what plants and animals need to live, then they are more likely to remember the differences.

They might try employing skills learned in one subject to record learning in another so that concepts in science are recorded in a poem or events in history are shown in a strip cartoon. Events in a story can be detailed on a time-line; speech bubbles could show different sides of an argument in any subject and mimes, puzzles and even jokes might be used to recall key facts in maths or DT. Personal creativity can often be developed by pupils working in pairs as they gain ideas from each other. For example, how might each of the following be used by pairs of pupils to record learning in an English lesson, a science lesson and a geography lesson?

- a journey stick (see Chapter 11);
- a game to record learning;
- puzzles and brain teasers;
- a collection of labelled objects.

How might each of the following be used by pairs of pupils to record learning in a maths lesson, an MFL lesson and a history lesson?

- a four-screen multimedia presentation;
- a treasure hunt;
- a quiz;
- a mime or short piece of drama.

Creative Challenge!
- How many ways to record learning have you planned for the next two weeks of work?
- Do they involve oral, practical, written, drawn, drama and digital options?
- How could you create a wider range of options?
- Which of these have you tried? Podcasts/cartoons/mnemonics/a paper model/mind map/digital film.

Creativity and differentiation

Students and teachers alike are often urged to differentiate learning activities in at least three ways in almost every lesson. This may be neither feasible nor desirable if it over-complicates a lesson or makes the workload unmanageable. Differentiation 'by outcome' is sometimes listed by the inexperienced, which in practice can mean none at all! Differentiation is perhaps best used as an aid to allowing children to record their learning in personally relevant and original ways. Some examples of differentiation in a Design Technology context are shown in Table 8.2.

Table 8.2   Practical ways to differentiate teaching

Method	Action
Support	Find different ways to consolidate and revise what has been learned
	Give more help, perhaps from a support assistant or another child
	Written support may be given by prompts and scaffolding. Adults might help with threading needles
Time	Allow different times for completing a task. Sometimes the more able in a subject require longer as they explore a more complex task they have devised
Questioning	Differentiate questioning to explore the ideas of less able or extend gifted and talented pupils, e.g. 'What was the hardest part of the work?' 'How could you improve the appearance of your toy?' or 'In what ways is your toy suitable for a 5-year-old child?'
	Less confident pupils might need a sentence start, e.g. 'I think that Mum would need . . .' 'What a person with arthritis might need would be . . .'
Grouping	To give support or to extend the most able. (Change groups regularly). Those who are most able on literacy or maths may be less capable in D&T
Outcomes (different objectives)	*Pupils have different task and different objectives*
	OR
	All children are asked to design a moving monster to act as a notice board, but one group must use series circuits and another use parallel circuits
Tasks (similar objective)	When *pupils work on different tasks but with similar objectives*
	Pupils of different abilities might work with different materials, or be required to work in more detail or with more explanation. The depth of response required may vary. If assessment has shown that Year 1 children have different levels of fine motor skills, one group could be helped to cut pieces of paper and card, while another group focuses on drawing round shapes or using a ruler to draw lines
	1. Give tasks with different levels of challenge to different ability groups., e.g. the less able design a flowerbed for a blind person, while the more able design a garden for a blind person.
	2. Change the materials used, e.g. one group use card and another wood/plastic. In sewing, less able children might use Binca and another group felt, while more able children can cope with material which will fray
	3. Less able children work to set task, e.g. to create a recipe for a healthy soup. More able children might devise recipe for someone on a diet/with a gluten/sugar intolerance diet, or to devise their own design challenge
	4. Vary the kinds of responses you require, e.g. individual, one response per pair, one response per group
	5. Vary depth of response required, e.g. write one example or write an example with a reason. Sketch and label two ideas . . . sketch four ideas and explain your favourite
	6. Vary ways in which responses are presented, e.g. choose whether to draw or write/model your idea.

Method	Action
Focus	All children work on similar task but teaching focuses on different aspects of that task, e.g. if children are creating advertisements for a torch they have designed. All children are asked to consider the use of colour and layout in their designs. With one group, the teacher focuses on the use of persuasive language while with another she focuses on layout or technical drawing skills
Level of structure	For some, the task is structured while others are given an open-ended task, e.g. pupils are designing a desk tidy, for an able group this is an open-ended task, while a less able group is given a list of tasks to do to support their planning

Using ICT for personal creative development

1   Regularly teach IT skills which can be applied in a range of contexts and suggest ideas for what these contexts might be. If you teach them how to construct tables, then provide opportunities for individuals to use them on stand-alone or laptop machines in citizenship, history or geography, while others are writing or drawing their response. Specialist software can help them create concept maps, flowcharts and presentations.

2   Make sure even the youngest children can take photos, which may be edited to personalize recording. Help them to use IT tools to research appropriately, draw, paint, collect and organize data and ideas.

3   Whatever the subject, when most of the class are recording with pencil and paper, individuals might use a computer, possibly with a differentiated template. Writing up science experiments could be done as a recipe, a magazine article, a cartoon strip, drama script, a news bulletin or poem, provided the required number of technical terms is used and explained. (These might be supplied in a word bank or as part of a template.)

4   Show pupils how to use computers to personalize their ideas in different ways through redrafting, making diagrams and concept maps, adding ideas to speech bubbles and creating timelines, diagrams and maps.

Developing personal creativity in the six Areas of Creative Endeavour

Some of these may be done in school, while others might be set as homework or holiday tasks (Table 8.3). In some cases, the ideas might be developed at home with just a drawing or a few words to record them and the outcomes trialled in school.

Table 8.3 ACE and developing personalized creativity in KS1 and KS2 pupils

ACE	Ideas to develop the creativity of individual KS1 pupils
1. Technological	1. Allow time for pupils to decide how a pop-up mouth design might be applied to a range of animals/monsters/robots/something else rather than everyone making a different coloured duck face OR teach several pop-up card techniques for pupils to apply in different contexts 2. Demonstrate several ways to make finger puppets and let pupils choose to use one or devise their own and add individual characteristics 3. Teach them how to make ice lollies from orange juice. Ask them to devise a new recipe perhaps by adding small pieces of fruit or using a smoothie/custard/sauce base
2. Artistic	1. Challenge pupils to take photos of their family and friends in ways which show their personalities 2. Demonstrate how pipe cleaners can be joined and shaped. Suggest that they make sculptures/models in this way 3. Show pupils how to use pictures and scraps from coloured magazines to make a paper collage. Ask them to make one at home. Suitable magazines might be sent from school if they are unlikely to be available at home 4. If a short rhyme is written as a class, ask individuals to invent a tune to go with it. E.g. Happy birthday to my friend, Birthday wishes I will send. Older children could add another two lines of rhyme and tune
3. Mathematical	1. How many sums can they make from the digits 1, 2 and 5? (Operations as appropriate.) Older pupils may use simple fractions and multiplication. (Other digits or specific operations may be suggested to help develop problem solving abilities and explore numerical relationships) 2. Create number sequences using calculations they have been taught 3. Challenge individuals to invent oral 'What am I?' shape challenges for their friends 4. How many ways can they find to measure a bottle of fizzy drink? (This could involve linear, capacity, weight as well as different measuring devices)
4. Linguistic	1. Let pupils use a puppet in 'Show and tell' sessions to talk, tell stories or discuss things which interest them 2. Give pupils cards with particularly interesting words which have to be incorporated into a piece of writing. Scintillating new words can inspire more original work 3. Challenge them to invent new verses for a familiar rhyme
5. Physical	1. Play music with strong rhythms, teach a few basic steps and arm movements for children to build into a personal celebration dance, e.g. for when their team wins 2. Teach basic gymnastic skills which can be put together in simple sequences 3. Devise balancing exercises to be done on a line or imagined tightrope. How long can they balance on one leg with their eyes closed? (Talk about safety considerations here)
6. Natural Philosophical	1. Start a collection of natural objects and find ways to classify them, e.g. leaves, photos of flowers, feathers, shells, stones, seeds 2. Invent a hearing/sight test to try out on family/friends 3. Think up some questions they would like to ask a giraffe (or other animal). Suggest some of the possible answers

ACE	Ideas to develop the creativity of individual KS1 pupils
1. Technological	1. Devise a way to help remember what to bring to school each day, especially on dinner money/PE days
	2. Demonstrate some basic ways to make a paper bag. Pupils to innovate on these designs and make their own gift bags from a wide range of papers and haberdashery
	3. Design/make a scarecrow from waste materials
2. Artistic	1. After reading relevant poem or teaching them about the features of minibeasts or other animals ask them to invent a new insect/dragon. This could form the basis of other modelling or literacy work
	2. Design a personal logo or heraldic device
	3. Use electronic keyboards to help pupils compose their own ring tones
3. Mathematical	1. Devise symmetrical patterns from both regular and irregular shapes
	2. Invent maths puzzles and challenges for friends
	3. Invent and use a personal set of Tangram-type shapes. Use to make a range of pictures and patterns. Can a friend recreate the original design from which it was made?
4. Linguistic	1. Encourage the keeping of personal diaries, not necessarily daily, but at least weekly, which include reflections, questions, interesting words or ideas they have found. These may be loose-leaf or electronic. Pupils should be able to keep them private if they wish
	2. Devise personal mnemonics to remember spellings e.g. *Never Eat Crisps, Eat Salad Sandwiches And Remain Young* helps to reminds us how to spell Necessary
	3. Create an interesting sentence which uses all letters of the alphabet. Use as handwriting and typing practice. It might be texted to the teacher/tweeted to the world
5. Physical	1. Teach basic ball bouncing and throwing skills for individual pupils to play on their own and build into a game of Tensies. (Do first ball action 10 times, second one 9 times . . . until the last and most difficult one is done only once.) Adding claps, waves turns and bouncing under one leg etc. should increase the complexity of each stage
	2. Devise as many ways as they can to aid relaxation, both standing, sitting and lying down
	3. Devise personal daily keep-fit routine (and use it!)
6. Natural Philosophical	1. Ask individuals to come up with the most interesting/important question they can about an aspect of the natural world. It might help to limit the questions to one area such as insects/plants/deserts or the planets. With practice they will be able to ask deeper and more philosophical questions about life, the universe and everything. It does not matter if you or they cannot answer these questions, but having ideas about where to look for answers, how to discuss them and what angles to consider for each may be more important than the answers themselves
	2. How many ways can they think of to dry something? E.g. a pair of wet shoes
	3. Talk about scavenger hunts and how to devise interesting questions. Combine the best ones for a scavenger hunt on the next school trip/other occasion, e.g. find something round/spiky/soft/blue/the leaf with the longest edge/something which was once alive/part of a tree/ an animal

(continued)

Table 8.3 *(continued)*

ACE	Ideas to develop the creativity of individual KS1 pupils
1. Technological	1. Design an ideal room in 2D using drawing or computer shapes. Make a model of it using a shoe box/grocery carton and waste materials 2. Show pupils how to make flying birds from stiff card or plywood. Help them to create their own bird/bat/insect/dragons which fly in a similar way 3. Help pupils to design and make an individual portable study. If a piece of good quality recycled card or plastic corriflute is used for the basic design, folders, pocket wipe clean writing surfaces, and personal posters or memo areas can be added. Children will learn many design skills as well as techniques for cutting and joining a range of materials. Handles may be integral or added
2. Artistic	1. Teach them to make tessellating pictures on the lines of the graphic artist Escher, and let pupils experiment with their own designs 2. Encourage pupils to make an individual portfolio of their art work or just one aspect of it, e.g. their computer art, experiments with chalk and pastel 3. Demonstrate some of the ways digital photos can be edited to improve them or create photo collage. This can be time-consuming but they could develop their skills either at home or in an out-of-school club. Challenging them to modify a photo in paint program to show the animal which might be their alter ego can produce very creative results
3. Mathematical	1. Compose a rhyme to help remember a mathematical rule. E.g. *To read a grid reference, remember this rhyme, first go along and then up the line* 2. Use a computer spreadsheet to work out a personal budget for a holiday/saving for something 3. How many ways can you find to record a problem involving ratios? E.g. it takes 2 parts orange juice and 3 parts passion fruit to make 2 fruit cocktails, what will be needed for 5 or 7 cocktails?
4. Linguistic	1. Record learning in any subject using their own cartoon characters and speech bubbles. A computer template can help with this 2. Teach homophones for pupils to use in the creation of riddles 3. Personal poems about a range of emotions and ideas can be stimulated through a pupil's response to open-ended questions with a surreal twist. E.g. Where does anger come from? What colour is it? What does it fear?
5. Physical	1. Work out how to get an extra 30 minutes exercise a day 2. Devise a trick using a skateboard/roller-blades/bike (homework) 3. Encourage pupils to take part in some extra-curricular sport such as swimming, gymnastics, life saving, orienteering or dance. The local library may have lists of local classes which are not available through the school
6. Natural Philosophical	1. Keep a question board/box for pupils to add challenging enquiry or reflective philosophical questions. Try to debate some of these in spare moments such as just before a break or in Circle time and thinking lessons 2. Encourage individuals to follow their own interests and devise questions which require personal consideration/internet/book research/scientific tests to answer 3. Ask each to invent a new animal or plant, make a booklet all about it with a labelled diagram and explanations of the life processes it uses

9 Creativity across the curriculum

Many methodologies have been proposed to develop pupils' creative thinking and learning skills, some of which involve a radical approach to the whole curriculum. This chapter looks at some of the methods which come under the umbrella term of the creative curriculum and examples of each strategy are given for teachers in Key Stage 1, Lower Key Stage 2 and Upper Key Stage 2. Ways to extend these to a whole-school approach are considered along with the problem of assessing their success and the growth of creative development in individual pupils.

The creative curriculum

Although this is a term in frequent use, there seems to be some doubt as to what exactly it means. The questions is raised in an on-line *Times Educational Supplement* forum 'Is it just that we've come back full circle and are teaching through topics again, or is there something more to it than that?' Replies indicate that many see it as topic teaching but with more hassle.

Once the National Curriculum (NC) was given to schools and supplemented by the QCA units, some teachers felt that this was a blueprint for all their planning and in a number of schools the creative element of teacher planning was lost. With it sometimes went the potential for creative learning which was not what was intended by QCA. The NC has always been a minimum not a maximum entitlement, and creative schools have used it as a basis for their own ideas with much success. However, it was not until the DfEE *Excellence and Enjoyment* report of 2003 that all schools were officially encouraged to do what the best schools had always done: 'take ownership of the curriculum' and be 'creative and innovative' in the ways they teach. Robert Fisher's article in the *TES* (7 March 2003) confirmed that: 'schools with the most imaginative and creative approaches to the curriculum tend to get both the best results and inspection reports'.

The *All Our Futures* report (DfES 1999: 2) argued that to meet the challenges of the twenty-first century, pupils' creativity needed to be developed. They acknowledged the need to nurture a curriculum which would develop young people's capacities for original ideas and action.

The creative curriculum is not a single curriculum, but an attitude towards curriculum planning. Gerver (2010) explained the creative curriculum is no different from any other curriculum. The creativity comes from the way it is implemented so that it is flexible, responsive to need and focussed on developing children's natural sense of enquiry, hypothesis and investigation.

The creative curriculum works when there is a whole-school approach to planning and teaching. With this approach, the Foundation subjects often provide the basis for a theme such as the Vikings or Habitats rather than a 'holes, gaps and cavities' (Richards 1973) approach common in the 1970s, when some topics made tenuous links to other subjects. In the creative curriculum, learning is based on a clear progression of skills in all subjects, but particularly literacy, numeracy and ICT which are then used for learning in other areas, so when diary writing is a literacy focus, there will be opportunities for the class to write diaries in another context soon afterwards. If they are learning about co-ordinates in maths, then mapping skills would be developed in a geographical or historical or biological context. In this way pupils make connections with prior learning. Burgess in his 2007 report, *Lifting the Lid on the Creative Curriculum*, showed that diverse approaches can result in highly creative schools which are recognized as successful by OFSTED. It is the way the curriculum is taught, not the subject or topic approach which is key to its creativity. Burgess lists the features of successful creative schools as those which:

- are child-centred;
- put skills before content;
- employ a slow organic approach which allows enough time for learning to be explored and consolidated;
- use flexible and dynamic curricula;
- have head teachers with a strong sense of professional confidence and autonomy and a shared vision of what they were doing and why with their staff;
- are characterized by a high level of communication and open debate so staff feel they have ownership of the teaching and learning process.

Nolan (2010) agrees that a creative curriculum will look different in every school. It is inspirational for both teachers to teach and for pupils to learn. It does not jump on bandwagons, but adapts and changes with new ideas, appropriate technology and in the light of improved pedagogies.

Creative teaching, creative learning and teaching for creativity

- *Creative teaching* involves teachers making learning more interesting and effective by using imaginative approaches in the classroom (Cremin, in Wilson 2007). It involves the creativity of the teacher.
- *Teaching for creativity* involves teachers developing children's creative strengths and 'empowering, encouraging and enabling children to be in control of activities' (Eaude, in Wilson 2007: 65).
- *Creative learning* involves learners using their imagination and experience to develop their own learning either collaboratively or through personal projects which engage them in critical evaluation of their learning. It has been termed 'a form of apprenticeship' (Craft, in Wilson 2007).

Suggestions for practice

Audit your school or class for the following features of the creative curriculum:

1. When do you work from children's questions or interests?
2. How often is self-evaluation used by pupils to aid learning?
3. How do you use the outdoor learning environment in your children's education?
4. In which subjects do you encourage learning through the creative arts?
5. When do you use a problem-solving or enterprise approach?
6. Do you have a flexible approach to timetabling so that pupils do not always have to stop work they find engaging to start a new lesson?
7. Can pupils work in teams on collaborative learning, perhaps with local adults on community based projects?
8. Which activities are open-ended?
9. When are risk taking and resilience developed?
10. Do you plan more for Creative Teaching, Creative Learning or Teaching for Creativity?

Investigative learning

There are several types of active learning based on constructivist theory, where groups of learners work in collaborative groups at authentic learning tasks with the teacher acting as a facilitator and assessor rather than as a didactic director of the work:

- In *Problem-based learning* (PBL) a problematic situation is usually presented by the educator, with learners identifying the nature of the problem before working independently in tutorial-supported groups, to present a solution. This approach is common in higher education, but is increasingly used in the primary school. The point of PBL is not just to solve particular problems, but to learn the problem-solving skills and practical skills and knowledge associated with the process. Enterprise education (see p. 134) might be seen as a form of problem-based learning.
- *Project-based learning* is also confusingly abbreviated to PBL and so here is given as PjBL. Questions and subjects for project-based learning are usually initiated by the learner, as is common in the Reggio Emilio approach (see p. 132), and these may or may not be problem-based.
- *Enquiry-based learning* (EBL) is an umbrella term for several types of teaching and active learning experiences, which may include PBL and PjBL, where progress is assessed by how well students develop experimental and analytical skills rather than how much knowledge they can recall. EBL was initially developed during the discovery learning movement of the 1960s and was cultivated in response to the perceived failure of more traditional forms of teaching, where learners were mainly required to memorize facts. It is based on Dewey's theory of inquiry (1938), the constructivist theories of Vygotsky (1978) and the self-regulated learning ideas of Zimmerman (1998) As noted by the HEA

Guide to Curriculum Design, 'EBL is perhaps more open to divergent ways of thinking about problems, more open to exploring and understanding different ways of perceiving the world and less concerned with providing firm solutions to problems that do not have simple or unique solutions' (Kahn and O'Rourke 2004).

Project- and problem-based learning

In project-based learning the teacher defines the task, while in problem-based learning, the outcome is not always apparent to the learners who have to define it as well as their own leaning needs before tackling a project. In some projects, with very young children, the teacher may keep the class as a large group for some aspects of teaching before small groups find ways to tackle the challenge. It is the enquiry process, not the solution finding which is most important here and basic literacy, numeracy and cross-curricular skills are taught as required. Bell (2010), a keen advocate of the PjBL, reported higher academic grades in both Britain and America for students engaged in these approaches to learning.

Characteristics of both PBL and PjBL:

- learning is driven by authentic learning tasks that replicate real-world activities;
- learning activities combine subject knowledge, creative and critical thinking as well as subject-based skills to solve problems;
- tasks can be motivating as they are seen as relevant and interesting to learners;
- assessment can be based on a practical tasks across a range of skills, enabling more useful assessment of competence than a pencil and paper test;
- both are ways of developing independent learning by offering students autonomy and choice in their learning.

During the course of a problem-based learning task, learners use the following steps:

1 Define the problem.
2 Brainstorm ideas.
3 Use 'triggers' from the problem scenario to define their own learning objectives.
4 Work out what must be done to solve it.
5 Acquire the necessary skills and knowledge for solving the problem.
6 Carry out the task.
7 Assess their progress.

During the course of a project-based learning task, learners use the following steps:

1 The pupil or teacher identifies a project to study.
2 Pupils are helped to ascertain the skills and knowledge they need to solve the problem.

3   Skills and knowledge teaching are given, which may involve trialling of potential solutions.
4   Completion of the work.

Private study may be part of both processes and there may be a presentation phase at the end to interested parties. Steps may be repeated as necessary in order to complete the project or find a solution.

The advantages of these methods of education are that they put the responsibility for learning on to the learner which can be motivating and empowering. They facilitate autonomy, and respect for others while fostering collaborative, social and communication skills that are greatly needed in today's society. Developing problem-solving techniques can help to develop the creativity of both groups and individuals. Of course, creativity and problem-solving are not identical. Not all problems require creative solutions or original thinking and many activities which do require creativity such as writing, drawing, sculpting, hypothesizing and inventing are not always seen as problem-solving.

Difficulties include the amount of time which is required for effective implementation of tasks, the training of teachers to give effective support, and ensuring adequate coverage of the necessary skills and knowledge required by set curricula. A concern with PBL is that learners may get frustrated by a perceived lack of direction from the educator, and that the tasks of facilitating and assessing may seem harder for the teacher than a more didactic approach. There may be issues with staffing small groups, timetabling and resourcing. Another concern with both forms of learning is that many skills acquired are not measurable by standardized tests. Assessing the quality of someone's thinking is problematic, although it may be attempted by assessing their actions and discussing their ideas with them. One solution is to provide a series of tasks so that learners will be given the opportunity to show their skills in several different areas such as communication or collaboration, as well as practical ones such as IT facility. Questioning as well as observation is an important part of the assessment process.

With the development of interactive IT applications new possibilities have opened up for independent learning of this type:

- The National Gallery in London uses Webquests which are problem-solving activities for primary pupils, using nine national museum collections to foster enquiry-based learning in a wide number of curriculum areas.
- A study in Singapore by Ang and Wang (2006) involving under-achieving students, looked at teaching science concepts by requiring pupils to use the computer program 'Active Worlds' to build 3D objects that could display information correctly about the solar system. Results showed that the students were unusually engaged in the learning task, achieving 100 per cent attendance, good behaviour, meeting deadlines and becoming very active in the learning process. It was suggested that 'Online gaming in a virtual learning environment (VLE) has great potential in motivating students in learning Science.'

These are just two examples of ways which ICT can enable a fresh approach to teaching and learning. If we can involve the technologies with which our pupils are familiar and which motivate them, in active learning we may be able inspire both teachers and learners with exciting educational opportunities.

Enquiry-based learning (EBL)

Enquiry-based learning employs investigations, problems, or case studies as a basis for individual and group projects. Research activity and fieldwork by learners is an essential part of the learning experience. Many schools already use some of these approaches in specific subjects so that fieldwork is one lesson in a series of geography or history sessions, while investigations are used routinely as a method of instruction in a science module. Some teachers work from pupil-based interests and questions to plan their whole curriculum along project work lines, while others set up problem-based scenarios to develop cross-curricular skills. Frequently case studies in Britain or in developing countries form the basis for a term's geographical learning, and increasingly schools favour pupils learning through personal or group projects which may form part of their homework scheme. Whichever method is used, independent research activity, along lines identified by groups or individuals, is likely to form part of the learning process. With EBL, these methods are central to most teaching and learning experiences.

Features of successful EBL

- Open-ended research questions and problems which allow a variety of responses or solutions.
- Both teachers and pupils engage in a collaborative learning process where teachers may not know all the answers.
- The learner is at the heart of the learning process and takes responsibility for seeking evidence and analysing it.
- Learning activities are structured to foster learner independence.
- A supportive teaching atmosphere which tolerates uncertainty and thinking time.
- The enquiry requires learners to draw on existing knowledge and identify their learning needs.
- A willingness by both teacher and learners to take risks and follow leads which may not always be productive.
- The teacher helps pupils to reflect on their learning through careful questioning.
- Digital technologies and resources are used in the creation, organization and sharing of knowledge.
- Learners are encouraged to present their findings in diverse but meaningful ways which engage an audience.

In some schools, the whole curriculum is taught along these lines with beneficial results.

Garner (2009) suggests that geography teaching is the ideal context for EBL as it uses the enquiry cycle of ask, plan, collect, record, analyse, discuss data, draw conclusions, and evaluate, and includes the development of higher-order thinking and reflection skills. It can connect with other cross-curricular concepts and skills, including development of attitudes and values.

Research by Chan (2010) found that teachers have conflicting views about the value of EBL. Some believed that teachers should be facilitators in students' learning; while others believed teachers should be knowledge transmitters. Some teachers felt that even in enquiry-based learning, the learning should be about finding the 'right answers'. Some teachers expressed the view that enquiry-based learning has its 'value in theory' but not the 'value in practice'. And even some of those who claimed to believe in the value of enquiry-based learning admitted they seldom used it with their classes. Several reasons were suggested for this: first, there was the fear of losing control of the class, second, the problems of assessing the learning in EBL, and, third, there were also cultural influences from the schools which demanded secure academic grades or lacked flexibility with timetabling or a culture reluctant to take risks. It was clear that the success of EBL is dependent on the attitudes of the school and the teachers involved.

Teachers who view learning as a process of knowledge construction will want to ensure that their teaching moves away from just the transmission of information towards the implementation of activities and environments which will develop pupils' curiosity and support their active learning. They will work through open-ended challenges which allow the genuine exploration and investigation of authentic questions and issues.

Suggestions for practice

Audit your planning to see in which subjects you currently use the following teaching and learning methods (T&L) (Table 9.1).

Table 9.1   A teaching and learning audit

T&L method	Contexts where we currently use this	Contexts where we could use this
Field-work		
Investigations		
Problem-based learning		
Project-based learning		
Case studies		
Individual projects		
Group projects		
Research activity		
Child-initiated projects		

Case study: Reggio Emilia

Reggio Emilia is a project-based learning approach that began in northern Italy after the Second World War when Loris Malaguzzi, a young teacher and the founder of the system, worked with the parents of this region to provide child care for pre-school children. This system puts into practice many aspects of the work of Dewey, Piaget, and Vygotsky. It is a collaborative approach to education involving the children, their parents and the teachers, each of whom has recognized rights and responsibilities as they co-construct knowledge. Parents are seen as the first teacher, the class teacher as the second teacher and the environment as the third teacher. Children are also encouraged to learn from their peers and regular reflection on their activities. Long-term projects, initiated by the children's interests are used as vehicles for learning.

The Reggio Emilia teacher does the following:

1. allows the children to ask their own questions, and generate their own hypotheses and to test them;
2. welcomes contradictions and uncertainties as starting points for exploring, discussing and debating;
3. provides opportunity to explore and record ideas and learning in many ways such as play, art, drama as well as writing, to represent thoughts and ideas;
4. provides opportunity for the children to communicate their ideas to others;
5. offers children, through reflection and metacognition, ways to reorganize concepts, ideas, thoughts and theories to construct new meaning for themselves;
6. is a keen observer, documenter, and partner in the learning process.

Daily documentation is a key element in the Reggio approach, to aid reflection, assessment and research. Through this child-centred philosophy children are encouraged to pursue their natural curiosity, creativity and critical thinking to explore, investigate, and experience. The Reggio example, based on the principles of respect, responsibility, and community, is one model of project-based learning, which has lessons for all educators interested in developing the creativity of children.

Suggestions for practice

Investigations may take no more than one lesson to complete, but if they are genuinely open-ended, they can be of great value whether pupils are budgeting for an event, looking at the properties of materials or researching the difference between living in one time and place with that in another.

Longer enquirers perhaps as part of a school or homework project and requiring a range of investigative skills might look at the following:

- Which type of animal would make the best pet? (Consider initial costs as well as regular care including feeding and vet's bills.)
- How has life changed in our area in the past 500 years?
- Where does our chocolate/newspaper come from?
- What are your clothes from and where do they go?
- What is the best way to grow plants?

A more open-ended approach might be:

- How can we show our families and friends what we have studied in school this term? (This could lead to creating a presentation, a display, film or publication such as a website or book.)
- Create a local newspaper or news programme.
- Redesign part of the school grounds for a need identified by the pupils.

Case studies

Try some real science

A study of bumblebees by a group of Devon children became the first primary school project to be published in a Royal Society scientific journal. The children, aged between 8 and 10, discovered that bees could be trained to recognize colour patterns. They worked with a professional scientist, but the paper was 'entirely conceived and written' by the pupils. The children tested bees to see if they could learn to use different colour patterns to find their way to sugar water, while avoiding salt water; see http://www.bbc.co.uk/news/education-12051883.

Introduce a multimedia challenge

In a London school, film-making was employed in each class as a tool to explore various aspects of the curriculum. Fourteen films were made as part of a 2010 project with subjects as diverse as 'Healthy Eating' to 'Golden Greeks', 'Spanish Numbers' to 'How to Make Paper'. Pupils used their films to explain and share their knowledge with other classes. Visit the Creative Partnerships site for more ideas, see http://www.creative-partnerships.com.

Enterprise Education

Enterprise Education involves helping young people to develop 'the skills and qualities they need to face their future with confidence' (www.rotherhamready.org.uk/). There are several models for this, some of which are one-off projects by individual classes or schools, and others which are organized nationally, such as MicroSociety. This 12-week simulation for Year 5 involves pupils in creating their own society and setting up the institutions required such as a government, a civil service, an economy, businesses, and a legal system. The project has been developed by My Voice London, the Education Business Partnership for Kingston and Merton, which provides the training and resources required for teachers to run the project.

Rotherham Ready

Another skill-based approach to Enterprise Education which involves creative teaching, teaching for creativity and creative learning is exemplified by the Rotherham Ready approach. In South Yorkshire, an area which has suffered from pit and industrial closure in recent years, Rotherham Ready began with the vision of equipping local school children with the enterprise skills they would need to make a success of their future and help create a thriving economy in the locality. They began by working with leaders from business and education to identify 13 key skills and qualities, one of which is creativity which young people need to face the future with confidence; these they called the 'Big 13'. These 'Big 13' are skills for school, home, work and business – a manifesto for approaching life successfully.

Rotherham Ready works with schools, colleges, businesses and the local university to embed these 13 skills into the classroom and get teachers and learners excited about using the language and embracing the concepts. Rotherham's success with this project has been recognized by the OFSTED report of 2011, which agreed with the Rotherham Ready approach that 'some young people will become entrepreneurs, but all young people will need to be enterprising'. The inspectors applauded the scheme's emphasis on involving all students, including those with learning difficulties and/or disabilities, and saw the project as a key influence in 'developing a more enterprising culture within an overall economic regeneration agenda'.

Although creativity is listed as just one of the 'Big 13', each of these skills embraces many aspects of the five Creative Endeavours, whether it is having to ask the right questions, make connections with skills taught in maths, literacy, ICT or science, see a problem as an opportunity, explore new ways of working or reflect on progress. The skills have been expanded to a six-level matrix so as to plan for and assess progress in each. What is impressive about this project is the way pupils are able to take control and use their initiative for much of their learning. Children in one school created characters to remind themselves of the 'Big 13' skills which led to one class writing a book *The Animals of Skillzville* to introduce the skills to younger pupils in the school. Other pupils have used the skills for data analysis, or to create a mythical enterprise animal or make mind maps to show how these skills link to other curriculum areas.

Rotherham has been acknowledged nationally as a centre for excellence in enterprise learning and was recently awarded the title of the 'Most Enterprising Place in Britain' by Enterprise UK, a campaigning organization set up by the British Chamber of Commerce, the Confederation of British Industry, the Institute of Directors and the Federation of Small Businesses, and with many local schools achieving Warwick Awards for excellence in Enterprise, Rotherham Ready is now reaching out to involve educational establishments and businesses in other areas of the UK.

Suggestions for practice

1. Find out more about the Rotherham Ready approach.
2. Look up other sources of information about Enterprise education. Try the Enterprise Village site at http://www.enterprisevillage.org.uk/. This is a free resource for primary, secondary and further education staff interested in enterprise education.
3. The Economics, Business and Enterprise Association is a professional association that provides support for teachers in schools and colleges and others involved in economics, business and enterprise education. It provides a wide range of resources, including video and web links to support teaching and learning, and professional networking opportunities, see www.ebea.org.uk.
4. Microsociety, developed by the Education Business Partnership for Kingston and Merton, is a project that promotes economic understanding for Year 5 pupils, and includes resources and training for teachers, see www.myvoicelondon.org.uk.
5. Young Enterprise activities aim 'to inspire and equip young people to learn and succeed through enterprise', see www.young-enterprise.org.uk.
6. Follow one of these approaches to plan an Enterprise Project in your school.

Mantle of the expert

www.mantleoftheexpert.com

The Mantle of the Expert (MoE) is a drama-based enquiry method of teaching invented and developed by Professor Dorothy Heathcote at the University of Newcastle on Tyne in the 1980s. It might also be seen as a form of problem-based or enterprise learning. This approach is based on the principle that young people learn best when they are involved in their learning, by experiencing the learning as experts who will acquire the skills they need as and when required. As adults we learn through everyday experience through our jobs whether as curators, clinicians or cooks; from our hobbies, such as gardening, reading and sport; and through daily activities like driving a car or household budgeting. We learn from our own experiences and from others about how to communicate and collaborate, how to use tools and technical terms, and how to solve problems and reflect on our success and failures. As adults, we learn from what others have written in books and published materials such as those on the Internet and it can be motivating and empowering for children to learn in this way as well.

The MoE approach sets up situations where children can learn as adults do in everyday contexts from and with others in activities which draw on and extend their existing expertise. MoE builds on children's natural appetite for play and pretend activities which involve running a fictional ethical enterprise in a way which develops a feeling of community and responsibility. In this enterprise the pupils take on the role of experts in a field chosen by their teachers, identified as one which will help develop the skills and knowledge they need while covering aspects of the national curriculum. As they do this they find they need to acquire maths, literacy and ICT skills as well as knowledge about their subject in a context which motivates them and where they can see the relevance. They have a real purpose for learning and discovering information and acquiring expertise which to apply to their project. MoE encourages creativity and critical thinking, develops teamwork, communication skills and decision-making. There is usually a fictional client involved who contacts the team for their services, perhaps as a business partner who wants help in setting up a garden centre, a museum curator wanting archaeologists to explore an Orkney burial mound, or a buyer wanting a new product for their shop. This means that the children are working for someone other than their teacher and this gives them a set of user needs with which they have to work. Reflection on their learning is an essential part of the process.

Activities may include the following:

- Mime and drama.
- Research.
- Learning to use a calculator, spreadsheet and create charts and tables.
- Learning to write for particular purposes, e.g. letters, reports, advertisement.
- Negotiation, discussion and debate.
- Creating and selling products.
- Using ICT for effective communication and recording.
- Presentations either personal or using multi-media.
- Critical evaluation and reflective discussion.

The teacher steps in and out of role, guiding their research, teaching skills as they are required, providing resources and altering the scenario so as to challenge, support and encourage the experts. MoE creates a context and a purpose for learning. Perhaps it is most valuable because there is a 'continuous goal of raising the students' awareness of how responsibility arising from the particular expertise is part of a value system' (Heathcote and Bolton 1996: 24).

The main difficulty for the teacher with this approach to teaching and learning is ensuring curriculum coverage and that all children are adequately supported with their personal learning needs. It may also be a problem to assess individual progress in collaborative working. Some children might be domineering and exclude those with less social status from participating fully, and the less confident might be tempted to get a free ride on the abilities of others without making a sufficient contribution. The teacher has to be adaptable to the suggestions of the children, able to conjure up resources as required and able to enter into the drama as a participant. Not all parents will at first understand that their children seem to be engaged in fantasy play rather than proper lessons for much of the time. It will take excellent communication, explanation and reflection from all involved to see the value of this creative way of working.

Examples from practice

- Examples of MoE projects can be found on http://www.mantleoftheexpert.com/. There are also links to the Bealings School which uses this approach and claims that 'almost any area of the curriculum could be taught through a Mantle of the Expert'.
- Treetop Transport was a Y1 and Y2 enterprise begun in response to lorry haulage company, asked for help to transport endangered animals to safety.
- Running a Bear Sanctuary was a Year 3/4 project which started from a story about dancing bears in Tudor times and went on to organize setting up a bear sanctuary.
- Giantlife Foundation was an organization formed by a Y5, Y6 class to promote better understanding of extremely tall people in modern times and also to research evidence of entire races of giants through history.
- To plan a term's work at Birley Spa Primary in Sheffield, staff choose the programmes of study they want to cover and then give the pupils a choice about the context in which they would like to do this. For a rocks and soils project, one class chose to work as geologists while another voted to be vulcanologists and were really impressed by their teacher's influence and organization when a volcano erupted in Iceland just two weeks into the project. The objectives are used flexibly so that the PoS can be covered differently within the same topic or in another context. The pupils took on a range of roles at different parts of the project being reporters, geologists, scientists, witnesses to an eruption or news presenters as required. They used e-mail to contact the media and were thrilled with the replies they received.
- Another time when teaching staff decided that work on plants would be appropriate, one class chose to be garden centre staff to learn about plants, while a parallel class were in a jungle camp challenge. Work on a World of Chocolate Cafe resulted in parents coming in to be served drinks and snacks in an end-of-term café. In each case the children identified the jobs which need doing with the teacher in a

managerial role as part of each drama. In this school, teachers sometimes uses a Dictaphone to record the children's reflections on their learning.

- MoE provides a system for harnessing children's natural inclination to play and to imagine. It develops their confidence as well as creative problem-solving and critical thinking skills. In this way, children see the usefulness of learning, and learn how to take responsibility for what and how they learn. They learn to think in new ways, empathize with others, create new ideas and theories, test them out and reflect on their progress. The MoE approach to teaching uses two complementary modes of creativity: the generative mode and the critically evaluative mode as described by Ken Robinson in the NACCCE report (1999). In a well-organized MoE, the work is purposeful with outcomes which are imaginative and of value.

10 Developing creativity across the curriculum

Using ICT to develop creativity across the curriculum

In this section we will look at the way ICT can develop the creativity of the child and the creative expertise of the teacher through the five creative behaviours.

Questioning and challenging ?

One of the most effective ways to learn is to ask questions. Children should be encouraged to practise this skill from their first days in school progressing from 'how?' and 'where?' to 'when?' and 'why?' to 'what if?' and 'how can?' All questions can have worth and may require different ways to find answers.

AREST
Questions can be answered using the acronym AREST (Jesson and Peacock 2011):

- **Ask** someone through e-mail, texting, web-cam, Skype, video-conferencing, blogging or social networking.
- **Research** answers using the Internet or CD-ROMs.
- **Experiment** to investigate ideas through data-logging, modelling to try out ideas or data-handling software to organize and make charts to help analyse data.
- **Simulation** on CD-ROMs and the Internet when first-hand tests are impracticable.
- **Think** around a problem, recording reflections on ideas, events and discussions using ICT to organize these in notes and lists and mind maps.

Digital technologies can be used in many contexts with each of these techniques and both help to answer and to stimulate further questions:

- In KS1 children asking 'How are my clothes made?' could put fabric samples under a digital microscope or visualizer. Seeing the world in this way or through the lens of a digital camera can prompt further questions. Challenges such as

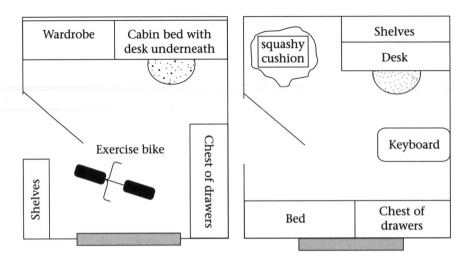

Figure 10.1 Alternative bedroom designs using computer graphics tools

'Do I live nearer to school than my friends?' can be answered through on-line maps. Unusual questions such as 'What if there was no green in the world?' might be checked out by taking the green out of digital photos.

- Children in LKS2 might want to know 'What did the Tudors have for breakfast?' and use a CD-ROM or the Internet to find out. Poems can be turned into stories and vice versa and the tenses changed more quickly with a word processor than by hand.
- Older pupils in UKS2 can be very motivated to design their ideal den or to redesign their bedroom to use the space more effectively (Figure 10.1). Try the CAD room planning programs from IKEA (http://www.ikea.com/ms/en_GB/rooms_ideas/splashplanners.html) or the graphics tools in Word, Textease or other WP programs.

Data-loggers can record the light, sound, movement and temperature levels round school with a view to making improvements, or see if the school pets are more active at night. A word processor can answer questions about how a different layout might affect a presentation, or help check spelling and grammar queries. Asking useful questions which help to sort items into categories can be developed using a binary (branching) database.

Making connections and seeing relationships

Several computer programs can help children make connections and see relationships. Both branching and standard databases can sort data according to its properties. Spreadsheets can be used as databases to classify and sort specimens according to what they have in common. Charts from these can show connections and relationships clearly.

In KS1 an interactive whiteboard (IWB) can be used to display sets of items for pupils to identify what they have in common or identify which is the odd one out. The children may have ideas which their teacher does not expect and explanations for these should be encouraged. Digital soundscapes can be made for stories and poems they enjoy either using digital sound files or recording their own percussion and tuned instrumental playing. This might be added to a reading of the text and turned into a podcast for the school website.

Pupils in LKS2 could use a computer cartoon template to record learning in science or RE or make a digital animated film to record learning in geography or citizenship sessions. Making connections and seeing relationships is a skill needed to create analogies and metaphors. The latter are useful to make complex ideas memorable and accessible. To encourage a variety of personal connections, a teacher could challenge the class to explain what anger is like in response to a picture of handcuffs, a fire, or a rat. Answers might be it is like handcuffs because it stops you doing things, a fire because it spreads easily and can hurt people, and a rat because it is often hidden and can eat up the good things in life. Any answer they can justify is valid. Pupils could create similar puzzles for their friends using clip art, e.g. a classroom is like . . .; a friend is like . . .; a story is like . . .

Pupils in UKS2 could use concept-mapping software such as Kidspiration to create a mind map to show connections between prior knowledge and recent learning. When searching for patterns in plant growth or changing materials, spreadsheets can show trends. Pupils should be encouraged to present their learning in many relevant and engaging ways including digital movies, podcasts, multimedia presentations, word processed posters and brochures to share with different audiences. They can share them with distant audiences through e-mails, e-zines, and virtual learning environments (VLEs). However, they should be warned about the dangers of sharing personal information on social networking sites.

Seeing things in new ways and envisaging what might be 👓

An important role of education is to help the learner to see things in new ways and from different points of view; to imagine possibilities, foresee problems and visualize solutions. 'What if?' is a higher-order thinking skill to develop.

KS1 children can be helped to imagine and then check what other people and places are like and use a web-cam to find out. Taking digital photos of a locality from the perspective of a baby, or a wheelchair user can develop consideration for others' needs. Children who find sums stressful may enjoy them as games on an IWB. Ideas can be trialled in a graphics programme and the artist experiment with 'what if' possibilities until satisfied with their design.

Pupils in Y3 and Y4, can use a paint program to adapt digital photos to show their personalities or disguise themselves (Figure 10.2).

Altering the colour levels of digital photos could show how the world appears to a colour-blind person or an animal which sees colours differently from people. Creating digital films about moral dilemmas enables children to work through 'what if?' alternatives in problematic situations.

Figure 10.2   Carys in disguise

Y5 and Y6 children can be challenged to envisage how the parts of the school might be improved and research options using digital maps and a graphics package to add new features. If they Twitter a traditional tale into 140 characters, what would be lost? What might be clearer? When data-handling they can manipulate data and choose the most appropriate chart.

Exploring ideas, keeping options open ⊕

Creativity is also about exploring different possibilities, keeping options open until a preferred solution is found while developing decision-making skills. Digital technology allows pupils to experiment with ideas while keeping all alternatives intact. Through play young children explore routes for a floor turtle to visit features on a floor map. Designs for cards, bookmarks or calendars, for different recipients, can be explored with a graphics package. A word-processing package empowers pupils to experiment with layouts. A spreadsheet allows options to be tried when budgeting. Simulation programs enable risk-taking without disaster or time wasting, e.g. when growing plants, although they should not replace practical investigations which are vital to the understanding of the way plants really grow and the time growth takes. The measuring jug and weighing simulations on the Interactive Teaching Programs site enable endless experimentation without spillage or weight lifting when learning to estimate and measure. It is fun to hear how a musical composition can sound with altered tempo or different instruments. Musical software can do this without spoiling the original composition. Tactical computer games allow learners to play with ideas, try out strategies and overcome problems. The design and use of avatars (Google this term to get free examples), or Virtual worlds such as Sim City or Barnsborough enable anything from an outfit to an alternative lifestyle to be explored. The latter, originally designed to improve boys' writing, is reported as having much wider beneficial effects.

In Y5 and Y6 groups of friends could use a wiki to collect uses for a digital camera. (Challenge them to find more than a hundred.) Control technology allows pupils to turn lights on or off, raise and lower barriers and sound warnings in response to instructions. Such activities will generate many problems to anticipate or solve where creative ingenuity is developed. Alternatives to writing up their learning might involve digital film, digital sound, presentation and graphics programs.

Reflecting critically on ideas, actions and outcomes

Reflection is an integral part of the learning process as we learn to assess what works and what does not, and ICT can help to structure this. Even young children can be helped to make an electronic portfolio of their progress which includes scanned images, photos, text and graphics in a presentation program. Pupils can type comments about what they found most interesting, most challenging and what they would like to do next. If a teaching assistant can help with assembling these, the task can be made manageable for a large class. An important part of the process is the child choosing the pieces and comments to add. A tape-recorder or digital recorder could also be used to record reflection and set targets.

Pupils with greater keyboard control could add speech and thought bubbles to digital text, photos and art work to review what they have learned and explain the most useful or enjoyable part of a session. Concept maps can record learning before and after a topic with reflective comments added. Reviews of school events can be shared on a class e-zine or VLE for relatives and carers to read. Word processing reviews allow editing and rewording of ideas. Few adults would now write an article by hand so we should allow pupils the same support we use. Avoid using a word processor just for fair copies: start and finish writing on a computer or start and finish by hand.

For pupils on a residential trip, a digital movie camera could be set up somewhere private for children to reflect, Big Brother-style, on what it feels like to be away from home. Podcasting requires descriptive and analytical skills with no visual clues to aid the listener's understanding. These can be created by children to explain their learning. Some schools now use blogs for pupils to review their learning, to add constructive comments on others' ideas. This might be for a single project, or as a regular electronic diary to show progression.

> The advantages of ICT to develop creative skills are its accuracy, speed and versatility. Alternatives can be explored and all choices kept until a final decision is made. Different versions can be saved and adapted for particular situations or recipients. ICT is not one technique: it can be visual, oral, aural, graphic, practical, diagrammatic, realistic or imaginative. ICT tools are certainly not the only way to develop creative skills, but they can go a long way to increase cooperation and communication, develop imagination, and increase enjoyment and to personalise and enrich the learning experience in the busy classroom. Along with the skills of an open-minded teacher, they can help pupils to question and challenge, to make connections and see

relationships to envisage what might be, to explore ideas, to keep options open and to reflect critically on their ideas, actions and outcomes.

(Jesson and Peacock 2011)

Computers can help develop children's thinking skills when used as part of a larger dialogue about thinking and learning (Wegerif 2002). The challenge for the teacher is to find ways to use the computer to encourage thinking and discussion between children.

Suggestions for practice

Table 10.1   Suggestions for IT use

Creative Endeavour	Year group	Suggestion
Questioning and challenging	KS1	How many different shapes of flower are there? Use a **visualizer** to compare shapes and parts
	LKS2	How fit am I? Use a **spreadsheet,** to record progress in keeping fit over half a term. Consider what elements comprise physical fitness and how each may be developed and measured during class PE
	UKS2	How can we use our classroom space more effectively? Use a **Graphics** program to try ideas
Making connections and seeing relationships	KS1	Create a **soundscape** for a story and add to a **podcast**
	LKS2	Use a **WP** to create strip cartoons to show learning in science or RE
	UKS2	Create a **mind-map** to show prior knowledge and recent learning in any subject. Use the information to make a **digital presentation** for parents' evening or a class exhibition
Envisaging what might be	KS1	**Use a webcam/e-mail** to find what the people are doing in other places
	LKS2	How could I disguise myself? Alter digital photos in **paint program**
	UKS2	**Twitter** a traditional tale or poem. What is lost and what might be enhanced?

Creative Endeavour	Year group	Suggestion
Exploring ideas, keeping options open	KS1	Use **Turtle graphics** to find the best route round a maze they have designed
		Create abstract art design for calendar/bookmark in **Graphics** program. Use basic design altered to favourite colours of recipient
	LKS2	Use **avatars on line** to create an alter ego. Bring it to life in a story
	UKS2	Design the perfect den with a friend. Use the **graphics program** and **e-mail** to communicate ideas
Reflecting critically on ideas, actions and outcomes	KS1	Create an **e-portfolio** with comments. Include scanned art work, word processed text, and photos of pupils in a range of activities. Speech or thought bubbles and captions can be added by child to say what was easiest/hardest/most interesting/most enjoyable and what they'd like to learn/do next
	LKS2	Record their experiences with **digital audio/tape** and comment on them
	UKS2	Use **blogs** to help pupils review their learning and to comment on other people's ideas

11 Developing creativity through subject teaching

Think out of the box, by all means, but serious efforts in-box must accompany for any suitable culmination.

(Yamamoto 2010)

This section is not intended as a complete guide to teaching any subject area. It simply aims to show how every subject has potential for both creative teaching and learning to develop both group and personal creativity. Whether you prefer a subject-, topic-, thematic or problem-based approach, the ideas in this section can be adapted. Aspects of every subject should be incorporated into a child's experience at some time in their primary education. Suggestions for each subject or age and ability group may be tailored for another. In each section, ideas are suggested, on a theme, so that for history the use of artefacts is emphasized, while with PE it is the invention of games and dances. It would be perfectly possible to put the artefacts with the RE or Geography section or the invention of games and dances into the Science or Maths section to support creative teaching and learning in those areas. Although there is a final section for ICT, this should be used as a tool in all subjects to develop creative ideas, and as innovative subject in its own right.

NACCCE (1999: 43) stated that 'sustained creative achievement involves knowledge of the field in question and skills in the media concerned', reminding us that sound subject and skills knowledge is necessary for creative development. Creativity does not occur in a vacuum but must be developed alongside the skills and knowledge for the subjects it enlivens. In maths teaching, there is a tradition of teaching basic skills and then providing problems which need those skills to solve them. Creative teaching does the same in all the other subjects so that teaching science, historical or geographical enquiry skills, for example, is followed by a challenge in which they can be applied.

The requirements of the National Curriculum's, literacy and numeracy hours should not be a barrier to creative teaching and learning. They are just a guide to the content of some lessons, not to the ways they must be taught. Creative teachers vary the approach from lesson to lesson. Opportunities for visual learning will include maps, diagrams, timelines, mind maps and displaying written words and pictures when describing things. A whiteboard can show maths concepts visually, display texts, list instructions and help those with a graphical preference for learning. Aids to auditory learning will include repeating new, difficult or key words and concepts aloud, using rhymes, paired talk and group discussion. P4C sessions can develop thinking skills and explore ideas from differing perspectives. Some learners enjoy using or creating recorded stories or podcasts, making oral reports, and presentations. To aid kinaesthetic learning, provide hands-on activities and experiments. Use field trips and outdoor activities wherever possible and try to employ regular role play and drama opportunities. These do not have to be extensive and might just involve a few seconds of mime to revise learning from a session. Frequent breaks allow for exercise and stretching, while 'soft thinking time' is required to mull over ideas.

The rest of this chapter offers you a rich range of ideas across a spectrum of subject areas which will help you implement some of the ideas contained in this book and develop creative teaching and learning to develop both group and personal creativity. Each subject area appears on a double-page spread and considers creative teaching and learning through:

Creative teaching and learning through Literacy

Creative teaching and learning through Maths

Creative teaching and learning through Science

Creative teaching and learning through Design Technology (DT)

Creative teaching and learning through History

Creative teaching and learning through Geography

Creative teaching and learning through Art and Design

Creative teaching and learning through PE

Creative teaching and learning through Modern Foreign Languages

Creative teaching and learning through Music and Drama

Creative teaching and learning through RE and Citizenship Education

Creative teaching and learning through ICT

Creative teaching and learning through Literacy

> It is better to have enough ideas for some of them to be wrong, than to be always right by having no ideas at all.
>
> Edward de Bono

The main aim for getting children to communicate must surely be to give them pleasure in the activity. Without enjoyment in speech and writing, as well as a willingness to listen to others' ideas, their work will be superficial and without real engagement. Creative writing is just one aspect of literacy; creating thinking, speech, and drama need to come first. All speech and writing is to some extent creative, but opportunities to innovate and take risks in school may be hidden behind barriers of objectives. Professional writers redraft many times: a laborious process unless they use a word processor. Despite the many computers in schools, some children rarely use one to take the tedium out of checking work. Although spelling and grammar are important, motivation needs to come first. The ideas here aim to engage, inspire and add relevance to children's lives. Writing for a purpose rather than exercises helps develop originality and a voice as they create for a particular audience.

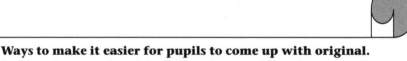

Ways to make it easier for pupils to come up with original.

1. Give advance notice of the writing they may do, so they can mull over some ideas.
2. Ask them to talk a story through with a friend before writing to sort out the main events.
3. Ask groups or pairs to write a story which answers a question such as 'Whatever happened to the groink?' or 'How did the monkey get its tail?'
4. Give interesting words or items which must be included in a poem, report or story.
5. *Lion, witch and wardrobe technique:* Let them choose random items from a set of lists which you or they have compiled so they each have a person, an animal and an item to include. This can be a useful starting point which is often hard to come up with on your own.
7. Encourage them to write to manufacturers, MPs, TV programmes, charities, or celebrities they admire and who are likely to write back.
8. Vary the stimulus, so that one day it might be a treasure chest, a piece of music, or a painting and another a letter, an article, a rhyme or the need to create a museum or presentation of some kind.
9. Set amusing challenges, e.g. Write instructions for how to trap a teacher.

Nonsense can make sense!

1. Read a nonsense rhyme or poem such as Jabberwocky to the class. Explore the meanings of some of the made-up words or nonsensical features.

2. Ask pupils to invent a new type of monster, name it, talk about it, draw it and add labels with made up words which describe it. For example, the wings might be blotious, the eyes, spobbly, and the skin scraurcous. Then they may be ready to write a story or poem about it.

Oral opportunities

Use role play and drama at all ages to give experience on which to build creative ideas and later writing.

Make the most of visits and visitors by making digital audio recordings. These can be used in podcasts and multimedia presentations.

Plan a live presentation to parents, or record a radio programme/TV show.

Turn a story/poem into a puppet show.

Work in pairs to make someone say yes/no.

Play 20 questions to find a mystery object where only yes/no can be said.

Devise debates and discussions on local and national issues as well as items in books, newspapers and magazines.

Let them apply what they have learned in one context to learning in another e.g. once pupils have been taught instructional writing, they could use this genre to write up science experiments as spells. When they can write a diary of their own activities, they could record geographical or historical events, or religious stories in this way. Poems can be used to record learning in science or maths, and cartoons are an engaging way to document many types of experience.

Be brave!

Try writing with the class under same conditions you have set them. Be prepared to share your ideas at the end of a 5- or 15-minute silent session. This can help keep the class on task as they see you are prepared to share the same process. To be really fair, let them choose your stimulus so you don't just read out something you have practised in advance. Real creativity involves bravery and risk taking.

Model the composition process with different genres as you comment on the way you choose words and redraft to improve sense and structure.

Set them enjoyable challenges such as writing:

- a treasure hunt

- instructions and rules for a game they invent

- riddles and jokes

- a blog

- contributions to a wiki, perhaps even adding or amending an item in Wikipedia

Encourage original layouts.

Creative teaching and learning through Maths

> Mathematics is a creative discipline. It can stimulate moments of pleasure and wonder when a pupil solves a problem for the first time, discovers a more elegant solution to that problem, or suddenly sees hidden connection.
>
> (DfEE/QCA 1999: 14)

Creative learning in maths is about finding a personal response to problems and ideas. Those who find it hard to express themselves artistically or through writing may have a talent for mathematical exploration so opportunities to explore and apply mathematical procedures should be offered through games, homework challenges and puzzles involving open-ended investigations. Briggs, cited in Wilson (2007: 100) offers a checklist for deciding what makes a 'good' problem-solving task.

A Problem-solving activity should be	*A Problem-solving activity should offer/present*
• accessible to all • possible to extend • possible to narrow • enjoyable	• a practical starting point • opportunities for mathematical discussion • a reason for children to record their ideas • opportunities for repetition without becoming meaningless both for teachers and children • clarity of underlying mathematics

Maths is a visual subject with patterns of numbers, shapes and symbols and if we can exploit this visual characteristic, we may be able to engage those who find abstraction difficult. Asking pupils to search for patterns is only useful if they then have to explain them. Devising rhymes to remember maths rules will help some, while manipulating maths materials and maths games will help others. Children who can use all learning styles are the most successful learners.

Challenges with potential for developing pupil creativity in Maths

KS1	How many ways can be found to sort a collection of bottles? E.g. capacity, weight, size, shape, cost.
LKS2	What interesting number patterns can be seen on a digital clock? E.g. 12:34 12:51 6:09 What differences would there be between 12 hour and 24 hour clocks?
UKS2	Find a way to estimate the number of leaves on a tree or the number of people in a crowd.

Ways to encourage enjoyable creativity in Maths

Allow enough time for solutions and new ideas
- Set open-ended challenges
- Ask open-ended questions
- Encourage diverse ways of working and recording
- Value original ideas

Ask pupils to solve number problems they devise by obtaining numbers from dice/spinners/other random ways. Vary ways to collect data, e.g. GPS, Wii, data-logging, sports results.

How many designs can they create by cutting a square of paper into two identical pieces? OR How many tessellating patterns can they create? Which shapes are best for this?

How many ways can a number be made using given digits/operations? Adapt this to the calculation strategies they know. It is a good start-the-day challenge.

Design wallpaper with a repeating/rotating pattern or two examples of symmetry.

Find patterns in number squares/create number patterns of their own.

Give open-ended challenges to suit each ability level, e.g. How many ways can they pay for an item which costs 20p or £1.00 or £5.76? Given them an answer and ask what the question might be.

Find ways for pupils to apply their math skills in other subject and cross-curricular projects. We should be teaching for the *pleasure* of using maths, not just the utility of the subject.

Writing maths trails can give relevance to class learning, by helping pupils make connections to what they see around them while helping them devise questions, and see things in new ways.

Older but less mathematically able pupils benefit from making booklets/poster/multimedia texts to teach younger pupils about aspects of maths, e.g. shapes/fractions.

Give a Countdown challenge to make a target number using four other numbers chosen at random and involving the fewest calculations in as short a time as possible.

Creative teaching and learning through Science

> Discovery consists of seeing what everybody has seen and thinking what nobody has thought
>
> Albert Szent-Gyorgyi, Hungarian scientist and Nobel Prize winner.

Not only children but many teachers see science as being about learning a set of facts and skills, rather than developing scientific theories, exploring ideas and discovering relationships. However, the five creative behaviours of questioning, making connections, seeing things differently, exploring ideas, and reflecting, describe sound scientific practice.

Science should be about excitement and exploring ideas: the pupil's ideas. For this to be meaningful, the questions need to come from the child not the teacher. Too often classes are told what to find out, how to do it and what the solution will be before they even start a test. Lacking enough time and equipment, groups are allocated tasks so that only a few actually get to test, measure or record. Creative science is when children work imaginatively, with a scientific purpose in mind which results in an outcome of value to them. This outcome needs to be a new understanding, may create new questions and it may or may not be recorded conventionally. Johnson, cited in Wilson (2009) suggest problem-solving, investigations and discussion to challenge thinking should be a regular part of science teaching to develop scientific understandings as well as understanding the nature of science.

Problem-solving challenges	Investigations	Discussions
What is the mystery powder?	How many ways can a group of items be sorted?	Why are many butterflies coloured the way they are?
What is the best way to make a paper plane?	Which is the best way to wash dirty clothes?	What is the most useful material in the world?
How can you develop a timing device?	Which animals live in our school grounds?	What is the best way to count plant types in a lawn?

Challenges with potential for developing pupil creativity in Science

KS1	On which surfaces do snails travel fastest? E.g. glass, sandpaper, plastic or something else?
LKS2	How can the descent of a marble on a tilted tray be slowed down? E.g. Try adding strips of card/pieces of plasticine.
UKS2	Devise a signalling system using lights or buzzers which will send a message in three different ways.

- Use a video, **CD-ROM** or simulation to study the Earth and its relationship to the solar system.
- Use the **Internet** to find out how the length of day and night/the seasons affects plant growth/animal behaviour such as migration in different parts of the world.
- Pupils can create a digital mind map of what they learn with **hyperlinks** to relevant websites/pages of information.

Ways to use ICT in Science

Pupils write brief responses to each question, here, about an animal, and then assemble them into a poem.

* What does it remind you of?

* How does it move?

* What does it eat?

* Where does it hide?

* What does it fear?

* What sounds does it make?

Ways to use e-learning in Science

- **Tables** can be a useful way of recording results for analysis.
- Use **data-loggers** to record changes in light, sound, temperature and movement investigations.
- A **simulation** program can explore what might happen to plants and animals in different situations.
- Use a **branching database** to sort, group and identify plants, animals and materials.
- Compare leaves, flowers, shells and materials using a **digital microscope** or **visualizer**.
- A **database** or **spreadsheet** can store data and produce charts for analysis.
- Use a **tape recorder** or **digital audio recorder** to record sound sources.
- **Hand-held devices** and **palm tops** can be used to collect data on field trips.

Record learning in Science through creative writing

- record the results of investigations.
- to make labelled diagrams e.g. of parts of a plant.
- record local building materials in the high street, a park or the school. Use to devise a materials trail for another class.
- record the changes in a shadow of a human sundial during a day.
- e-mail photos of local wildlife to another school to compare habitats.
- record plant growth through using **freeze frame animation/time lapse** photography or look at videos on YouTube which show this.

Use a **digital camera** to:

Creative teaching and learning through Design Technology (DT)

Genius is one percent inspiration and ninety-nine percent perspiration.

(Edison)

> ## We can design by doing, dreaming and drawing.
> The process does not always have to start on paper. Many inventors develop ideas in their heads or by making mocking-up prototypes. Young children especially prefer to design as they make. This is fine with materials which can be recycled and with construction kits. Whatever the construction methods or subject knowledge taught, the design and make task which follows should be an open-ended one, which allows each child to develop ideas from their imagination. DT should involve both creative and critical thinking skills with evaluation at each stage of design and production. It should also involve being resourceful with resources so as to minimize waste.

Design Technology is a subject which is much misunderstood and often taught badly by a generation of teachers who were never taught it themselves. Too often the design element is reduced to decorating someone else's design and the technology is unchallenging. The primary school is an ideal place for pupils to learn to cook, sew, saw, construct, but above all to consider user needs and solve problems. These may be organizational problems about the most effective way to store and give out resources; conceptual problems which involve coming up with new ideas such as what sort of game could be made to revise learning in science; or constructional problems when making a toy to amuse a sick child. A more positive and proactive approach is to think of DT as a possibility-finding subject rather than a problem-solving one. It is inherently creative because it involves the imagination, is purposeful and involves originality and creating items or systems of value. Through DT, pupils can learn to see problems as opportunities and develop a creative approach to life so they grow up working out everyday challenges, making their own toys and amusements, and finding the most effective ways of doing things for themselves. They will learn to cope with uncertainty, take sensible risks and adapt ideas and techniques they have been taught.

Challenges with potential for developing pupil creativity in DT

KS1	Design a home for a fantasy figure who has special powers or needs (Identify these first). It might be a dragon, a magician, a fairy or a super-bat.
LKS2	Design three different outfits for a pop star to wear to a show, in a race and relaxing at home.
UKS2	Create a pulley to lift a load from a toy lorry to a ship.

Creative work comes from pupil's interests and relevant contexts. Children of all ages could design **dens** made from large recycled card packing cases.

I've seen nursery children in an award-winning school using power tools under close supervision to make dens and play equipment from large pieces of wood. Parents or grandparents might be able to supervise children doing this in small groups.

Older children could design and make
- a play mat for a younger child.
- a picture book with moving parts to tell a story/explain a scientific process.
- a paper glider which will travel a long way.
- tasty soups, tapas, breads and biscuits by adapting basic recipes.
- jewellery from papier-mâché/waste materials.
- Science/maths/sculpture trails.

Younger children could design and make . . .
- finger puppets to illustrate a nursery rhyme.
- salads, fruit kebabs, vegetable snacks.
- dragons/dinosaurs/monsters/zoo animals from strips of newspaper and flour and water paste over rolls of newspaper.
- cards with moving parts.
- an invented pet and a home for it.
- simple mobiles.
- models to go with favourite stories.

Involve whole classes with:
- Enterprise activities with products/presents to sell.
- Games based on board games, dominoes, or games they know.
- Finding ways to improve the organization of the indoor/outdoor playtimes to reduce conflict and increase enjoyment.
- Redesigning parts of the school ground for wildlife, as quiet areas, outdoor science areas or small theatres.

* Pupils could redesign the classroom for a particular activity or a new class. Following discussion about user needs the layout might be modelled in wooden or plastic bricks, waste materials or on a computer using graphics scaled to fit the room. measurements.

* Designing an exhibition or museum or display might be a whole class project or just a challenge for a couple of pupils wanting to put up their own display about an area of interest.

* Give DT design challenges for monthly homework tasks.

How many ways can they design and make?
- a home for a mini-beast.
- a moving vehicle for a particular purpose.
- a card animal which stands up.
- a model for an advertisement which uses a cam.
- the lightest bridge which will span 30 cm and hold 200g weight
- tall structures from straws/rolls of newspaper.

Creative teaching and learning through History

From the experience of the past we derive instructive lessons for the future.

John Quincy Adams, sixth American president, 1025

History requires creative teaching to make the past feel as real as the present. It needs creative learning to keep its messages alive and for children to see their relevance for today. Historical enquiry not only can enrich the present but also give us a new perspective on today's problems. To do this we need to question our sources of information and try to piece together the evidence we have along with our own ideas and experience. This can involve tolerating uncertainty while asking questions, making connections, exploring ideas, coming up with theories about the way people behaved, and explaining our ideas. By studying the way people have reacted to their circumstances, we can begin to understand their motives and develop imagination and empathy. Divergent thinking should be imbued with creativity and logic to develop multiple ideas about why people may have acted in the way they have or what part an artefact may have played in the past. History is a subject which embraces every other subject as we study the art, religion, writing and inventions in the past as well as the events which accompanied them.

In any subject we need to teach skills and then provide a challenge for their application which has multiple options. A way to help children understand that history involves changing interpretations of the past through inference and deduction is to provide them with documents and artefacts from which they can work out information about an event or a person's life. Creative teaching requires pupils to use skills from all subjects to discover and present their findings in engaging ways: perhaps in an electronic poster, or as an oral presentation with a visualizer to share the artefacts they are explaining.

Challenges with potential for developing pupil creativity in History

---

KS1	What questions would you like to ask an historical figure? What would you tell them about your life?
LKS2	Using a set of picture of artefacts from the time studied, what can the class tell about the people who lived then? What questions would they like to ask them? (A good way to start a project).
UKS2	Design a board game which uses facts from the period being studied. (A good way to end a project).

Create Timelines
- On a computer
  - Using a table
  - Using a spreadsheet
  - Using a commercial version
- With a line of children and labels
- With string across a room
- With points along the playground/ along a school corridor
- Ordered objects

  How will you create yours?

Artefact activities for all ages

- Play **odd one out** using sets of pictures or artefacts. With no single right answer the emphasis is on creative but realistic explanations.

- Order or **from most to least** in terms of age, fragility, interest or another way devised by pupils.

- **Find the pairs** Match objects or pictures into pairs and explain the link.

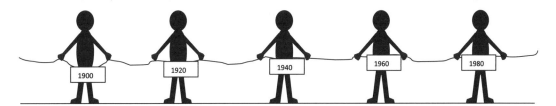

Arrange **visits** from grandparents so that children can make connections between their own lives and those of people who have grown up in different circumstances. This helps pupils to see how swiftly history is made. Prepare some questions in advance and get permission to record the visit using digital media. Letters of thanks and an invitation to see the resulting work are always appreciated and motivating for the class.

Role play . . . Can help to make sense of the past if it is well informed. It is best to have a well-briefed adult, possibly the teacher, in role to introduce and answer questions about a historical figure.

If Florence Nightingale arrives with a plain apron, cap, lamp, some bloody bandages as well as a bucket and mop these would provide useful starting points for children to question her about her life. She might bring a letter from home or a map showing how far she has travelled.

Role plays run in historical locations by teams of experts can be valuable in helping pupils to engage with contemporary issues and involve themselves physically with life in the past.

Use treasure chests

. . . to motivate as well as inspire questions and curiosity.

Fill an old suitcase or old box from a car boot sale or a treasure chest you have made from a cardboard box, with items which have relevance to an historical topic. Challenge the class to find the relevance of each and perhaps add some more challenges of their own.

Discuss **moral dilemmas** which people have faced:
- What might you do if you were given a slave?
- What would you say to a brother who wanted to join the Crusaders?
- Should people always do as they are told by their leaders?

Creative teaching and learning through Geography

> Geography makes us aware that we must think globally.
>
> Bill Giles, BBC weather-man

Studying geography gives us a sense of who we are and where we fit into the world. It is more than knowledge and understanding about places and people and being able to read a map. We all have what Bale (1987) terms 'private geographies' which are our schema of how we relate to the world. It is a socially important subject for pupils to study so that they 'live as responsible global citizens, able to act responsibly for a sustainable future' (Martin 2004).

The activities we teach should help our children to create connections and understanding between themselves and others and link the personal with the local and the global. To do this they need to learn to ask and answer questions about the world around them, explore ideas to seeing things in new ways, and reflect on how their changed understanding has implications for their actions. They should learn to look with criticality on the way it is organized and imagine more equitable and effective ways to do this. 'Through imagining other possible worlds, to consider how conflicts and issues might be resolved, and the parts individuals and groups might play in this process' (Martin 2004). Geographical teaching can benefit from problem-, project- or enquiry-based learning.

Link your school to others around the world through programmes such as *Commenius.com*. This can give many new angles to develop creative work as pupils plan what to ask and what to share about their countries. My school swapped information with schools in Hungary, Germany and Finland. We made DVDs of our local areas to share as well as games about local wildlife and books about local customs. These projects gave real purpose to their learning and developed many creative skills in technology, design, research and writing.

Challenges with potential for developing pupil creativity in Geography

KS1	Take photos which show your school as a happy place. Then take photos that imply it is like a prison (Locks, gates and bars are often in evidence).
LKS2	Devise a scavenger hunt for someone to use at the sea-side. This might include pictures, and items found on the shore E.g. something hard, or pink or rough, something beginning with S, part of an animal or plant, something very old.
UKS2	Look at the National Trust's list of 50 things to do before you are 11 and ¾. These involve different ways of interacting with the countryside. Pupils to devise their own wish list suitable for their locality and life style. **https://www.50things.org.uk/**

Collections are a stimulating and addictive way to find out more about an area. Starting a photographic collection of wild flowers, or pressed leaves, or shells, or feathers or stones can all start an interest in an aspect of local or even national geography which can last a lifetime. I have just found my 682nd wild flower in Britain on a botanical treasure hunt I started in primary school.

Planning a holiday for themselves or a family member, whether at home or abroad requires creative planning, questioning and budgeting skills as they consider others' needs and views.

Use national and local **news items** to stimulate interest in geographies of other peoples and places. They are a great way to identify issues, stimulate questions and make connections.

Older pupils could plan a **marketing campaign** to put their locality on the tourist map.
Younger children might use **digital film** to make a brochure of their home or street or school.

A **journey stick** is a way of recording a journey round a locality by attaching items of significance to a stick or rope in the order in which they were found. The items should represent places of interest or significance which were seen. The final piece can be digitally photographed and pasted into a document for further comments if required.

A **treasure hunt** is a great way to help children notice details in buildings and local flora which might otherwise be missed. Photos of significant items can be included to aid identification.

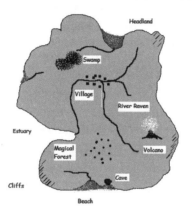

Teach them investigation skills in school in a way which will make them want to find out more at home and perhaps even make their own local study or **holiday diary**.

Map reading is a life skill which everyone should learn. It is enjoyable, useful and has great creative potential if children are given the opportunity to make their own maps for different purposes.

To teach children about physical features on a map, show them how to paint a map of somewhere such as India or Haiti on-screen using the brush and flood fill tools. They can add and label specific geographical features using the pencil and text tools. Use with creative writing or compass work in maths. Keys can explain geographical features. Young children love to make maps of imagined places. Adding caves, mines, forests, swamps, mountains, headlands and volcanoes gives opportunities for imaginative development as well as understanding of geographical terms. These can be used as the starting points for stories.

Help pupils make connection with where they go on **holiday** and what they see on **TV**. Many children travel the world with little idea of exactly where they have been.
Keep world, European and British maps handy to share information about places they go or they see on TV. Tell them about travel programmes which will be on in the week.

Creative teaching and learning through Art and Design

> Art and design is not just a subject to learn, but an activity that you can practise: with your hands, your eyes, your whole personality.
>
> Quentin Blake, Children's laureate

Although Art and Design are most often thought of as areas for creativity to flourish, too often in schools there is little genuine exploration and too much copying of others' ideas. Children need time to generate ideas, explore, review, and discuss them, to develop their ideas and personal creativity. Finding enough time to do this can be a challenge, but artistic homework tasks involving pencils, and biros or collages from the cards, wrapping paper, magazines and newspapers found in many homes can help. Most PCs have a simple art program on them in the Accessories menu and many have programs for editing photos as well. Those without a home computer could try out these programs in their local library. Pre- and post-school and playtime clubs can provide extra artistic experience. An art or craft task before registration can be a popular and creative way to start the day. A balance of teaching correct techniques and practising them imaginatively for enjoyment needs to be found.

Teach pupils:	Challenge them to:
How to cut, fold, pleat, quill, frill, and fringe a range of papers	Apply the techniques to create a collage in a relevant context, e.g. a rainforest collage
Photo-editing and digital painting	Create photographic collages, and alter digital photos to create new works of art
How to slot one piece of card into another with two slits	Make simple sculptures from card using this method
How to use mixed media to make a collage	Make a picture to go with music they enjoy
A range of techniques, e.g. with chalk/charcoal or ink	Show how they feel through a painting or drawing, about a particular situation
How to use straws and pipe-cleaners or plasticine or clay to make models	Design a new animal that has never been seen before
Box-building and papier-mâché techniques	Create their own monsters and robots

Challenges with potential for developing pupil creativity in Art and Design

KS1   Design a necklace, wristband or crown from salt dough/seeds/shells/aluminium foil and card.

LKS2   Use a digital camera to capture patterns e.g. in leaves, stones, buildings, clouds, flowers and bark.

UKS2   Copy a full length portrait of yourself into a paint programme. Rub out the background and paint in a new one.

Beach art could include:

- Sand castles

- Sand and shell sculptures

- Stone sculptures.

This sculpture from wood off-cuts, was created as a way to record the features of insects following a science session about living things.

Creating sculptures from driftwood and roots develops skills in exploring and adapting shapes using surforms, saws and drills.

Show pupils how to take photos from unusual angle such as above or below a subject and encourage them to experiment with different subjects and locations. These could be displayed in a 'Guess what?' competition.

Help pupils to explore the potential of wire sculpture, starting with pipe-cleaners for KS1 and then using pliers and wire cutters with older children.

Make sure you provide enough space for this so no one gets hurt. I believe that it is our job as teachers not to avoid potentially risky situations, but to show how to enjoy them safely.

Creative teaching and learning through PE

> The health of nations is more important than the wealth of nations.
>
> Will Durant, American writer, historian, and philosopher

Although creativity is not the first word which springs to mind when describing organized sports and games with strict rules, few would deny the ingenuity of sportsmen such as Beckham and Bothum, the innovative dancing of Darcy Bussell, or the originality of skaters, and gymnasts. Boys are often motivated to dance after watching YouTube clips of the percussion-based show Stomp. Imaginative teaching is necessary in PE to personalize sets of skills from which the less athletic or uncompetitive may feel alienated.

As much time as possible in a PE session should be devoted to practising the activity so that learners get adequate exercise. This can mean sharing inspirational film clips with teaching points before the session and then trying, evaluating and modifying them in the session. Appropriate warm-up activities can first be modelled by the teacher before individual pupils lead either small groups, or even the whole class. A follow-my-leader warm-up with each child having the opportunity to devise ways of moving for the others to follow gives opportunities for personal innovation, and leaders change on a given signal. Creative learning involves pupils both as individuals and in groups building on skills they have been taught to create their own dances, games, keep-fit and gymnastics routines. The teacher should encourage innovation and responsible risk taking, as well as artistic and technical development. Some dance, gymnastic and games activities can be adapted for use in water so that children can work out new movements in the swimming pool to develop their confidence and agility in water. Out of doors, timed treasure hunts, fitness trails, perhaps with items to record, obstacle courses, and orienteering activities all offer opportunities both in their creation as well as the tactics and decision-making involved by groups following them.

Challenges with potential for developing pupil creativity in PE

KS1	Develop a dragon dance in small groups and combine to make a large one.
LKS2	Invent a relay game which involves different ways of moving.
UKS2	Create a street dance/zumba routine from basic steps. (Find ideas on line for this if required.)

As many pupils travel widely these days it might be useful for them to devise **a keep-fit routine** to be done sitting in a car or plane seat. Planning these in groups can help to develop a wide range of ideas for arm, leg, head and joint movements.

These much not annoy other passengers!

Create **a dance** which uses a scarf/hoop/skipping rope/ribbon or football.

PE challenges to develop fitness and creativity for all ages

Ask pupils to **devise an obstacle course** to be used on sports day.

They might use a computer and graphics tools to represent each stage.

A class, or even a whole school, could be challenged to create **a fitness trail** around the playground, or the school grounds if possible. Instructions for the exercises to be performed at each station could be word-processed with added diagrams and laminated.

It might be possible to get a grant to help making any necessary apparatus, or local parents and volunteers could help pupils to make it.

Show classes how to develop different football or netball skills and ask small groups to plan **team games** and tactics which use them. These can be taught to the rest of the class and used in playtimes.

Groups could invent new **team games** with small apparatus such as skipping ropes, or beanbags. If they can organize the sharing and tidying of these at playtimes, their use can reduce playground conflict and boredom as well as increase physical fitness.

Teach pupils a basic set of dance steps such as those involved in salsa, country dances, line dances or jive.

Let them practise these in small groups and then **devise a new country dance or salsa routine** which they can teach to the whole class. This activity can be very popular with even reluctant dancers when they become the dance teachers.

Use a **graphics program** to design fitness trails/potted sports activities, which will develop stamina and flexibility.

Use **Wii technology** to motivate less confident pupils who are familiar with them in a home setting. These can give experience of unfamiliar sports such as tennis/bowling.

Use **digital photos** and films of their PE activities to identify ways to improve control and coordination.

Create a class **keep-fit plan** on the interactive whiteboard. Record PE times, after-school opportunities to keep fit, and look at ways to keep fit at playtimes. Add local opportunities such as swimming and sports clubs.

Creative teaching and learning through Modern Foreign Languages teaching (MFL)

An essential aspect of creativity is not being afraid to fail.

Edwin Land

The main aim of teaching MFL in the primary school has to be getting pupils to enjoy the MFL experience and there is much more to this than teaching vocabulary and grammar. Effective teaching promotes a positive attitude to learning languages, gives instruction in some of the skills necessary for learning languages and promotes intercultural understanding, which is a vital asset in our increasingly global society. It is not important which language is taught but how it is done.

Few primary schools have specialist MFL teachers and many instructors are learning only just ahead of their classes, which takes courage. Most children would prefer a sensitive teacher who makes the learning enjoyable to an expert who does not. Pupils need confidence to try out their language skills without fear of failure and ridicule for poor grammar or pronunciation. A creative teacher will provide conditions which promote low anxiety levels to give pupils the courage to have a go, often employing activities which are enjoyed in other contexts. Using puppets, drama, and role plays can develop speaking and listening skills in any MFL. Younger children will enjoy class shops using money, weights and measures vocabulary or information offices which give verbal directions. Playing games of Scrabble, cards, snakes and ladders or anything which requires oral communication may be adapted to an MFL. Songs and rhymes use repetition to good effect and older pupils can create their own. Be creative with your IT resources and check out blogs and wikis to which older pupils can contribute and note the best language apps available on the Internet. Learners can use the **Internet** to find out about life in other countries through focused questions and key words.

Challenges with potential for developing pupil creativity in Modern Foreign Languages

KS1	Create a Pet Parlour or vet's surgery to give advice about sick toy pets.
LKS2	Set up a French shop, to sell items in Euros if possible.
UKS2	Role-play a travel agency in France.

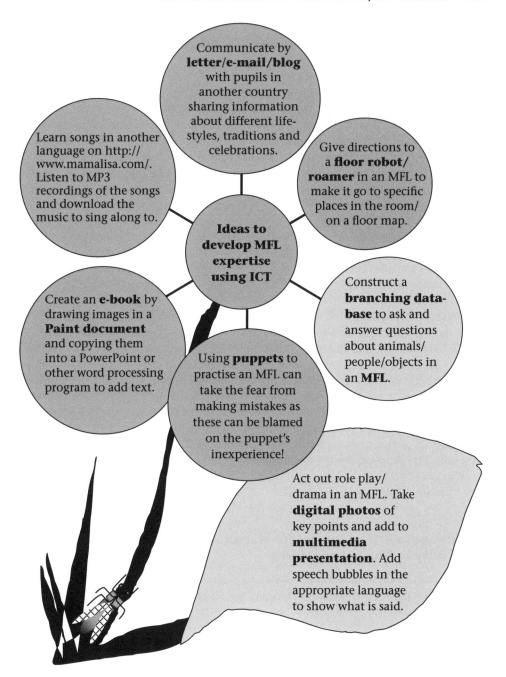

Communicate by **letter/e-mail/blog** with pupils in another country sharing information about different lifestyles, traditions and celebrations.

Learn songs in another language on http://www.mamalisa.com/. Listen to MP3 recordings of the songs and download the music to sing along to.

Give directions to a **floor robot/roamer** in an MFL to make it go to specific places in the room/on a floor map.

Ideas to develop MFL expertise using ICT

Create an **e-book** by drawing images in a **Paint document** and copying them into a PowerPoint or other word processing program to add text.

Construct a **branching database** to ask and answer questions about animals/people/objects in an **MFL**.

Using **puppets** to practise an MFL can take the fear from making mistakes as these can be blamed on the puppet's inexperience!

Act out role play/drama in an MFL. Take **digital photos** of key points and add to **multimedia presentation**. Add speech bubbles in the appropriate language to show what is said.

Creative teaching and learning through Music and Drama

> Creativity is allowing yourself to make mistakes. Art is knowing which ones to keep
>
> Scott Adams, cartoonist

Music and drama can be exploratory learning mediums as well as subjects in their own right. Both involve active learning, exploring ideas and emotions. Children who find difficulty with a literary approach to the world may find these aural and kinaesthetic approaches more engaging. Making music or developing a drama can be used to develop ideas in any subject but both should also be developed as disciplines in their own right.

Music is the most daunting subject for many teachers with its own language: a code which may confuse the non-specialist. However, there is help on the Internet for those of us who do not play a musical instrument with on-line keyboards, digital sound files and musical activities to be adapted as required. The resulting compositions and soundscapes can be saved as podcasts and added to multimedia presentations or web-based publications.

Drama as a process rather than a final performance can be a way of exploring ideas, representing views and remembering key points. In maths, the key features of a graph can be made memorable by getting pupils to represent the vertical and horizontal axes, and the bars which can be stretched or lowered to represent different data. They can be timelines with labels, actions and artefacts. Through drama, learners can improvise ways to represent scientific concepts such as how circuits or life cycles can be represented. Plenary mimes can be improvised to recall key facts from a history or geography sessions. Dramatizing a poem, story or a piece of music or a painting will develop their questioning, connecting, exploring and reflecting skills as they learn to see things in new ways. As drama deals with emotions, it should be handled with sensitivity. It must be clear which parts of the lessons are drama and which are real life, and winding down activities are useful to make the break.

Challenges with potential for developing pupil creativity in Music and Drama

KS1	Take a well-known tune such as London's Burning or Twinkle Twinkle, and add new words.
LKS2	How many ways can a new rhythm be added to a familiar song?
UKS2	Compose, using keyboards or percussion and voices a short introduction to a favourite programme.

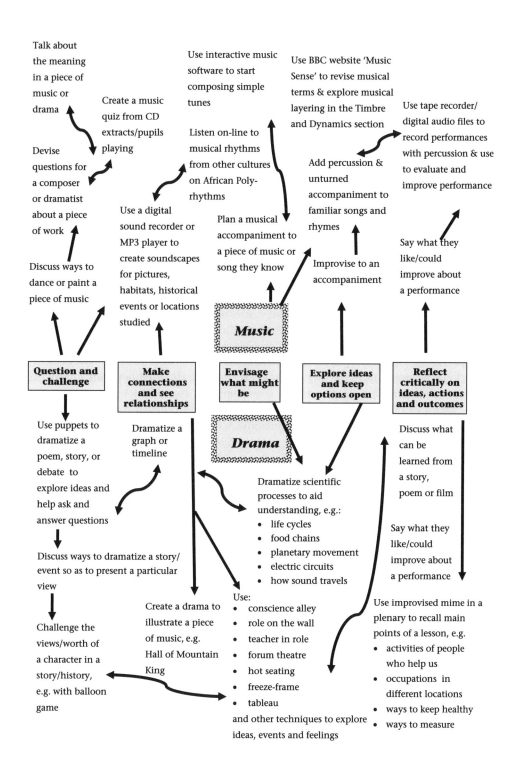

Creative teaching and learning through RE and Citizenship Education (CE)

> Creative CE is about looking at our social world with critical eyes, identifying what we would like to improve, and then developing realistic, appropriate ideas and plans
>
> (Claire and Wooley 2009)

The teaching of RE is concerned not just with passing on cultural understanding and traditions, but with asking ultimate questions so as to understand our place in the universe and develop our moral values. A creative teacher will make RE sessions stimulating through a variety of approaches offering pupils a range of ways to explore and record their learning. Some RE lessons can be sensory experiences with incense, candles, religious music, and flowers or through examining ceremonial clothes and religious artefacts. As they study the lives of religious leaders, children can develop all five creative behaviours as they consider ultimate questions, explore ideas, connect these with their own experience, see things in new ways and reflect on these ideas. Storytelling to illustrate a point or encouraging reflection is traditional in most religious traditions. Care must be taken with Islamic and Sikh stories where questioning may not be felt to be appropriate by believers. In instances where this is suitable, retelling or dramatizing stories in a new context or using art, calligraphy or creative writing can aid understanding of complex ideas.

CE can be taught from starting points in all subject areas whether pupils are looking at issues of respect, personal identity or social equality. Issues which arise from literature, current or historical events can provide a context for developing questions and looking at things in new ways. Scientific advance can raise moral concerns. We are teaching the citizens of a forthcoming world. CE involves developing the processes of creative and critical thinking so that our children can deal with issues we have not yet had to consider.

Challenges with potential for developing pupil creativity in RE and Citizenship

KS1	Why is Harry Potter a hero? Discuss what makes someone a hero or a villain.
LKS2	List questions you would like to ask God, the prime-minister, a world faith leader.
UKS2	Decide on the 5 most important rules for your life

  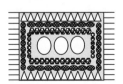

Create **concept maps** to show ideas about responsibility, community, joy and sadness. The advantage of using ICT is that the text boxes are easily moved to reorganize ideas. Add clip art symbols where appropriate.

Redraft religious stories using a word processor, to tell them from another view-point. This can help pupils to consider issues of right and wrong, explore questions and consider different opinions.

Create a children's charter explaining their rights and responsibilities.

List ultimate or moral questions they would like to discuss in large speech bubbles and use to stimulate class discussions.

Update a parable to a present-day context to give it relevance. Act it out concentrating on the ideas and empathy rather than the standard of performance and being word perfect.

Create **multimedia presentations** of stories or factual accounts of learning about a religion. Add text, images and sound files to create an engaging presentation. Photos and scanned images of children's art can be inserted. Word and picture banks can differentiate this activity.

KS1 pupils can use **speech bubbles** and photos of themselves to explain ways in which they can help others. E.g. I share my ball, I listen to friends when they have problems, I help with the dishes at home. Thought bubbles can compare what they think with what they might say.

Create a cartoon strip or storyboard to explain the traditions which are important to a particular religion/set of beliefs. Talking through **puppets** or **role play** can help pupils explore difficult ideas while feeling less vulnerable to criticism.

Draw or collage pictures about festivals and celebrations. Add text to explain what is happening in the pictures. Individual pictures and captions could be put together to make one long story on the wall, e.g. a creation story.

Creative teaching and learning through ICT

> Success is on the far side of failure.
>
> Thomas Watson Snr, President of IBM, died 1956

When planning a term's work, teachers should aim to include elements from each of the four aspects of ICT study. These are:

- finding things out;
- developing ideas and making things happen;
- exchanging and sharing information; and
- reviewing, modifying and evaluating work as it progresses.

There is a wealth of technology available to develop creative ideas and opportunities in teaching and learning. Consider which of the following you currently use and which you might be able to learn more about and make use of.

Audio tour of a location
Avatars
Blog/e-mail/Wiki
Branching database
Brochure/Poster using word banks
Cartoon
CD-ROMs/talking books
Concept map
Control technology
Data-logging
Digital audio recorders
Digital film or Animation
Digital microscope/visualizer
Google Earth and Multimap
GPS software
Graphs and charts from a spreadsheet
Hand-held gameboys
Hand-held PDAs
Hyperlinked story/presentation
Interactive/hyperlinked presentation
Labelled diagram
Maps created in paint/draw program
Photo-copier/scanner

Photos altered in photographic program
Pictures created in paint/draw program
Podcast
Poem . . . shaped or word processed
Puzzles and games created in graphics program
Questionnaire
Quiz
Simulation software
Slideshow presentation
Soundscape
Story
Survey
Table
Template
Timeline
Treasure hunt
Turtles/pixies/roamers
YouTube clips and videos
Virtual worlds
Webcam
Wii
Word processed articles/reports

Use concept maps, flowcharts, diagrams, graphs, graphics and texts to simplify complex ideas for the reader. These could be used as part of a brochure, magazine, **multimedia presentation**, website, oral presentation or report.

Use **video conferencing** facilities to discuss issues with people from other schools. Establish ground-rules for taking turns. Develop clear diction and microphone technique. Use **video** to record role play of drama developing conciliation techniques.

Show KS2 pupils how to use spreadsheets to make **function machines** to add or find the difference between two numbers. These can be decorated in an art session to look like complex machines. Pupils can change the formula to create different types of sum. This one uses the formula: =IF(C5+E5=G5, "well done", "try again") in the cell next to the Try Again cell.

Once they know the formula, they can experiment with other function machines. I have found this very motivating for less confident mathematicians.

Create a class **e-zine** or class/school/club website. Try http://www.schools.ik.org/ for free hosting and templates and awards.

Use a screen with a grid to create symmetrical pictures. One pupil could draw half a house/face for another pupil to complete. Mistakes are more easily corrected than with paper and pencil.

Use a screen **turtles** to create a maze. Each child to navigate through the maze designed by partner. Partner to give directions using maths language to reinforce directions and angle vocabulary.

Use **e-mail** and **digital photographs** to communicate with pupils in another school about scientific investigations, e.g. comparing habitats.

Take digital photos, video clips, sound recordings and add key terminology using **'Windows Movie Maker'** to make a film about a project. This might be about significant inventions in the past and/or about their own experiments

Let KS1 pupils combine words and pictures when sorting and grouping familiar living things according to observable features and properties. A **word bank** with clip art would be useful for this. For poor readers, use a program such as **Clicker** or **Textease** which can read the words aloud to the pupils on selection.

Help pupils to draw a simplified floor map of a locality with which they are familiar (e.g. the island of Struay from the *Katie Morag* series). Mark places they know on the map. Show the class how to program a **roamer** or **floor turtle** to visit places on the map. The roamer could be dressed as a postman and pupils work in groups to devise a sequence of instructions to send it on from one location to another.

Appendix 1
Help sheet

Example of prompt sheet I used with a Y5 class to remind them of some of the possibilities for their personal projects. This could be adapted for other year groups and projects.

Personal project on Ancient OR Modern Egypt

Here are some of the ideas we discussed to make your project enjoyable and interesting. You can get information from travel brochures, books, CD-ROMs and the Internet. Remember to write it all in your own words.

Give yourself a tick/mark out of 5 for each of the following features you feel you do well. Don't feel you have to do them all, they are just the ideas we discussed. The ideas in **bold** are the most important to include.

1. Contents (write this last when you know what you have done)
2. **Introduction**
3. Map with labels
4. Timeline
5. Labelled diagrams/pictures
6. Information about different topics
7. Newspaper style report/diary section
8. Poem/acrostic
9. Did you know? section
10. Pictures drawn, copied, traced or cut from magazines
11. Games, e.g. word search/crossword
12. Alphabet of Egyptian things (A = Anubis, B= Beetle) (scarab) etc. . . with definitions
13. How to make section e.g. hieroglyphics/papyrus/models
14. Poster page
15. Puzzles
16. Quiz
17. Table of facts
18. Graphs and charts
19. **Conclusion** (what I learned/found most interesting/enjoyed section)

Glossary
Bibliography (evidence of book/Internet/CD-ROM/newspaper research)

Appendix 2
Feedback proforma

To be completed on a computer for personal projects.

Dear

I really enjoyed reading your project on .... I did not know that ....
.... Your work on .... was especially interesting. I like the way you
have .... Another idea might be to ....

I hope you enjoy your next project as much as I enjoyed reading this one.

Well done for all your hard work!

It is useful to have about three variations on this so with the added details, everyone has
a personal response.

Appendix 3
Websites which support creative development

Materials from the *Creativity: Find it! Promote it* project have been archived by the government at:

http://tna.europarchive.org/20080528123629/http://www.ncaction.org.uk/creativity/index.htm

There are pages on:

- What is Creativity?
- Why is creativity so important?
- How can you spot creativity?
- How can teachers promote creativity?
- How can heads and managers promote creativity?

There are examples of creativity in action, and links to relevant sites and resources.

The Creativity Culture and Education site (CCE) has links to research evidence to support a creative approach to teaching:
http://www.creativitycultureeducation.org/

The following sites may be of interest for developing both child and adult creativity. Some of these sites have a commercial interest in the topic.

The *Thinking Together* website explains the philosophy behind teaching children to think as well as providing links to resources and other publications:
http://thinkingtogether.educ.cam.ac.uk/

SAPERE (UK society for philosophy for children):
http://www.sapere.org.uk

Robert Fisher has compiled a useful set of resources and links at;
http://www.teachingthinking.net/

http://www.mantleoftheexpert.com/is a central location for information and resources on Mantle of the Expert. It would be useful to anyone interested in using and developing MoE as an approach to teaching and learning.

http://creativityforlife.com/includes sections on personal creativity as well as creativity at work and welcomes contributions from other developers in this area.

http://creativityinschools.com/showcases and creative learning projects implemented in schools across the UK by Pablo Productions Ltd who offer support for creative teaching and learning through digital creativity, and drama.

http://www.creative-partnerships.com/schools-of-creativity/has archived examples of creative work done by schools in many curriculum areas.

http://creativitygames.net/offers weekly challenges for developing creative ideas.

The website Creativity and Innovation Techniques A–Z may appeal to those who like lists of ideas to try. http://www.mycoted.com/Category:Creativity_Techniques

The Mindtools site has a similar list designed to develop adult creativity, some of which might be adapted for use with children. http://www.mindtools.com/pages/main/newMN_CT.htm

Mike Fleetham's Thinking Classroom is a teachers' website with original high quality classroom resources and training for all ages and subjects. Many resources and a monthly on-line magazine are free but for a small charge you have access to even more. http://www.thinkingclassroom.co.uk/Home.aspx

http://www.brainstorming.co.uk/contents.html is aimed mainly at adults with an engaging selection of puzzles, quotes, articles, some free software to try out together with a useful set of evaluated links to other sites.

Appendix 4
Ideas for design challenges weekly/monthly

These ideas can be used to stimulate creative development with groups or individual pupils. They might be used as part of topic work in class, for homework or holiday activities. Even if a whole class is not able to respond to such challenges, those who do can benefit enormously and the desire to join in spreads as interest from one task sparks an interest in other areas. The results may be drawn, modelled, or recorded digitally. Ideas from one Key Stage might be adapted for the other.

Ideas for KS1

Create:	Designs to draw and make
1. Something to protect a dragon's egg 2. A game with marbles 3. Make a plasticine pet and a home for it. Decide what care it needs 4. Create a robot from scrap materials 5. Invent, draw/model and label a plant with special properties 6. A skittle game with plastic bottles 7. A way to tidy a toy box/cupboard/shelf 8. A bird feeder 9. A space capsule to tell aliens about your life 10. A present for someone	1. A really scary scarecrow 2. Designs for cards using flaps, sliders and moving parts 3. A puppet from a glove/sock 4. Perfect pet and a home for it (e.g. potato mouse) 5. Paper collage using magazines and newspaper 6. A fantasy shoebox garden 7. A festive decoration
New foods to design	Sporty challenges
1. A playtime snack 2. A summer salad 3. A new drink 4. A breakfast cereal from oats, fruits, nuts and seeds. Use supermarket ingredients	1. A keep fit dance 2. A gymnastic routine 3. A game with a ball 4. Develop a marching routine

Ideas to explore	*Word/writing challenges*
1. Would you rather be rich or good looking? 2. What are the most important things everyone needs to learn? 3. What would be the best/worst things about having no clocks? 4. What would you most like to ask the queen or another famous person? 5. How could we stop people from dropping litter?	1. Invent new words and their definitions 2. Write an acrostic about yourself 3. Make a spell to turn anything you like into chocolate/gold. What might be the consequences? 4. Create an alphabet around an area of interest. A is for . . . B is for . . . 5. Design badges for friends and family using a word processor if possible. 6. Make a labelled diagram of an alien and its space ship 7. List what might be found in a wizard's pocket
Investigations *These would work best after skills are taught in similar contexts in school*	*Play areas* *These might be paper plans or constructed as part of the classroom/in a bedroom/in the garden at home*
1. Where do snails like to live? 2. Which food trays make the best boat? 3. Which kitchen tools make the best musical sounds?	1. An undersea cave 2. A magician's castle 3. A fairy/superhero den 4. The flight deck of a plane or rocket

Ideas for KS2

Create:	*Designs to draw and make*
1. Game for the garden/someone ill in bed/to use on a journey 2. A new type of transport 3. A thief-proof device to protect a diamond 4. A new animal/dinosaur/insect/mini-beast 5. A kit of equipment for a detective/dragon hunter/sports person/gardener 6. Treasure island map 7. A ring tone for a mobile phone 8. Board game which builds on sporting knowledge/something learned in school 9. A toy for a baby 10. A present for someone	1. An ideal garden (could be modelled on a plate/created digitally) 2. A litter bin with special features 3. Designs for cards/posters 4. Puppets from junk materials 5. Paper collage using magazines and newspaper 6. Model dragon/dinosaur from waste materials 7. Improve your image. (Use a digital camera and simple photo-editing program.) There are many free editing programs on the Internet. E.g. http://pixlr.com/
New foods to design	*Sporty challenges*
1. A low fat snack 2. A winter salad 3. A fruit or vegetable cocktail 4. A super soup	1. A keep fit exercise routine 2. Dance 3. Game with a ball 4. Develop a juggling routine

Ideas to explore	Word/writing challenges
1. Is it ever right to steal?	1. Make a collection of interesting place names
2. How should I spend/share my pocket money if I had £5.00 a week?	2. Invent your own collective nouns
3. How would the way we treat animals change if they could talk to us?	3. Write an information leaflet about something which interests you
4. What would you most like to ask the prime minister/someone else?	4. Invent a crossword/word puzzle to share with friends
5. Which historical person would you most like to invite to your home? What would you want to show or ask them?	5. Make up your own secret code
	6. Create mnemonics to help you remember facts/difficult spellings

Investigations *These would work best after skills are taught in similar contexts in school*	Play areas to plan *These might be drawn by hand or on a computer, but are best built for real in the playground, bedroom or garden at home.*
1. Which animals live in your garden or local park?	1. A detective's headquarters
2. How far can a paper plane fly?	2. A boy's den/a girl's den
3. What were school days like for your grandparents?	3. A pirate's cave
4. How many ways can you record what you do on holiday? (Include drawing, modelling, writing and digital media)	4. A space base

References

Abdallah, A. (1996) Fostering creativity in student teachers, *Community Review*, 14: 52–9.

Alexander, R. (2009) *Independent Cambridge Review*. London: Routledge.

Amabile, T. (1988) A model of creativity and innovation in organizations, in B.M. Staw and L.L. Cunnings (eds), *Research in Organizational Behaviour*. Greenwich, CT: JAI.

Amabile, T.M. (1996) *Creativity in Context*. Boulder, CO: Westview Press.

Amabile, T.M. (1997) Motivating creativity in organizations: on doing what you love and loving what you do, *California Management Review*, 40(1): 39–58.

Anderson, L.W. and Krathwohl, D.R. (eds) (2001) *A Taxonomy for Learning, Teaching and Assessing: A Revision of Bloom's Taxonomy of Educational Objectives*, Complete edition. New York: Longman.

Ang, K. and Wang, Q. (2006) A case study of engaging primary school students in learning science by using Active Worlds, in R. Philip, A. Voerman and J. Dalziel (eds) *Proceedings of the First International LAMS Conference 2006: Designing the Future of Learning* 6–8 December 2006, Sydney: LAMS Foundation, pp. 5–14. Available at: http://lamsfoundation.org/lams2006/papers.htm.

Arthur, J., Grainger, T. and Wray, D. (eds) (2006) *Learning to Teach in the Primary School*. London: Routledge.

Atkinson, E.S. (1994) Key factors which affect pupils; performance in technology project work, in J.S. Smith (ed.) *IDATER 94*, Loughborough: Design and Technology, Loughborough University, pp. 30–7.

Bale, P. (1987) *Geography in the Primary School*. London: Routledge & Kegan Paul.

Bandura, A. (1986) *Social Foundations of Thought and Action*. Englewood Cliffs, NJ: Prentice-Hall.

Beetlestone, F. (1998a) *Learning in the Early Years: Creative Development*. Leamington Spa: Scholastic.

Beetlestone, F. (1998b) *Creative Children, Imaginative Teaching*. Oxford: Oxford University Press.

Bell, S. (2010) Project-based learning for the 21st century: skills for the future, *The Clearing House*, 83: 39–43.

Bhatia, T.K. and Ritchie, W.C. (2008) The bilingual mind and linguistic creativity, *Journal of Creative Communications*, 3(1): 5–21.

Björkman, H. (2004) Design dialogue groups as a source of innovation: factors behind group creativity, *Creativity and Innovation Management*, 13(2), available at: http://www.blackwell publishing.com/pdf/Bjorkman_Jun04.pdf.

Bloom, B.S. and Krathwohl, D.R. (1956) *Taxonomy of Educational Objectives: The Classification of Educational Goals, by a Committee of College and University Examiners. Handbook 1: Cognitive Domain*. New York: Longmans.

Boden, M. (2004) *The Creative Mind: Myths and Mechanisms*. London: Routledge.

Burgess, T. (2007) *Lifting the Lid on the Creative Curriculum*, NSCL report, available at: http://www.nationalcollege.org.uk/index/docinfo.htm?id=17281 (accessed 5 Nov. 2011).

Buzan, T. (1991) *The Mind Map Book*. New York: Penguin.

Chan, D. and Zhao, Y. (2010) The relationship between drawing skill and artistic creativity: do age and artistic involvement make a difference? *Creativity Research Journal*, 22(1).

Chan Hok On, A. (2010) How do teachers' beliefs affect the implementation of inquiry-based learning in the PGS curriculum? A case study of two primary schools in Hong Kong, thesis submitted for the Degree of Doctor of Education in the University of Durham, School of Education, available at: http://etheses.dur.ac.uk/320/1/The_thesis_of_Angus_FINAL.pdf?DDD29 (accessed 16 August 2011).

Claire, H. and Wooley, R. (2009) What has creativity go to do with citizenship education? In A. Wilson (ed.) *Creativity in Primary Education*, Surrey: Learning Matters.

Claxton, G. (2002) *Building Learning Power Helping Young People Become Better Learners*. Bristol: TLO.

Claxton, G. (2003) *Creativity: A Guide for the Advanced Learner (and Teacher)*, available at: http://www.guyclaxton.com/documents/New/A%20Guide%20for%20the%20Advanced%20Learner.pdf (accessed 12 Oct. 2011).

Claxton, G. (2011) Claxton's BLP site, available at: http://www.buildinglearningpower.co.uk/blp/What_is_BLP.html.

Claxton, G., Lucas, B. and Webster, R. (2010) *Bodies of Knowledge: How the Learning in Science Could Transform Practical and Vocational Education*. Winchester: University of Winchester Edge Foundation.

Cohen, J. and Ferrari, J. (2010) Take some time to think this over: the relation between rumination, indecision, and creativity, *Creativity Research Journal*, 22(1): 68–73.

Compton, A. (2010) The rise and fall of creativity in English education, *Educational Futures*, 2(2).

Craft, A. (1996) Nourishing educator creativity: a holistic approach to CPD, *British Journal of In-Service Education*, 22(3): 309–22.

Craft, A. (2000) *Creativity Across the Primary Curriculum: Framing and Developing Practice*. London: Routledge Falmer.

Craft, A. (2001) *An Analysis of Research and Literature on Creativity in Education*. London: QCA.

Craft, A. (2002) *Creativity and Early Years Education*. Continuum Books.

Craft, A. (2003) The limits to creativity in education: dilemmas for the educator, *British Journal of Educational Studies*, 51(2): 113–27.

Craft, A. (2005) *Creativity in Schools: Tensions and Dilemmas*. London: Routledge.

Craft, A., (2001). Little c creativity. In A. Craft, B. Jeffrey, M. Leibling, (Eds.). *Creativity in education*. London: Continuum.

Craft, A. (2002) *Creativity in the Early Years: A Lifewide Foundation*. London: Continuum.

Craft, A. Gardner, H. and Claxton, G. (2008) *Creativity, Wisdom and Trusteeship*. Thousand Oaks, CA: Corwin Press.

Cropley, P. (2001) *Creativity in Education and Learning: A Guide for Teachers and Educators*. London: Kogan Page.

Csikszentmihalyi, M. (1990) *Flow: The Psychology of Optimal Experience*. New York: Harper and Row.

Csikszentmihalyi, M. (1996a) *Creativity: Flow and the Psychology of Discovery and Invention*. London: HarperCollins.

Csikszentmihalyi, M. (1996b) *Creativity: The Work and Lives of 91 Eminent People*. London: HarperCollins.

Dawkins, R. (1976) *The Selfish Gene*. Oxford: Oxford University Press.

Deakin-Crick, R., Broadfoot, P. and Claxton, G. (2004) Developing an Effective Lifelong Learning Inventory: The ELLI Project, *Assessment in Education*, 11(3), available at: http://www.ellionline.co.uk/research.php.

De Bono, E. (1967) *The Use of Lateral Thinking*. London: Jonathan Cape.

De Bono, E. (1999) *Six Thinking Hats*. Harmondsworth: Penguin.

Dewey, J. (1938) *Logic: The Theory of Inquiry*. New York: Henry Holt.

DfEE (1999) *The National Curriculum*. London: HMSO.

DfEE (2006) *Emerging Good Practice in Promoting Creativity*. London: TSO.

DfEE (2007) *Pedagogy and Personalisation*. London: DfES Publications.

DfEE/QCA (1999) *The National Curriculum: Handbook for Primary Teachers in England and Wales*. London: DfEE/QCA.

DfES (2003) *Excellence and Enjoyment: A Strategy for Primary Schools*. London: Department for Education and Skills.

Downing, D. and Lamont, E. with Newby, M. (2007) *HEARTS Higher Education, the Arts and Schools: an Experiment in Educating Teachers*. Slough: NFER. Published in May 2007 by the National Foundation for Educational Research, The Mere, Upton Park, Slough, Berkshire SL1 2DQ.

Ellis, S., Barrs, M. and Bunting, J. (2007) Assessing Learning in Creative Contexts: An action research project, led by the Centre for Literacy in Primary Education with Lambeth City Learning Centre and CfBT Action Zone Centre for Literacy in Primary Education, available at: www.clpe.co.uk/_file/tb7aJAzEwO_50421.pdf (accessed 6 Nov. 2011).

Faulkner, D. (2006) *Excellence, Creativity and Innovation in Teacher Education: EXCITE!* Phase II Report Open University and Synectics World.com.

Feldhusen, J.F. and Goh, B.E. (1995) Assessing and accessing creativity: an integrative review of theory, research, and development, *Creativity Research Journal* 8(3): 231–50.

Feldman, D.H., Csikszentmihalyi, M. and Gardner, H. (1994) *Changing the World: A Framework for the Study of Creativity*. Westport, CT: Praeger.

Fisher, R. (1996) *Stories for Thinking*. Oxford: Nash Pollock.

Fisher, R. (2003) Creativity in schools, *TES*, 7 March.

Fisher, R. (2007) Creative minds: building communities of learning for the creative age, available at: http://www.pantaneto.co.uk/issue25/fisher.htm (accessed 11 October 2011).

Fisher, R. and Williams, M. (eds) (2004) *Unlocking Creativity: Teaching Across the Curriculum*. London: David Fulton.

Fryer, M. (1996) *Creative Teaching and Learning*. London: Paul Chapman Publishing.

Fryer, M. (2003) *Creativity Across the Curriculum: A Review and Analysis of Programmes Designed to Develop Creativity*. London: QCA.

Galton, P. et al. (1999) *Inside the Primary Classroom Twenty Years on*. London: Routledge.

Galton, F. (1869) *Hereditary Genius: An Inquiry into Its Laws and Consequences*. London: Macmillan.

Gardner, H. (1983) *Frames of Mind: The Theory of Multiple Intelligence*. New York: Basic Books.

Gardner, H. (1993) *Creating Minds: An Anatomy of Creativity Seen Through the Lives of Freud, Einstein, Picasso, Stravinsky, Eliot, Graham, and Gandhi*. New York: Basic Books.

Gardner, H. (1997) *Extraordinary Minds: Portraits of Four Exceptional Individuals and an Examination of Our Own Extraordinariness*. New York: Basic Books.

Gardner, H. and Hatch, T. (1989) Multiple intelligences go to school: educational implications of the theory of multiple intelligences, *Educational Researcher*, 18(8), 4–9.

Garner, W. (2009) Enquiry as a pedagogical approach within the context of primary geography, available at: www.geography.org.uk/download/GA_Conf09RPGarner.ppt (accessed 16 August 2011).

Gerver, R. (2010) *Creating Tomorrow's Schools Today: Education – Our Children – Their Futures*. London: Continuum International Publishing Group.

Guilford, J.P. (1950) Creativity, *American Psychologist*, 5(9): 444–54.

Hardiman, P. et al. (2003) *Interactive Whole Class Teaching in the Literacy and Numeracy Lessons, University of Newcastle on Tyne: A Report for the Economic and Research Council*. London: ERC.

Hargreaves, D. et al. (2005) *About Learning: Report of the Learning Working Group*. London: Demos.

Harris, R. (2010) Creative Thinking Techniques, available at: http://www.virtualsalt.com/crebook2.htm (accessed 21 October 2011).

Heathcote, D. and Bolton, G. (1996) *Drama for Learning: Dorothy Heathcote's Mantle of the Expert Approach to Education*. Connecticut: Greenwood Press.

Hennessey, B. (1996) Teaching for creative development: a social-psychological approach, in N. Colangelo and G. Davis (eds) *Handbook of Gifted Education*, 2nd edn, Needham Heights, MA: Allyn and Bacon, pp. 282–91.

Higgins, S., Baumfield, V. and Leat, D. (2001) *Thinking Through Primary Teaching*. Cambridge: Chris Kington.

Honey, P. and Mumford, A. (1983) *Using Your Learning Styles*. Maidenhead: Peter Honey Publications.

Jesson, J. and Peacock, G. (2011) *The Really Useful ICT Book: A Practical Guide to Using Technology Across the Primary Curriculum*. London: Routledge.

Kahn, P. and O'Rourke, K. (2004) *Guide to Curriculum Design: Enquiry-Based Learning*. London: HEA.

Kerka, S. (1999) *Creativity in Adulthood*. ERIC Digest No. 204. ERIC Clearinghouse on Adult Career and Vocational Education.

Kirschenbaum, P. (1998) The Creativity Classification System (CCS): an assessment theory. *Roeper Review*, 21(1), 20–6.

Kolb, D.A. (1984) *Experiential Learning*. Englewood Cliffs, NJ: Prentice-Hall.

Langer, E.J. and Moldovenau, M. (2000) The construct of mindfulness, *Journal of Social Issues*, 56(1).

Lipman, M. (1991) *Thinking in Education*, New York: Cambridge University Press.

Lucas, B. (2001) Creative teaching, teaching creativity and creative learning, in A. Craft, B. Jeffrey and M. Leibling (eds) *Creativity in Education*. London: Continuum.

Martin, F. (2004) Creativity through geography, in R. Fisher and M. Williams (eds) *Unlocking Creativity: Teaching across the Curriculum*. London: David Fulton.

Maslow, A.H. (1943) A theory of human motivation, *Psychological Review,* 50(4): 370–96.

Mauzy, J. (2006) Managing Personal Creativity *Design Management Review* Vol. 17 No. 3.

McGuinness, C. (1999) *From Thinking Skills to Thinking Classrooms: A Review and Evaluation of Approaches for Developing Pupils' Thinking*. London: DfEE (Research Report RR115).

McGuinness, C. (2000) ACTS (Activating Children's Thinking Skills): A methodology for enhancing thinking skills across the curriculum, available at: http://www.tlrp.org/pub/acadpub/Mcguinness2000.pdf (accessed 11 November 2011).

Moon, J. (1999) *Learning Journals: A Handbook for Academics, Students and Professional Development*. London: Kogan Page.

Moyles, J. (1992) *Organising for Learning in the Primary Classroom*. Buckingham: Open University Press.

NACCCE (1999) *All Our Futures*. London: DfEE.

NACCCE (1999) *All Our Futures: Creativity, Culture and Education*. Suffolk: DfEE.

Nolan, A. (2010) *The Creative Curriculum: A Definition*. Fifth Element Systems Limited, available at: http://www.vthelement.co.uk/papers/creative_curriculum.pdf (accessed 14 August 2011).

Novak, J.D. and Canas, A.J. (2006) The Theory Underlying Concept Maps and How to Construct and Use Them, available at: http://cmap.ihmc.us/Publications/ResearchPapers/TheoryUnderlyingConceptMaps.pdf (accessed 21 October 2011).

OFSTED (2003a) *Improving City Schools: How the Arts Can Help*. London: DfES.

OFSTED (2003b) *Raising Achievement through the Arts*. London: DfES.

OFSTED (2003c) *Expecting the Unexpected: Developing Creativity in Primary and Secondary Schools*. London: DfES.

OFSTED (2010) *Learning: Creative Approaches That Raise Standards*. London: DfES.

OFSTED (2009) *Gifted and Talented Pupils in School*. London: DfES.

OFSTED (2011) *Economics, Business and Enterprise Education*. London: DfES.

Osborn, A.F. (1953) *Applied Imagination: Principles and Procedures of Creative Problem-solving*. New York: Scribners.

Pashler, H., McDaniel, M., Rohrer, D. and Bjork, R. (2009) Learning styles: Concepts and evidence, *Psychological Science in the Public Interest*, 9: 105–19.

Piaget, J. (1948) *To Understand is to Invent*. New York: UNESCO.

Plowden, J. (1967) *Children and their Primary Schools, Report of the Central Advisory Council for Education in England*. London: HMSO.

(QCA) (1998) *National Curriculum 1998: The Next Steps in Developing the School Curriculum*. London: QCA.

QCA (2004) *Creativity: Find it! Promote it*. Available at: http://tna.europarchive.org/20080528123629/ http://www.ncaction.org.uk/creativity/index.htm.

Rasulzada, F. and Dackert, I. (2009) Organizational creativity and innovation in relation to psychological well-being and organizational factors, *Creativity Research Journal*, 21(2–3): 191–8.

Rego, A., Machado, F., Leal, S., and Pina e Cunha, M. (2009) Are hopeful employees more creative? An empirical study, *Creativity Research Journal*, 21(2–3).

Rhodes, M. (1961) An analysis of creativity, *Phi Delta Kappan*, 42: 305–10.

Richards, R. (1973) *Science 5/13: Holes, Gaps and Cavities*. London: Macdonald Educational.

Rose, J. (2009) *The Independent Review of the Primary Curriculum: Final Report* (The Rose Review). London: DCFS.

Runco, M.A. (1996) Personal creativity: definition and developmental issues, *New Directions for Child Development*, 72: 3–30.

Runco, M.A. (2003) Education for creative potential, *Scandinavian Journal of Educational Research*, 47(3).

Scottish Government (2004) *A Curriculum for Excellence*, available at: http://www.ltscotland.org. uk/understandingthecurriculum/whatiscurriculumforexcellence/ (accessed 11 October 2011).

SEED (2006) *Promoting Creativity in Education: Overview of Key National Policy Developments Across the UK*. Available at: http://www.hmie.gov.uk/documents/publication/hmiepcie.html.

Seltzer, K. and Bentley, T. (1999) *The Creative Age: Knowledge and Skills for the New Economy*. London: Demos.

Shedd, J. (1928) *Salt from My Attic*. Portland, ME: The Mosher Press.

Sheridan, D. (2010) When clapping data speaks to Wii: exertion interfaces, physical creativity and performative interaction. Paper presented at 'Children's Playground Games and Songs in the New Media Age: Interim Conference', 25th February 2010, London Knowledge Lab, London. Available at: http://projects.beyondtext.ac.uk/playgroundgames/uploads/sheridan_ playground_interim.pdf (accessed 12 October 2011).

Shneiderman, B. (2000) Creating creativity: user interfaces for supporting innovation *ACM Transactions on Computer-Human Interaction*, 7(1): 114–38.

Simonton, D.K. (2003) Scientific creativity as constrained stochastic behavior: the integration of product, process, and person perspectives, *Psychological Bulletin*, 129: 475–94.

Spendlove, D. (2005) Creativity in education: a review, *D & T Educational: an international Journal*, 10(2).

Spindler, G.D. (1983) Anthropologists view American culture, *Annual Review of Anthropology*, 12: 49–78.

Sternberg, R.J. (ed.) (1999) *Handbook of Creativity*. Cambridge: Cambridge University Press.

Sternberg, R.J. and Williams, W. (1996) How to develop student creativity, available at: http:// ozpk.tripod.com/000000creat (accessed 17 October 2011).

Sternberg, R.J. and Williams, W. (2011) *Teaching for Creativity: Two Dozen Tips*, available at: http:// www.cdl.org/resource-library/articles/teaching_creativity.php (accessed 31 October 2011).

Swartz, R. and Parks, S. (1994) *Infusing the Teaching of Critical and Creative Thinking into Content Instruction: A Lesson Design Handbook for the Elementary Grades*. California: Critical Thinking Press and Software.

Tatarkiewicz, W. (1980) *A History of Six Ideas: An Essay in Aesthetics*. Trans. from the Polish by C. Kasparek. The Hague: Martinus Nijhoff.

Torrance, E.P. (1966 1974) *Torrance Tests of Creative Thinking: Norms-technical Manual*. Princeton, NJ: Personnel Press.

Vygotsky, L. S. (1978) *Mind in Society: The Development of Higher Psychological Processes*. Cambridge, MA: Harvard University Press.

Wallace, B. (2010) Thinking Activity in a Social Context, available at: http://www.tascwheel.com/ (accessed 11 November 2011).

Wallas, G. (1926) *The Art of Thought*. New York: Harcourt Brace.

Wegerif, R. (2002) *Thinking Skills, Technology and Learning: A Review of the Literature for Nestafuturelab*. Milton Keynes: Open University (available at http://www.nestafuturelab.org/reviews/ts01.htm).

Wegerif, R. (2010) *Mind Expanding: Teaching for Thinking and Creativity in Primary Education*. Maidenhead: Open University Press.

Wilson, A. (ed.) (2007/2009) *Creativity in Primary Education*. Surrey: Learning Matters.

Wiltermuth, S. (2008) Dominance, complementarity and group creativity, Stanford University, available at: http://opimweb.wharton.upenn.edu/documents/seminars/Dissertation%20 Proposal%201.pdf.

Yamamoto, K. (2010) Out of the box: the origination and form in creativity, *Creativity Research Journal*, 22(3): 345–6.

Yeh, Y-C. and Wu, J.J. (2006) The cognitive processes of pupils' technological creativity, *Creativity Research Journal*, 18(2): 213–27.

Youssef, C.M. and Luthans, F. (2007) Positive organizational behavior in the workplace: the impact of hope, optimism, and resilience, *Journal of Management*, 33(5): 774–800.

Zawada, B. (2009) Linguistic creativity and mental representation with reference to intercategorial, available at: http://hdl.handle.net/10500/1965 (accessed 12 October 2011).

Zimmerman, B.J. (1998) Developing self-fulfilling cycles of academic regulation: an analysis of exemplary instructional models, in D. H. Schunk and B. J. Zimmerman (eds) *Self-Regulated Learning: From Teaching to Self-Reflective Practice*. New York: Guilford, pp. 1–19.

Zimmerman, B.J. and Schunk, D.H. (eds) (1989) *Self-Regulated Learning and Academic Achievement: Theory, Research and Practice*. New York: Springer-Verlag.

Index